Brownbread
and
War

Roddy Doyle was born in Dublin in 1958. His first
novel, *The Commitments*, was published to great acclaim
in 1987 and was made into a very successful film by
Alan Parker in 1991. *The Snapper* was published in 1990
and has been made into a film, directed by Stephen
Frears, for the BBC's *Screen Two*. His third novel, *The
Van*, was shortlisted for the 1991 Booker Prize. His
latest novel, *Paddy Clarke Ha Ha Ha*, is published in
hardback by Secker & Warburg.

By the same author
and available in Minerva

The Commitments
The Snapper
The Van

Brownbread
and
War

RODDY DOYLE

Minerva

A Minerva Paperback
BROWNBREAD AND WAR

War first published in 1989
by Passion Machine Limited
45–46 Hardwicke Street
Dublin 1 *

Copyright © Roddy Doyle 1989

Brownbread first published in 1992
by Martin Secker & Warburg Limited

Copyright © Roddy Doyle 1987

This collection first published in Great Britain 1992
by Martin Secker & Warburg Limited
This Minerva edition published 1993
by Mandarin Paperbacks
an imprint of Reed Consumer Books Limited
Michelin House, 81 Fulham Road, London SW3 6RB
and Auckland, Melbourne, Singapore and Toronto

Reprinted 1993 (twice), 1994 (twice), 1995

Copyright © Roddy Doyle 1992
The author has asserted his moral rights

A CIP catalogue record for this title
is available from the British Library

ISBN 0 7493 9751 9

This book is dedicated
to Paul Mercier

Contents

Introduction   1

Brownbread   3

War   95

Introduction

In November 1985 a friend of mine, Paul Mercier, invited me to watch a rehearsal of his new play, *Wasters*. Rehearsals took place in a smelly old hall behind Cranby Row. It was a horrible Monday night. I'd just discovered that one of my boots was leaking. My glasses were wet and foggy and I'd no tissues to wipe them. I sat steaming and half-blind on a chair with a wobble and waited, and tried to make my face look like it was happy to be there.

Then it started.

It was fast and funny and wonderful but that wasn't it: for the first time in my life I saw characters I recognised, people I met every day, the language I heard every day. It was like watching an old cine-film; I could point out people I knew and remember them saying what they said. The way they dressed, walked, held their cans of lager – it was all very familiar. I'll never forget it.

I don't remember if it was still raining when I was going home.

Studs, Paul Mercier's next play, was even better. I saw it five times in its three-week run. It was the story of a Sunday morning soccer team. Eleven players in black body-stockings and too-long shorts danced, ran and slow-motioned their way through the rounds of the Cup into the final, and lost. They were eleven men I knew. And the manager, I knew him as well. I was upset when they lost although I knew they would. *Studs* was perfect. It's my favourite play.

These two plays were produced by the Passion Machine, a company founded by Paul Mercier, John Sutton—another friend—and John Dunne. They were performed in the SFX Centre (the renamed St Francis Xavier Hall—it was blessed by the Pope in 1957, by telegram). It wasn't a theatre. It was used for heavy-metal gigs, bingo, martial arts competitions, talent shows, civil service exams, auctions, Irish dancing. It had none of the things we expect to see in a good theatre—clean toilets, spacious bars, young men and women dressed in black talking meaningful shite during the intermission.

—It's quite good but is it theatre?

—Well, it's pure music hall really, isn't it?

—Exactly.

It was a dump. I loved it. I saw The Clash there, Madness, The Pretenders, Echo and the Bunnymen. I saw Whitesnake fans from

Cork getting sick outside it. Two police motorbikes were set on fire outside—I didn't see that. A punk poet, onstage, tried to open a fire extinguisher with a sledge-hammer—I didn't see that either. I saw enough though. Things happened at the SFX. Most of all, I went to the plays. The Passion Machine made a theatre out of it; no frills or messing—a good stage and bad seats. I loved going there. I hadn't been to many plays. I'd been to none more than once. I went to *Wasters* four times, *Studs* five, and the next one, *Spacers*, four times. I'd never seen anything like them. They were brilliant; all written and directed by Paul Mercier.

After four plays by Paul, the Passion Machine wanted to produce the work of other new writers. They asked me to write a play. I'd just finished writing *The Commitments*; it was June 1986. I was about to start *The Snapper*. I'd never thought about writing a play. It had never been an ambition. If I hadn't been asked—if I'd been asked by anyone other than Paul Mercier and John Sutton—I'd never have written one. I was very proud of my friends. I admired what they were doing—the plays themselves, their efforts to bring a new audience to the theatre, even their policy of serving intermission wine in plastic cups—without a licence. I was given the chance to be involved, and it was hard to stay calm. I was going to write a play; Paul Mercier was going to direct it. I was scared as well. I didn't think I could write anything remotely as solid as *Studs*. I was right; I couldn't. But I loved writing *Brownbread* and, later, *War*. I loved the whole thing—the rehearsals, everything.

I don't remember where I got the idea for *Brownbread*, three lads kidnapping a bishop. I felt that I needed a good excuse to keep all the characters in the one room onstage for two hours, and then I was writing dialogue for the lads and the bishop holed up in an upstairs bedroom. It made sense. *War* was inspired by a pile of pub quizzes I took part in, always on Monday night, in the Foxhound Inn, in Kilbarrack, and the Cedar Lounge, in Raheny. For about a year I read the papers and watched The News only with next Monday in mind. There was a volcano in Columbia; I didn't give a shite about the dead, I just wanted to remember the name of the mountain. I had a list of African presidents, emperors and prime ministers. Ouagadougou was the capital of Burkina Faso; Ruby shot Oswald; Bolton won the FA Cup in 1958. I never made the big time—Anne Brontë wrote *Agnes Grey*—I never won a trophy, cash or even a kettle-jug. I wasn't hopeless, though; I did win two tins of biscuits, a pocket calculator and a piece of paper that entitled me to one free visit to a fitness centre. Father Damien's leper colony was called Molokai.

Dublin, March 1992.

2

Brownbread

CHARACTERS

The Lads	**Ao Farrell** **John Murray** **Donkey**	All 19
The Hierarchy	**Bishop Treacy**	Late 40s
The Parents	**Mr Farrell** **Mrs Farrell** **Mrs Murray**	Early 40s Early 40s Mid 40s
The Police	**Plain-clothes Guard** **Uniformed Guard**	Mid 30s Late 20s
The Marines	**Lt George Bukowski** **Private Crabacre**	Early 40s Early 20s
The Media	**Maurice Murphy**	A TV journalist; late 20s
The Voices	**Hawker One** **Hawker Two** **Young Boy**	Women; late 30s 11 or 12
	Nuala	TV continuity announcer; early 20s.
	Pat Kenny **Charlie Bird** **Dave Fanning**	*Real* RTE broadcasters
	Ronald Reagan	President of the United States of America; early 100s.

Brownbread was first staged at the SFX Centre, Dublin, in September 1987.

Director	Paul Mercier
Producer	John Sutton
Designers	Anne Gately and Paul Mercier
Lighting	Pat Byrne
Sound Effects Recording	John Dunne/Shay Fitzgerald
Ao	Berts Folan
Donkey	Lawrence Lowry
John	Stephen Dunne
Bishop Treacy	Gerard Byrne
Mr Farrell	Brendan Gleeson
Mrs Murray/Mrs Farrell	Stephanie Dunne★
Uniformed Guard/Maurice Murphy/Private Crabacre	Charlie O'Neill
Plain-clothes Guard/ Lt Bukowski	Alan Archbald
Pat Kenny	Himself
Dave Fanning	Himself
Charlie Bird	Himself
Nuala	Sile Nugent
Ronald Reagan	Paul Nolan
Hawkers	Phil McCaughey/Stephanie Dunne
Young Boy	Roddy Doyle

★ Charlotte Bradley replaced Stephanie Dunne for the second half of the play's run.

Act One

PART ONE

Bo Diddley sings 'You Can't Judge A Book By Its Cover'. As the lights go up the music fades.

*A front upstairs bedroom in a terraced corporation house, in Barrytown, a suburb of north Dublin. The room is on a platform some feet above stage level. Characters on the stage are on the street outside the house. Characters on the platform are in the bedroom. The bedroom is on stage-right. The back wall and right wing-side wall have 'bedroom' wallpaper. A window looking onto the street is in the left wing-side wall. The front wall is missing, allowing the audience to see into the bedroom. The bedroom door is in the back wall. It is **Donkey**'s parents' bedroom. There should be a double bed, perhaps a dressing-table or wardrobe, at least one chair, and things that immediately mark it as a married couple's bedroom—a picture of a child with big sad eyes, a Dunne's nylon dressing-gown, a radio etc. The street outside the room can be indicated by a bollard, a wall etc.*

*Enter **Donkey**, a young man of about eighteen who could be mistaken for a thick but definitely isn't. He hurries into the room, looks around to see that everything is in order. He runs over and closes the wardrobe: he doesn't want the lads to see his ma's clothes. The inspection over, he goes back to the door and looks out.*

Donkey Will yis hurry up!

Donkey *rushes over to the window and looks out. He speaks to himself.*

Donkey What're *you* lookin' at, yeh nosey bitch? That's righ'. Get back in there an' polish your fuckin' ornaments.

Donkey dashes back to the door and looks out. He sees that the lads are on the stairs.

Donkey Hurry up, will yis. ——Kick his hand there, go on.

*We hear a screech of episcopal pain offstage. **Donkey** sniggers, shocked and delighted. He sees the lads and the **Bishop** are getting close to the door. He takes one last look around. Enter **Ao** and **John**, bursting in; hauling the **Bishop**. Ao and John are the same age as **Donkey**. The*

7

Bishop *is in his late forties, and is dressed in full regalia. He is resisting, but not very convincingly. He carries one hand as if it is very sore.*

Ao This way, eh —Your Bishop.

John Wipe your feet.

The **Bishop** *is shoved onto a chair and* **Ao** *starts to tie him with washing-line cord.*

Donkey Missis Moloney saw us.

Ao Fuck her, so wha'. She'll only be jealous.

The **Bishop** *is struggling to get out of the chair.* **Ao** *draws back to punch him.*

Ao Go on.

The **Bishop** *stops struggling.* **Donkey** *sniggers.*

John (*to the* **Bishop**) Go on. See wha' happens.

Bishop I —I really must protest.

Donkey (*after a short pause*) Fuck off.

Donkey *is obviously delighted that he can say this and get away with it. The other two lads laugh as well, a bit shocked.*

Bishop (*scared*) This is outrageous.

Ao (*agreeing*) It is alrigh'.

Ao *starts to blindfold the* **Bishop**.

John What're yeh doing' tha' for?

Ao So he won't be able to recognise us.

John Wha'!?

Ao *thinks about this very quickly.*

Ao Fuck it. I knew we'd do somethin' wrong. I fuckin' knew it. ——We'll just have to kill him.

The **Bishop** *yelps.* **Donkey** *points at the* **Bishop**; *a way of asking the others if they heard it too. They laugh.* **Ao** *continues blindfolding the* **Bishop**.

Ao May as well do it anyway. ——Is tha' too tight for yeh, Your Bishop?

Bishop ——No.

Donkey It will be if yeh mess, righ'.

A siren is heard offstage, left.

John Jaysis! Already?

The three lads rush to the window and look out. **Donkey** *puts his back very dramatically to the window wall; something he's seen done loads of times on 'Miami Vice'.*

Ao I didn't think they'd be this quick. ——Here they come; look it.

John Yeow! Look at them. Culchies Anonymous.

Ao (*counting*) One, two, three ——fuckin' hell.

Donkey *moves away from the wall and looks out.*

Donkey Rapid! ——We're on the map now lads, wha'. ——Jaysis! Missis Dixon's flowers! She'll go spare when she sees tha'.

More sirens are heard.

Donkey They're all wearin' anoraks, look.

Ao They're bullet-proof vests.

All three dive for the floor, **John** *letting go of a quick roar.*

John We're brownbread now.

Bishop Hello?

Ao (*from the floor*) Howyeh.

Bishop Em ——if you release me now, I'm sure I can ——

Donkey No way.

Ao No.

Donkey *has a gun. This is the first time the audience sees it. He points it at the* **Bishop**.

Donkey D'yeh see this?

Bishop (*scared*) No.

Donkey Well, it's a gun. A real one, righ'. An' if yeh shout or scream or ann'thin' I'll shoot the face off yeh.

The three lads are still lying on the floor. **Donkey** *finds it all very thrilling.*

Donkey This is the business, wha'.

Ao *creeps to the window and peeps out.*

John Mind your forehead.

Ao They know we're in here.

John (*matter-of-factly*) Brownbread, I'm tellin' yis.

Donkey Fuck up you, will yeh.

John *and* **Donkey** *face each other on the floor.*

John Are you talkin' to me?

Donkey Yeah.

They start pushing each other on the chest, as if getting ready to fight.

Donkey Come on!

Ao Here! Stop tha', will yis.

Donkey *and* **John** *stare each other out of it for a while.*

Ao Get the Bishop down there in case they shoot him.

Donkey Let them.

Donkey *and* **John** *put the chair down sideways on the floor, with the* **Bishop** *still tied to it.*

John Pass the saw please, Donkey.

The **Bishop** *is terrified.*

Donkey (*copping on*) Certainly. Which one d'you want? The chainsaw or the hacksaw?

John Oh, the hack. The hack. It's better crack with the hack.

Enter from left, very carefully, the two Guards; both wearing bullet-proof jackets. The **Uniformed Guard** *has a megaphone. The* **Plain-clothes Guard** *has a walkie-talkie. Both men move slowly, crouched.* **Uniform** *keeps looking behind him, as if making sure that the rest of the force is still there. He's nervous but he sniffs promotion. He's there because the house is on his 'manor'.* **Plain-clothes** *looks as if he's done this sort of thing before; he creeps forward very smoothly. He studies the house in front of him. Both men are from places far from Dublin.*

Plain-clothes (*into the walkie-talkie*) What's the beef on the house?

The walkie-talkie crackles back briefly.

Plain-clothes (*annoyed*) I know it's a corporation house.

Donkey Have another look.

Ao Fuck off.

Donkey Chicken.

Ao Fuck off.

John *makes hacksaw noises into the* **Bishop**'*s ear.*

John You won't say annythin', sure yeh won't?

Bishop (*squeaks; then coughs*) No.

The walkie-talkie crackles.

Plain-clothes (*into the walkie-talkie*) Try the roof.
(*To* **Uniform**.) The middle of the terrace. They couldn't have picked a worse place.

Uniform (*unsure*) Yes ——.
   (*Then more confidently.*) Stupid; stupid.

Plain-clothes You'd better establish contact.

Uniform *doesn't really know what he's just been told to do.* **Plain-clothes** *points to the megaphone.*

Plain-clothes Talk to them, okay.

Uniform Oh, right.

John What's happenin'?

Donkey Missis Dixon's beatin' the shite out o' them.

Uniform *turns on the megaphone; not sure how to operate it.*

Uniform (*into the megaphone*) Hello. ——Hey, you lads there in number thirty-seven. Over.

The lads look at each other. Ao nods. He opens the window and yells, without showing his face to the Guards outside.

Ao We *have* a television licence.

The lads laugh, delighted.

Donkey Fuckin' great.

John Television licence. Fair play to yeh.

Uniform (*into the megaphone*) Okay. ——Now. ——Do you by any chance have Bishop Treacy in there with you? ——Over.

Ao Yeah. Over.

Uniform (to **Plain-clothes**) They have him. I knew it.
   (*To left wing; shouts*) They have him alright.

He feels very important and successful.

Uniform (*into megaphone*) Right, lads. I think you'd better bring him down quick before you get into trouble.

Ao Yeah, sure. No problem.

Donkey Go home, you, and milk your cows!

The walkie-talkie crackles.

Plain-clothes (*into the walkie-talkie*) Only the upstairs front. Good.
   (*To* **Uniform**.) Find out if they've harmed him.

Uniform Okay; right. ——Roger.
   (*Into the megaphone.*) Is the Bishop alright?

Ao Yeah. He's not too bad.

Donkey *makes hacksaw noises and saws the* **Bishop**'s *leg with his hand.*

Uniform (*into the megaphone*) Have you harmed him in any way?

Ao Not yet.

Uniform (*to* **Plain-clothes**) He's okay. Thank God for that.

Plain-clothes See if they're armed.

Uniform *doesn't know what to do.*

Plain-clothes (*exasperated*) Ask them.

Uniform Roger.
> (*Into the megaphone.*) Are you toting any hardware, lads?
> (*Turns off the megaphone.*) Eh ——over.
> (*Turns the megaphone back on.*) Over.

Ao Wha'!?

Donkey Hardware!?

Plain-clothes Just ask them are they armed, okay.

Uniform (*into the megaphone*) Are you armed?

Ao Yeah.

John (*in a Harlem accent*) We sure are, motherfucker.

Plain-clothes (*to* **Uniform**) What with.

Uniform (*into the megaphone*) With what?

Ao A gun.

Plain-clothes (*suddenly more alert*) Jesus!

Uniform (*into the megaphone*) What make of a gun?

Ao (*impatient*) A gun. A gun tha' shoots bullets. A bang bang.
> (*To the lads.*) For fuck sake, wha'.

John Tha' poor sap is out of his league here.

Uniform (*into the megaphone*) How do we know you really have a gun? You could be having us on.

Donkey (*roars*) We'll shoot the Bishop an' throw him out the window. ——An' then yis'll fuckin' know.

The **Bishop** *whimpers, although he tries not to.*

Donkey Stop whingin', you.

John The Soldier's o' Christ, wha'.

Ao Leave him alone. Don't mind them, Your Bishop. They're only slaggin' yeh.

Donkey Arse licker.

Ao Fuck off, you.

Plain-clothes This *is* your 'manor', isn't it?

Uniform Yes, it is. From the shops down to —

Plain-clothes Okay. ——You said you knew them.

Uniform Oh, I do know them. Only too well.

Plain-clothes They're just fuckin' kids. Get them down here with the Bishop so we can go home, for Christ's sake, okay. Do you think you could manage that?

Uniform Right. ——Right.
(*Into the megaphone.*) Right, lads.

Ao Will yeh play a request, Larry?

The lads laugh.

Uniform Very humorous. ——Now lads, you know me —.

Donkey Yeah; you're the bollix tha' took our ball off us.

Ao Yeah; an' yeh bet up my little brother just cos he called yeh a redneck.

Plain-clothes *grabs the megaphone from* **Uniform**.

Plain-clothes (to **Uniform**) Give me a name.

Uniform Eh ——what?

Plain-clothes What are they called!?

Uniform Oh. One of them's a Farrell.

Plain-clothes What's his *christian* name?

Uniform *obviously doesn't know*.

Plain-clothes For Christ's sake!

Donkey I wish they'd do somethin'. This is gettin' boring.

Plain-clothes *doesn't bother using the megaphone*.

Plain-clothes Right gentlemen, enough is enough, okay. Bring the Bishop down and we'll forget all about this.

The lads hear footsteps above them, on the roof.

Donkey The cunts are in the attic!

The lads, panicky for the first time, don't know whether to stay on the floor or to stand up.

John Oh shite! We're definitely brownbread now.

Ao They're on the roof.

Plain-clothes You made a mistake, okay, but as long as the Bishop's okay it's not too serious.

Donkey (*to the* **Bishop**) Here, you. This is your fault.

Donkey *crawls towards the* **Bishop**, *to give him a dig.*

Ao Hang on.
(*Roars.*) Get your men off the roof, righ', an' out o' the house or the Bishop's a dead priest.

Ao *nods to* **Donkey,** *and* **Donkey** *pulls the* **Bishop**'*s ear. The* **Bishop** *roars.*

Ao (*roars*) Tha' was the Bishop there. Know wha' I mean?

Plain-clothes (*into the walkie-talkie*) Get them back.
(*Roars.*) Okay; they're going.

Donkey (*to* **Ao**) Again?

Ao Hang on a minute.

They hear the feet on the roof retreating.

Ao They're goin'.

John *is a bit more nervous than the other two.*

John Fuckin' hell. I thought we were dea —brownbread there.

Plain-clothes Okay; they're gone. Is the Bishop okay?

Uniform I don't think they'd really hurt him.

Plain-clothes *stares him out of it.*

Uniform I'd be very surprised if they really hurt him.
The walkie-talkie crackles.

Plain-clothes (*into the walkie-talkie*) Keep them there.

Ao (*roars*) He's grand.

Plain-clothes I want to talk to him, okay.

Donkey He's busy.

Plain-clothes (*annoyed, but trying to sound concerned about the lads*) Look, for Christ's sake, okay.

Uniform For Christ's sake, lads!

Plain-clothes What the hell's going on here, okay? ——Okay.
Look; you've got yourselves into some serious shit here and I, for one, want to get you out of it. So come on, okay.
(*To* **Uniform**.) The "We're all in this thing together" approach.

Donkey (*roars*) Fuck off!

Uniform (*a little bit triumphantly*) It doesn't work with this crowd.

Exit **Uniform**.

John (*imitating* **Plain-clothes**) I, for one, want to get you out of it, okay.

The walkie talkie crackles. **Plain-clothes** *listens.*

Donkey Okay.

Ao Okay.

John Okay.

Donkey (*to the* **Bishop**; *grabbing his ear*) Okay?

Bishop Okay.

Donkey Okay.

Plain-clothes (*roars*) Okay —

The lads laugh.

Ao (*roars*) Okay.

Plain-clothes Look; look. I'm on your side, okay —. Right?

Donkey I don't think so.

Ao Oink oink.

Enter **Uniform**, *crouching, and eating a sandwich.* **Plain-clothes** *is lost for a moment: he'd expected the lads to soften.* **Uniform** *wordlessly and very tentatively offers* **Plain-clothes** *a bite from his sandwich.* **Plain-clothes** *ignores it.*

Plain-clothes (*to* **Uniform**) We'd better establish the bastards' firepower. We might be able to take a run at them.

Uniform Good idea. It's *Aidan* Farrell.

Plain-clothes Have you only the one gun, ——Aidan?

The lads are surprised.

John Jaysis!

Donkey Someone's after rattin'.

John (*imitating* **Plain-clothes**) Okay, Aidan?

Plain-clothes Come on, Aidan. Speak to me. Have you only the one gun?

Ao Yeah. But we've only the one bishop as well.

Donkey Nice one, Ao.

John (*correcting* **Donkey**) Aidan.

Plain-clothes Okay; let's have a look at it.

Donkey No.

Ao *takes the gun from* **Donkey**.

Donkey Give us it back after, righ'.

Ao *carefully shows the gun at the window.*

Uniform It looks real enough. ——Black, like.

Plain-clothes (*to* **Uniform**) It looks like a Browning 9mm. Where the fuck did they get that? Any idea?

Uniform Em, ——it's hard to say.

Plain-clothes (*roars*) Where did you get that little baby?

John (*roars*) In a lucky bag.

Donkey Nice one.

The walkie-talkie crackles.

Plain-clothes (*into the walkie-talkie*) The Provos don't use them.

The walkie-talkie crackles.

Plain-clothes (*into the walkie-talkie*) Okay; right.
(*Roars.*) Can you prove it's the real thing without plugging the Bishop.

Ao *goes carefully to the side of the window. The other lads move so that they can see out.*

Ao D'yeh see tha' light over there at the corner? Outside Mooney's

Uniform (*the local expert; points*) That one there.

Plain-clothes I know.
(*Roars.*) I see it.

Ao Keep watchin' it.

Ao shoots, and there's an almighty bang.

Uniform (*roars*) It's still there.

Ao That's cos I missed it.

Plain-clothes (*the expert*) It's a Browning alright.

Uniform (*agrees*) Tis.

Plain-clothes Jesus Christ.
(*Into the walkie-talkie*) See if you can locate the bullet.
(*Roars.*) Right, Aidan. Let's talk. Come on. Why are you doing this?

Donkey (*to the lads*) That's a good question.

John (*to the lads*) Cos we're fuckin' eejits.

Plain-clothes (*roars*) Aidan —

Offstage **Ao's da,** **Mr Farrell,** *is arriving. He can be heard roaring.*

Plain-clothes (*into the walkie-talkie*) What's going on?

Farrell (*offstage*) I'm his da I'm tellin' yis. ——No, not the Bishop's da. ——Let me through there, pal, please.

Ao Oh fuck. Here's me ol' fella.

Ao dives from the window. **John** *and* **Donkey** *enjoy watching* **Ao.** *They giggle to each other.*

The walkie-talkie crackles.

Plain-clothes (*into the walkie-talkie*) No; don't let him through. I'm trying to —

Enter **Mr Farrell,** *a big man in his early forties. He hasn't had his dinner, so he's angry and impatient.*

Farrell (*to* **Uniform**) Eddie Farrell. Aidan's father. Are they up there, are they?

Uniform That's right.

Plain-clothes (*into the walkie-talkie*) For Christ's sake!

Farrell (*to both Guards*) My Jaysis, wha'. ——They kidnap a bishop an' then they bring him back to one o' their own houses!

Plain-clothes (*smooth; in control*) I'm sorry, Mr Farrell. You'll have to go back behind the —

Farrell (*roars*) Aidan! Aidan Farrell!

John Hate tha', Ao.

Bishop Excuse me.

The lads ignore him. **Ao** *pretends to have a nervous breakdown.*

Farrell Aidan!

The walkie-talkie crackles.

Plain-clothes (*into the walkie-talkie*) No; we'll see what happens.

Farrell Aidan! I'm fuckin' talkin' to yeh!

The lads laugh, to themselves. They like **Mr Farrell.**

Ao (*after a pause*) Howyeh, Da.

Farrell Howyeh!? Wha' d'yeh mean 'Howyeh'!? ——I come home for me fuckin' dinner an' —an' I find your mammy with her nerves in frits. An' your sisters in the hysterics an' —an' no fuckin' dinner. ——So fuck off with your Howyeh. Even the dog was throwin' a wobbler. ——Howyeh! ——An' Charlie Bird in the front fuckin' garden wantin' to interview me!

Donkey Your da's a mad spoon, Ao.

Ao (*roars*) Sorry, Da.

Bishop Excuse me.

17

Farrell Sorry!? Sorry, he says. ——Get down here, yeh little bastard, an' give back tha' Bishop.

Bishop Excuse me.

Plain-clothes You should listen to your father, Aidan.

Donkey (*roars*) You should get lost, pig.

Uniform (*to* **Plain-clothes**) What can you do!

Farrell Donkey. ——Yeh eejit, yeh. What's your mammy an' daddy goin' to say when they find ou' you've been using their house for kidnappin' bishops in?

Donkey It's alrigh', Mister Farrell. They're on their holidays. They won't be back for a week. I'll have it cleaned up ——(*It begins to dawn on* **Donkey** *that it won't be that easy.*) —Oh fuck.

Bishop Excuse me!

Donkey Wha'?

Bishop May I go to the toilet, please?

Donkey (*barks*) No. ——An' come here; if yeh wet the carpet I'll crease yeh.

Donkey *looks around, making sure that the room is tidy. The walkie-talkie crackles.*

Plain-clothes (*into the walkie-talkie*) Tell her they'll wipe their feet. Just get them in.
(*To himself, aloud.*) For Christ's sake!

Uniform *raises his eyes to heaven, agreeing with* **Plain-clothes**.

Farrell Well; are yeh comin' down or wha'?

Ao No Da. Sorry.

Donkey We're beyond the point of no return, Mister Farrell.

Farrell Wha'? Have yis killed the Bishop?

Donkey No.

Farrell Well then; what's your problem? Just bring him down an' we can all go home for the dinner.

Uniform Ah now, it's not as simple as that —

Plain-clothes *thumps* **Uniform**, *to get him to shut up*.

Ao Sorry, Da.

The walkie-talkie crackles.

Plain-clothes (*into the walkie-talkie*) About time. Make sure they stay hidden.

18

Farrell Ah, Aidan; for Jaysis sake.
(*To both Guards.*) He's never done annythin' like this before.

Donkey, *looking out of the window, sees snipers on a roof across the street, offstage.*

Donkey Here! Your men on the roof!

He dives to the floor. The other two follow.

John Oh Jaysis!

Ao (*to* **John**) If you say we're brownbread I'll fuckin' trounce yeh.

Farrell What's the story?

Mr Farrell *sees the snipers on the roof.*

Farrell Oh good Jaysis!

Mr Farrell *hides behind the Guards.*

Donkey They were aimin' at us.

Ao (*being brave*) Billy Mooney's pigeons'll start shitin' on them.
——Where are the curtains?

Donkey In the fuckin' washin' machine.

Plain-clothes (*into the walkie-talkie*) For Christ's sake!

The walkie-talkie crackles.

Plain-clothes (*into the walkie-talkie*) Finished her hoovering!?

The walkie-talkie crackles.

Plain-clothes (*into the walkie-talkie*) Get them off the roof!

Farrell (*to* **Uniform**) Yis aren't goin' to shoot them, are yis?
They're only young fellas.

Uniform Ah no, no. This isn't —

Farrell Miami?

Uniform Yes.

Ao Get your rifles off o' Flanagan's roof or we'll hurt the Bishop.

Donkey *crawls over to the* **Bishop**.

Donkey (*as if to a cat*) Here, Bishop, Bishop, Bishop.

Plain-clothes (*roars*) They're gone. They're gone. It was a mistake.

Mr Farrell *looks to make sure. He has never trusted the Guards.* **Ao**
looks out. The other two watch, half expecting his head to be blown off.

Ao They're gone.

John Where but?

Ao I've an idea.

Farrell (*roars*) Here; why don't yis stick the Bishop in front of the window.

Ao Jaysis! That's wha' I was goin' to say.
(*Roars.*) Hey, Da; that's wha' I was goin' to say.

Farrell Is tha' righ'? That's gas.

The lads carry the **Bishop** *on the chair over to the window and park him there with his back to it.*

Ao There y'are, Your Bishop. Fresh air.

Donkey *gives the fingers to the snipers opposite.*

Donkey Yah! Come on. Come on. Shoot now, yis cunts!

Plain-clothes (*furious*) You're under arrest, Mister Farrell —

Farrell You lay a finger on me, pal, an' the Bishop gets it.
(*Roars.*) Amn't I righ'?

Donkey Yeah. That's righ'.

Bishop This is ridiculous.

Ao I couldn't agree with you more, Your Bishop.

Plain-clothes Mister Farrell. ——My advice to you is to talk to that fuckin' son of yours —

Farrell Wha' d'yeh think I've been doin'? Only youse went and ruined it by stickin' your snipe —your fuckin' snipers up on Flanagan's roof there I'd've hadden them down by now.

Plain-clothes (*through his teeth*) Talk to them.

Farrell I will. I fuckin' will. Just don't crowd me, righ'.

Uniform (*to* **Plain-clothes**) You can see now where they get it from.

Ao What's goin' on?

Donkey Your da's rowin'.

Farrell Aidan.

Ao Da.

Farrell Aidan; why are yeh doin' this?

John (*to the lads*) We'll have to think o' somethin'.

Farrell Arc yeh in the IRA, Aidan?

Ao No way. They're saps.

Donkey Ah here!

Exit **Uniform**. **Plain-clothes** *is listening to the walkie-talkie.* **Mr Farrell** *tries to listen in now and again.*

20

Farrell Or tha' other shower. The I.N. ——yeh know. Whatever they fuckin' call themselves.

Donkey rolls up his sleeve and shows the tattoo he did on himself at the back of the class when he was in second year.

Donkey (*pointing to the tattoo*) Eire nua. Eire bleedin' nua.

John You'd die for Ireland, wouldn't yeh?

Donkey I would in me brown.

Ao (*to Mr Farrell*) No.

Farrell Well, why then?

Ao (*after a pause*) Jobs.

Donkey Wha'!? I don't want a fuckin' job.

Farrell Could yis not look in the paper like everyone else? Or go down to ANCO or somethin'? Jaysis, Aidan, if everyone on the dole started kidnappin' bishops the country'd be in a right fuckin' state. Jaysis, there'd be no one left to say mass.

Donkey I don't want a fuckin' job.
(*To* **John**.) Do you?

John *shrugs.*

The walkie-talkie crackles.

Plain-clothes (*into the walkie-talkie*) Can they get through the wall quickly?

The walkie-talkie crackles.

Plain-clothes (*into the walkie-talkie*) Good. Get back to me if they hear anything interesting, okay.

Ao We just had enough, Da, yeh know. We just had it up to here.

Ao briefly shows his head at the window and puts his hand to his forehead, showing how far he's had it up to.

John Take it easy, Ao. I'll start cryin'.

Donkey Who'd feed me horse?
(*Roars.*) Here! Mister Farrell. Will you feed me horse?

Farrell No, I won't feed your fuckin' horse.

Donkey (*hurt*) Okay. ——Okay. If yeh don't feed me horse then I'll shoot the Bishop.

Farrell Ah, shoot the jaysis Bishop an' we can all go home.

Plain-clothes (*into the walkie-talkie*) Anything yet?

The walkie-talkie crackles.

Plain-clothes (*into the walkie-talkie*) Good. ——Okay.

John (*to the lads*) If yis don't send us up a few brassers we'll shoot the Bishop, wha'.

Ao Good thinkin'. ——Jaysis, Your Bishop, I don't think you're goin' to get out o' here alive.

Bishop (*very bravely*) I put my trust in God.

Ao Then he'd better feed Donkey's horse.

The walkie-talkie crackles.

Plain-clothes (*into the walkie-talkie*) Two sugars. Thanks.

Mr Farrell *hears this.*

Farrell Aidan. Are yeh not goin' to come down?

Ao We can't.

Farrell What about your mammy, Aidan? Have yeh thought about her at all?

Donkey (*to the lads*) That's below the belt, that is.

Farrell (*when no answer comes from* **Ao**) Ah, Aidan. ——For God's sake.
(*Loses temper.*) Yeh fuckin' selfish little bastard yeh! I'm fuckin' starvin'!

Plain-clothes (*taking over*) You can't blame your father for losing his temper, Aidan. ——We all appreciate your problem. I was on the dole myself for quite a while —

John No, you weren't.

Plain-clothes I was —
(*Starting again.*) Look; we all know what you're going through, okay.

John (*imitating* **Plain-clothes**) Okay.

Plain-clothes *is furious but he controls himself.*

Plain-clothes I've three kids myself and —

Donkey Are they bastards as well?

John (*laughing*) Nice one, Donkey.

Ao (*to the lads*) He's goin' to fuckin' kill us when he catches us.

Plain-clothes *now makes one last effort to be 'reasonable'. While he speaks the lads are concentrating on noises they hear from next door. At first* **Mr Farrell** *makes signs and noises of agreement as he listens to* **Plain-clothes**. *But he quickly becomes confused. He raises his*

22

shoulders, and stares at **Plain-clothes** *as if trying to decide if he's a bit odd.*

Plain-clothes Okay, slag away. I don't mind. ——Look. —— Look. ——There's nothing *we* can do about your —— employment thing now. *We're* not the government, you know.

Farrell Exactly.

Plain-clothes Personally, I'd love to say; yeah, sure, we'll get jobs for you. It'd be great. I often worry. About my own kids, you know; what's going to happen them after they leave school. I have a college fees policy, with Irish Life. But to be honest, ——I don't know if Dave is really college material. He's a great little slogger —(*He remembers who he's talking to, and why.*) —— So you know, we know what you're going through. But, let's face it, you've committed a serious fuckin' crime here. Abduction. False imprisonment. It's no joke. We can't let —

John What's the noise?

Donkey Wha'?

They go to the front wall.

Donkey Missis Brady.

John She must have a big gang o' men in there with her.

Donkey Yep; that's Missis Brady alrigh'.

Ao It's the pigs.

John Listenin'.

Donkey (*in a loud 'dumb' voice*) Hey, lads; what'll we do with the bits o' the Bishop we can't get into the bucket?

Ao We'll eat him.

John Rapid! I bags his kiddleys.

The walkie-talkie crackles.

Plain-clothes (*into the walkie-talkie*) What d'you mean they're not listening to me!?

Farrell Aidan! Aidan!

Bishop I think your father wants to speak to you.

Ao Thanks.
    (*Roars.*) Wha'?

Farrell Will yeh listen to the man here, for Jaysis sake.

Ao Sorry. ——Go on.

Plain-clothes (*more formal —a bit hurt because the lads haven't been listening to him*) There's going to be no deals done.

Ao Hear tha', Your Bishop?

Plain-clothes At the moment you've got abduction and false

23

imprisonment under your belt. That's serious. The longer you stay up there the more serious it gets. The longer you keep the Bishop the more serious it gets. Touch the Bishop —

Donkey *gently touches the* **Bishop** *with a finger; and the* **Bishop** *jumps.*

Plain-clothes —and you'll be old men before —

The walkie-talkie crackles.

Plain-clothes (*into the walkie-talkie*) Yoh; talk to me.

The walkie-talkie crackles.

Plain-clothes (*into the walkie-talkie*) Interesting. Let her through. (*To the lads.*) Which one of you is Jonathan?

Ao (*puzzled*) None of us.

John (*To himself*) Oh fuck.

Ao Bishop. Pardon. What's your name?

Bishop Fergus.

John It's me.

Donkey Wha'!?

Enter **Mrs Murray**, **John**'s *mother; an appalling, overpowering person. Everything about her should scream 'I am middle class and it is the right way to be!'.* **Uniform** *follows* **Mrs Murray**, *trying desperately to look in charge; showing her the way although she's in front.*

John (*shattered*) Oh no. ——Oh no.

Mr Farrell *studies* **Mrs Murray**, *interested and puzzled. She was good looking once;* **Mr Farrell** *thinks so anyway. He's seen her before.*

Donkey The state of *her*.

Plain-clothes Missis Murray?

Mrs Murray Yes.

Plain-clothes (*pointing*) Your son is up there.

Plain-clothes *offers* **Mrs Murray** *the megaphone.*

Mrs Murray No, thank you. ——Jonathan!

John Oh no, ——please.

Ao What's goin' on?

Donkey Yeah.

Ao Is tha' your ma?

Mrs Murray Jonathan.

Plain-clothes Jonathan, your mother wants to talk to you.

Donkey What's this 'Jonathan' shite? Your name's Johnner.

Mrs Murray Jonathan, show yourself at the window, please.

Farrell (*to* **Mrs Murray**) Howyeh.

John I'm not talkin' to her.

Ao *sort of understands.*

Ao (*roars*) He's not here.

Mrs Murray (*pointing offstage*) He must be. That's his bicycle.

Farrell (*to* **Mrs Murray**) Yeh prob'ly don't remember me.

Mrs Murray Jonathan; answer me, please.

Ao (*to* **John**) Go on.

Farrell (*to* **Mrs Murray**) Yeh called round to our place a while back. Collectin'. For a sale o' work or somethin'.

Mrs Murray *looks at* **Mr Farrell** *for the first time.*

Farrell We —the wife —gave yeh a can o' pineapple chunks.

Mrs Murray (*coldly polite*) Really? Yes, I think I —

Farrell I said we'd been hangin' onto them till Bob Geldof called round but I was only messin'. D'yeh remember me?

Mrs Murray (*only too well*) Yes.

Farrell Eddie Farrell. ——My young fella's up there with your young fella.

Mrs Murray (*trying not to sound too appalled*) Really?

Farrell Right little bastards, aren't they?

John *is now at the window, looking at the space in front of* **Mrs Murray**; *not at her.*

Plain-clothes There he is, Mrs Murray.

Uniform Up there, Mrs Murray; look.

Mrs Murray (*giving out; furious*) Jonathan.

John Hello, ——Mam.
  (*Trying to save face.*) Howyeh, Ma.

The **Bishop** *giggles.*

John What're *you* laughin' at?

Mrs Murray Well? ——Would you like to explain yourself, please.

Ao *and* **Donkey** *watch, fascinated. They're discovering that they don't know* **John** *as well as they thought they did.*

John We're protestin'–ing, Ma—Mam.

25

Farrell Me arse.

He looks to **Mrs Murray**, *expecting her to agree.*

Mrs Murray Don't be ridiculous. About what, please?

Farrell They're lookin' for jobs, if yeh don't mind.

John *is still acutely embarrassed: he's been found out.*

Donkey (*looking out; to* **John**) You said your ma did cleanin'.

Mrs Murray Is what this man says true, Jonathan?

John ——Yeah.

Mrs Murray That's ridiculous. You're going to college in October. (*To* **Plain-clothes** *and* **Mr Farrell**.) He's repeating three subjects in Leeson Street. He nearly got the points last year but he failed Irish. The teacher was never in.

Farrell Go 'way.

Ao (*to* **John**) You told us —

John I'm not. ——Shite!

Uniform I'd a teacher like that.

Mrs Murray Jonathan; get down here at once.

Farrell Yeah. ——An' bring the Bishop with yeh.

John (*seeing the lads looking at him; pleading*) I'm adopted.

Ao Don't start.

Mrs Murray Jonathan!

John Fuck her; I hate her!

Ao (*roars*) Hang on.

Farrell Tha' was my young fella. Aidan. He's never done annythin' like this before. ——The poor oul' Bishop must've got a terrible fright all the same.

Ao (*to* **John**) What's the story?

John (*close to tears*) It's her. ——She's an awful fuckin' snob.

The walkie-talkie crackles.

Plain-clothes (*into the walkie-talkie*) A row? Good.

The walkie-talkie crackles.

Plain-clothes (*into the walkie-talkie*) Okay. Good idea. (*To* **Mrs Murray**) Excuse me, Missis Murray. Do you think you could talk a bit more to Jonathan, okay?

John *looks as if he could start crying.*

26

Mrs Murray I most certainly could. Jonathan; I don't intend staying here all day. Now I really think that you've mortified myself and your father enough for one day and I'm sure Bishop Treacy has had quite enough of this childishness so if you don't mind would yourself and your friends ——and, by the way, I don't know what sort of a crowd you've got yourself involved with ——.

Ao Get your act together; come on.

John I'm alrigh'. ——She's ruinin' everythin'. Why won't she let me live me own life?

Donkey Tell her to fuck off.

Ao Shut up, Donkey.

Donkey That's what I'd tell my ma.

Ao Yeah would in your bollix. ——

Plain-clothes (*into the walkie-talkie*) Anything yet?

The walkie-talkie crackles.

Mrs Murray I mean, you used to have quite nice friends. Donal. He was a very nice boy. I knew when I said you could go to that bloody disco thing I was making a mistake. I said it to Des. When you gave up the Sea Scouts ——. I'm sure the people here are very *nice* people but they're —just —not —your —type.

Ao This is pat'etic. We're goin' to give up cos your ma says you're to go home.

John No; no way. I'm not goin' down. An' I'm not goin' to *college* either. I don't care. Me bollix. An' I didn't *nearly* get the points. I got seven.

Farrell (*to* **Plain-clothes**) Hey; would your mot talk as much as tha'?

Plain-clothes She wouldn't be let.

They laugh; 'man's' laughter. **Uniform** *tries to join in.* **Mrs Murray** *stares them out of it.*

Mrs Murray You were always easily led. Always. That's your big problem. You've no mind of your own. If they told you to stick your head in the oven you'd do it. You've even picked up that —*accent*. —— And don't for one minute think that you're not going to college. Because you are.

Donkey Gerry Delaney said you were one o' the biggest thicks in your class.

John I know. I fuckin' know. But she won't believe me.

Ao Will yeh pass the Leavin' this time?

John Not at all. I haven't a clue.

Mrs Murray (*to* **Mr Farrell**) He's going to do a Communications degree in Rathmines.

Farrell Oh lovely. Very nice.

Plain-clothes (*into the walkie-talkie*) Are they giving up yet?

The walkie-talkie crackles.

Plain-clothes (*into the walkie-talkie*) Jesus; the rest of us are.

Mrs Murray Now, I'm sure Bishop Treacy has more confirmations to do today so come down this minute, please.

Ao Well then. What's your problem?

John Ah —. She'll buy a fuckin' college or somethin'. Or get me da to build one in the back.

Donkey Yeh told us your da was dead!

John (*embarrassed again*) Ah Jaysis ——. I'm sorry, righ'. ——I —

Ao (*in authority*) Righ'; come on. Tell her to go an' shite. ——Go on.

Donkey Rapid!

Ao Go on.

John I can't.

Ao Are yeh one o' the lads or wha'?

Donkey Yeah.

Mrs Murray Jonathan!

The lads and the **Bishop** *are braced.*

Mrs Murray Jonathan!!

John Go —— Go an' shite, Ma.

The lads cheer, laugh and pat **John** *on the back.* **Mr Farrell** *laughs.*

John Go an' shite, Ma!

Farrell Jaysis, Missis; that's a terrible cheeky pup yeh have there.

John Just go an' shite!

Mrs Murray How —dare —you!

Plain-clothes (*into the walkie-talkie*) How are things in the room?

The walkie-talkie crackles.

Plain-clothes (*into the walkie-talkie*) Shit!

The walkie-talkie crackles.

Plain-clothes (*into the walkie-talkie*) Leadership qualities!? Shit!

John I'm not comin' down, an' I'm not goin' home, an' I'm not goin' to college, an' go an' shite.

Donkey Yeow!

Mrs Murray Get down here this minute!

John No.

Donkey Yeow!!

Mrs Murray You just wait there. I'm coming up.

John *grabs the gun from* **Donkey.** *His new bravery and terror clash, and he becomes hysterical.*

John (*grabbing the gun*) Give us tha'!

Mrs Murray *strides towards the house.* **John** *roars, and shoots. The* **Bishop** *roars: the gun goes off right beside his head.* **Mrs Murray** *is hit in the foot. She roars, screams, falls, screams and roars.*

Farrell Oh, good fuck!

Exit **Mr Farrell** *and* **Uniform,** *in a hurry.*

Plain-clothes *throws himself on the ground. He looks up. He gets up and goes, hunched, to* **Mrs Murray.**

Plain-clothes (*loud*) Okay; okay. ——Okay. ——Okay.

Mrs Murray *is screaming, crying, roaring, screaming.* **John,** *at the window, is blubbering. The* **Bishop** *is trying not to.* **Donkey** *is fascinated, appalled and delighted.*

Donkey Did he hit her? Did he hit her? ——For fuck sake!

Bishop (*mumbling*) Oh blessed Mary, mother of Jesus, intercede on my behalf —

Ao Shut up!

John (*loud, but to himself*) Now. ——Now.

Ao He's after shootin' his ma. ——You're after shootin' your ma.

Mrs Murray *is, understandably, making a lot of high-pitched noise.* **Plain-clothes** *is looking at her wound, trying to quieten her.*

The walkie-talkie crackles.

Plain-clothes (*into the walkie-talkie*) Can they do it in time?

The walkie-talkie crackles.

Plain-clothes (*into the walkie-talkie*) Okay; stand by.

Ao *and* **Donkey** *look at each other. They laugh nervously.* **Ao** *is wondering if he should get the gun from* **John.** **John** *looks as if he's daydreaming, staring out the window.*

Ao You're not goin' to shoot her again, are yeh?

John *looks at* **Ao** *but he doesn't answer, as if he doesn't know what he's been asked. He looks out the window again. The* **Bishop** *is still mumbling.*

Ao She's learnt her lesson.
  (*To the* **Bishop**.) Would you ever shut up.

Plain-clothes (*roars*) Stretcher!
  (*To the lads.*) We're taking her off the street, okay. Don't shoot, okay.

Enter **Uniform**, *pushing a stretcher on wheels.*

Uniform It's only me lads; don't shoot. —Eh; here we are.

Uniform *and* **Plain-clothes** *load* **Mrs Murray** *onto the stretcher.*

Uniform Oh God, you can see the bone!

Mrs Murray *screams, and* **Uniform** *covers her mouth.*

Plain-clothes (*into the walkie-talkie*) Right. Go for it.

Immediately hammering is heard coming from behind the back wall, although the lads don't notice it at first.

John (*roars; half crying*) Why wouldn't yeh let me get tints in me hair? ——Wha' did yeh do with me communion money, yeh wagon? ——Why wouldn't yeh give me a dog for me birthday? ——The collected works o' Charles fuckin' Dickens!

John *braces himself to shoot at* **Mrs Murray** *again as the Guards scoot offstage with her on the stretcher.* **Ao**, *then* **Donkey**, *lunge at him. They get him to the ground.* **Ao** *gets the gun from* **John**. *All the while, the* **Bishop** *is very agitated; terrified. Then, sprawled on the ground, the lads notice the banging next door. Men on the other side are trying to hammer through.* **Ao** *is the first to realise what is happening.*

Ao What the fuck!

Ao *gets up with the gun in his hand and dashes to the window.*

Ao (*roars*) Here! Get your men ou' —

When **Ao** *looks out the window he sees the snipers across the street, hanging out of windows, aiming at him.* **Ao** *dives. He then stands up in the corner to the side of the window and puts the gun to the* **Bishop**'s *head.*

The hammering continues.

Ao (*roars; almost in a frenzy*) Get your men to stop knockin' the wall down an' get your men out o' Flanagan's or I'm goin' to shoot the Bishop! ——Now, righ'! ——Now!!

The **Bishop** *has had it: he begins to wail.*

John (*on his knees*) It looks like we're brownbread now an'annyway.

The hammering stops.

Silence.

The **Bishop***'s wailing becomes faint.* **Ao** *very carefully looks out the window.*

Ao Gone.

Donkey Oh, thank Jaysis.

Donkey *begins to giggle. The* **Bishop** *is crying and snuffling.* **Ao** *lifts the* **Bishop***'s cassock and puts it to his nose.*

Ao Blow.

The **Bishop** *blows.*

Sam the Sham and The Pharaohs sing 'The Hair On My Chinny Chin Chin'.

The lights go down quickly.

PART TWO

It is night outside the bedroom, and quiet. The odd light or faint siren from offstage suggests the presence of the Guards. **Ao** *and* **John** *are onstage.* **John** *is wearing the* **Bishop**'s *mitre.* **Ao** *is lounging on the bed.* **John** *is sitting on the floor, leaning against the wall. Some tin trays, the remains of a Chinese take-away, are lying around. There are also some four-pack cans of lager.* **Ao** *and* **John** *are relaxing, looking at the ceiling or floor; not talking.* **John** *very softly sings an adaptation of 'The Smurfs' Song'.*

John (*sings*) Do we wear our hats in bed?
　　No, we ride our mots instead —

John *stops singing.* **Ao** *scrapes the last of the goo from his tray and swallows it. He throws the tray onto the floor.*

Ao Tha' was grand. ——I'll tell yeh one thing; I was fuckin' starvin'.

John Yeah.

Ao (*to* **John**) Kidnappin' gives yeh an appetite alrigh', wha'.

John Yeah. ——An' shootin' your ma.

Ao *laughs.*

John I shouldn't've done tha'.

Ao Ah, she'll be alrigh'. Don't worry abou' it. ——She was lookin' for it an'annyway.

John Yeah. I suppose so. ——I'm sorry abou' ——lyin', yeh know.

Ao Forget abou' it. I don't blame yeh.

Plain-clothes (*from offstage; through a megaphone*) We can't see the Bishop. Where is the Bishop?

Ao *goes to the window.*

Ao (*roars*) He's in the jacks.
　　(*Roars.*) Donkey; how's the Bishop?

Donkey (*from offstage, right*) He'll be ou' in a minute.

Ao (*roars*) He'll be ou' in a minute.

John He's just wipin' his arse.

Ao (*roars, but he can't finish because he's laughing*) He's —— He's ——

*A flush is heard offstage, right. Enter **Donkey** through the bedroom door, leading the **Bishop** who is still blindfolded.*

Ao Good man, Your Bishop. Are yeh feelin' better after tha'?

Bishop Yes, thank you.

Ao Good. The oul' Chinese goes through yeh like a greyhound on skates, wha'.

Donkey He wants to know will we take the blindfold off him. Cos they all know who we are.

*The **Bishop** is put sitting down, and tied.*

Ao No funny stuff, righ'?

Bishop No; no.

Ao Okay?

The lads nod.

Ao Okay.

John (*imitating **Plain-clothes***) Okay.

Donkey *removes the blindfold.*

Donkey Howyeh.

Bishop (*blinking*) Eh, ——hello.

*The **Bishop** sees that it is dark outside.*

Bishop Good evening.

Donkey (*like an English butler*) Good evening.

Donkey *picks up a can of lager.*

Donkey (*to the **Bishop***) D'yeh want some?

Bishop No; no. ——Just a little swallow, perhaps.

Donkey Yeh may as well.

Donkey *pours some lager into the **Bishop**'s mouth.*

John Be careful, Donkey. He might bite yeh.

Donkey (*to the Bishop*) There.

Donkey *wipes the **Bishop**'s chin with his sleeve.*

Bishop Many thanks.

Ao One'll do him, Your Bishop.

Donkey (*to the **Bishop***) Would yeh mind if I called yeh Fergus?

Bishop Em, ——no.

Donkey Just as well for yourself.

John (*thinking of something brilliant*) Here!

John *sings his version of Paul Simon's 'You Can Call Me Al'.*

John (*sings*) I can call you Fergus
          And Fergus when you call me
          You can call me —Donkey —

Donkey Ha ha; nice one.

Donkey *starts to do the saxophone sounds from 'You Can Call Me Al', and* **Ao** *joins in.* **Ao** *does Chevy Chase's elbows routine from the promotional video, and nudges the* **Bishop***, trying to get him to join in. Then they stop.*

Ao (*after a pause*) It's calmed down a bit now.

Bishop Yes.

Ao Just as well, wha'.

Bishop Yes.

Ao I don't know abou' you but I'll tell yeh one thing. I couldn't live life at tha' pace all the time.

Bishop No.

Ao I'd've shotten yeh there, yeh know.

Bishop Yes, ——I know.

Donkey He would've. So would I'ave.

Ao No offence, like.

Bishop No; ——none taken.

Donkey D'yeh want some more, Fergus?

Bishop No. ——Thank you. It's a bit awkward.

John We could tie his legs —. We could tie your legs while you're drinkin'.

Ao Good thinkin'.

Donkey He might try an' leg it.

Ao No, he won't. Sure yeh won't?

Bishop No; ——no.

Donkey Yeh'd better not.

John *unties the* **Bishop**'s *hands, and then ties his legs to the legs of the chair.* **Donkey** *picks up a four-pack.*

Donkey Why do they call them six-packs when there's only four in
them?

John turns to **Ao**, *to laugh at* **Donkey**. *But* **Donkey**, *who had been
joking, catches* **John** *at it.*

Donkey Hah! Yeh bollix.
    (*Looking around.*) The mess in here.

Donkey *starts tidying up the tin trays, and finds some spilt goo on the
floor.*

Donkey Ah Jaysis, yis sloppy cunts yis! Which one o' yis done
    tha'?

John The Bishop. ——Leave it. It looks like one o' your da's puke
    stains.

Donkey Would I be able to get down to the kitchen for a J-cloth?
    Wha' d'yeh think?

Ao Don't be thick. The pigs are in the kitchen. Leave it. ——
    You're a rebel.

Donkey So's me ma.

John (*imitating* **Donkey**) Give us a J-cloth or we'll shoot the
    Bishop.

Donkey Fuck off, you.

John *finishes tying the* **Bishop**'s *legs. The* **Bishop** *tries his best to look
as if he's enjoying the crack.*

John There y'are.

Bishop Many thanks. ——Thank you.

Donkey (*handing the* **Bishop** *a can*) There's a can o' leg opener for
    yeh, Fergus.

Ao (*amused*) Take it easy, will yeh.

Bishop Thank you very ——em —

The **Bishop** *holds and studies the can as if he's never seen one before;
looking for the way in.*

Donkey There's a yoke at the top.

Bishop Ah, yes.

Donkey Yeh pull it.

Bishop Yes.

The **Bishop** *manages to open the can.*

John Well done.

Ao *goes over to the window.*

Ao (*roars*) Excuse me.

Plain-clothes (*from offstage*) We hear you.

Ao Thanks very much for the dinners.

Plain-clothes (*from offstage*) Okay.

John (*imitating* **Plain-clothes**) Okay.

Ao *jumps onto the bed.*

Ao (*lifting his can*) Cheers.

Donkey Cheers.

Bishop Cheers.

John (*in a Cockney accent*) Cheers, my son.

Ao Yeh know why they gave us these, don't yis?

John To get us locked.

Donkey Take more than tha' to get *us* locked, wha'.

Ao Fuckin' sure.

Donkey Did they get them in H. Williamses?

Ao How would I know!?

Donkey I was only wonderin'. ——D'yis know your woman tha' works in the off-licence in H. Williamses, do yis? ——Tina.

John Ah, she's gorgeous, she is. I'd give her me last Rolo.

Ao Who is she?

John (*winking at* **Ao**) Tina. ——From H. Williams.

Ao Oh, yeah. She's the one tha' scrapes the muck off the spuds, isn't she?

Donkey Fuck off, you. I bought me first flagon off Tina. I seen her on the DART there Saturday.

John Yeow!

Donkey Fuck off.
(*Bewildered.*) She was with tha' sap, Paddy Delaney. ——Daley Thompson Delaney. ——D'yis remember in school when he broke his bollix doin' the long jump?

They laugh. **Ao** *nudges the* **Bishop,** *and the* **Bishop** *joins in.* **Donkey** *sees him.*

Donkey What're *you* fuckin' laughin' at!?

Ao *and* **John** *roar laughing.* **Donkey** *points at the* **Bishop.**

Donkey You watch your step, pal.

John Don't mind him, Your Bishop. He's in love.

Donkey Fuck off. At least I didn't shoot me ma.

Ao Your ma's in Spain, yeh sap. You'd want to be a good fuckin' shot.

Donkey Fuck off.

John (*in a TV quiz show presenter voice*) Ao, are you ready to play 'Blockbusters'?

Ao Yes, Bob.

John What F.E. always falls in love with young ones that are older than him and are goin' with young fellas that are bigger than him?

Ao (*thinking hard*) Em ——F.E. ——F.E. ——Ah! Fuckin' Eejit!

John Yesss!

John *and* **Ao** *do the 'Blockbusters' music.*

John Tha' was a close one, Ao.

Ao Gosh yes, Bob. A bit too jolly fuckin' close. Did I win annythin'?

John Yes indeed, Ao.

Ao Not another trip to Singapore, is it?

John No. You have a choice.

Ao Yeah; go on.

John You must choose between a set of encyclopaedias or —— your hole off Whitney Houston!

Ao (*in agony*) Oh, decisions, decisions, decisions!

John We'll have to hurry you up, Ao.

Ao Hang on a minute, Bob. Is Whitney Houston tha' young one tha' works in the off-licence in H. Williams?

Donkey Fuck off. ——They're like kids, aren't they, Fergus?

John (*sings a version of the 'Skippy' theme*) Tina —Tina —Tina the bush kangaroooooo! —Tina —Tina —

Ao *laughs, and bounces like a kangaroo while* **John** *sings; and sticks his teeth out.* **Donkey** *laughs, because he's already made an eejit of himself by admitting that he fancies Tina.* **John** *makes Skippy noises, and sticks his teeth out; implying that Tina is prominent in the teeth department.*

Donkey Ah, that's not fair.

John She'll staple Paddy Delaney's lips together.

Donkey *enjoys that remark.*

Ao Were yeh ever in love yourself, Your Bishop?

Bishop (*trying to be 'nice'*) Ah no. ——No.

Donkey You're not a pig's ear, are yeh?

John Jaysis!

Bishop I'm sorry, eh, Donkey. I don't understand.

Donkey Are yeh a queer?

Bishop I most definitely am not! ——I —

Donkey Yeah? Go on. Tell us.

Ao (*to* **Donkey**) Leave him alone.
   (*To the* **Bishop**.) He's only slaggin' yeh.

Donkey There was a priest here once. ——Here. An' he was a
   queer.

Ao Shut up, Donkey.

Donkey Well, he was. Father —

Ao Donkey!
   (*Pointing to the* **Bishop**; *secretly*.) He's his boss.

Donkey Oh, yeah. ——Ah, he wasn't too bad. He oney —

Ao Donkey!

A short pause, punctuated by the odd giggle from the lads.

Ao (*enjoying himself*) Were yeh ever on the DART, Your Bishop?

Bishop No, I ——. No.

Donkey Were yeh not!? ——Jaysis.

Ao It's very good.

Bishop I believe so.

Ao It's a very efficient and reliable service.

Donkey Yeow!

John It's a rapid transit system.

Donkey *leans over and thumps* **John**.

Donkey Were yeh ever in a plane?

Bishop Yes.

Donkey So wha'?

The lads laugh.

Donkey D'yeh think you're great, do yeh?

Ao He's only messin', Your Bishop. Don't mind him.

Donkey Were yeh ever in Blackpool?

Bishop Blackpool in England?

Donkey Oh, good Jaysis! I give up.

John Were yeh ever in Africa?

Bishop Yes.

Donkey Is it anny good, is it?

The lads laugh.

Bishop Em; I don't know if I'd really describe it as —

Donkey Are there anny good disco bars?

*The **Bishop** smiles and forces himself to laugh.*

Ao Were yeh ever in a disco, Your Bishop?

Bishop No.

Donkey Yeh haven't missed much.

Ao *and* **John** *grin at each other.*

John (*sings*) Tina —Tina —

Donkey Ah, lay off.

Bishop I wonder, lads —

Donkey Wha' d'yeh do after your tea?

Bishop Eh ——; I'm not sure what you mean, Donkey.

Donkey Do yeh go ou'?

Ao Don't be thick, Donkey. He's a sap, Your Bishop.
(*To* **Donkey**.) I suppose yeh think he sits on the wall outside
his gaff an' smokes, do yeh?

Donkey No!

Ao Wha' then?

Donkey I was only wonderin' wha' he does; that's all.

Ao Mind your own fuckin' business. Would you like it if the
Bishop started askin' *you* questions like tha'?

Donkey I couldn't give a shite.

John D'yeh follow football, Your Bishop.

Bishop Oh, yes.

John Who d'yeh follow?

Bishop Carlow.

The lads crack up. Nothing is said for a while except:

John Carlow!

(*Pointing to the* **Bishop**.) It's life Jim but not as we know it
—not as we know it —not as we know it —

The three lads (*sing*) There's klingons on the starboard bow
—starboard bow —starboard bow —

Bishop Would you mind, lads, if I ——. If we were to stop this
now —

Ao (*definitely, but humorously*) No.

Donkey No way.

Bishop (*retreating*) Alright.
(*Advancing.*) But, lads, ——do you not see how you're ——
walking yourselves into quite dreadful, dreadful trouble?

The lads shrug and look at each other, and shrug.

Bishop A period in jail.

The lads shrug.

Bishop Ten years?

No reaction.

Bishop You'll be unemployable.

The lads grin, looking at the **Bishop** *as if he's a bit simple.* **Ao** *laughs.*

Bishop (*retreating*) Alright. ——But d'you mind me asking —.
Why did you, eh, *kid*nap me?

The lads sit up: this could be fun. They look to **Ao** *for the answer.*

Ao Well, we had the gun, an' you were in Barrytown doin' the
confirmations, an' there was nothin' on the telly; yeh know;
snooker or cricket —

John Or 'Live At Three' with Derek an' Thelma.

Ao So we said, "Fuck it; let's kidnap him". ——An' that's it
really.

John Yeah; that's it.

Bishop Oh. ——So, Ao, you did it because you had nothing else to
do. Is that right?

Ao No; not really.

The **Bishop** *looks lost.*

Ao I'd say we'd've done it annyway. Even if there had been
snooker on.

Donkey Snooker's borin'.

Bishop You did it because you were bored.

Ao ——No.

Bishop You said something about jobs to the police.

Ao I just *said* tha'. ——That's just an excuse, like. ——I wouldn't mind a job but. The few bob, yeh know.

John Yeah.

Ao I'm sick o' buyin' me kaks in Dunnes. Three pairs a year.

Donkey My ma buys my kaks.

Ao In Dunnes.

Donkey Yeah.

Ao (*proving his point*) There.

Donkey Where else would yeh get your kaks?

John *laughs.*

Ao (*explaining to the* **Bishop**) Donkey doesn't want a job.

Bishop (*nicely*) Why not?

Donkey I just don't.

John It'd force him to change his lifestyle.

Donkey Yeah; that's it.

Bishop (*to* **Donkey**) You have a horse.

Donkey Sort of. I've shares in one.

The lads laugh. The **Bishop** *is lost.*

Bishop (*starting again*) The gun.

Donkey It's a real one.

Bishop Yes.

Donkey (*pointing to* **John**) Ask his ma.

Ao You want to know where we got it, don't yeh?

Bishop Yes ——

Ao Ah, ha ha!
(*After a pause.*) We found it.
(*Suspecting the* **Bishop** *doesn't believe him.*) Swear to God.

John On the bible.

Ao We found it in the field. ——Beside the shops. It was under an ol' pram, yeh know.

As **Ao** *explains, the* **Bishop** *looks more and more lost.*

Ao In a plastic bag. With the bullets, in an oily cloth. Donkey was lookin' for his golf ball an' *he* found it.

Donkey I found me golf ball as well.

Bishop And you didn't bring it to the Guards.

Donkey No way. They'd've kept it. ——Johnner shot a cat with it yesterday.

John I wasn't aimin' at it. It got in the way. I meant to hit O'Driscoll's jacks window.

Bishop Why?

Donkey (*as if it was a stupid question*) Cos Billy O'Driscoll was in there.

Bishop Oh, ——I see. You don't like Billy O'Driscoll.

Donkey We do. He's dead on.

*The lads are really enjoying the **Bishop**'s efforts to understand them.*

Ao He was sittin' down, so the bullet wouldn't've hit him.

John We were doin' him a favour. Frightenin' the shite ou' of him.

*The **Bishop** joins in in the laughter.*

Bishop So ——. Let me see. You decided to abduct me because you had a gun.

Ao (*not convinced*) Sort of; yeah.

Donkey An' the free gaff.

Bishop (*lost*) Gaff?

Donkey *stands up to get a can and discovers that he has a dead leg.*

Donkey Jaysis!
(*Walking 'like an Egyptian'.*) Walk like a Cambodian.

Ao Don't mind him, Your Bishop.

Ao *now tries to explain to the **Bishop** the thrill of doing something you shouldn't do.*

Ao Did yeh ever rob ann'thin'?

Bishop No.

Donkey Wha'? Never?

Bishop Well, no; no.

Donkey Yeh lyin' bollix.

John Not even an orchard?

Bishop Yes; well, yes. I did takc apples from an orchard. ——On more than one occasion.

Ao Good man.

Donkey There now.

Bishop That's hardly 'robbing' as such.

Donkey Robbin's robbin'.

John (*slagging* **Donkey**.) That's true wha' Donkey said. Robbin's robbin'.

Donkey Fuck off, you.

Ao (*to the* **Bishop**) D'yeh remember runnin' away from the orchard?

Donkey Yeah; with the apples down your jumper.

John Or even up your jumper.

Donkey *wonders if he has just been slagged.*

Ao D'you remember it?

Bishop Yes.

Ao It was great, wasn't it?

Bishop (*pleased*) Yes.

They all grin.

John D'yeh know O'Neills, do yeh; the shoe shop place on Talbot Street?

Bishop ——I think so.

John We robbed a Doc —a boot —out o' there; one; only one o' them. An' we legged it down Talbot Street. An' your man was after us all the way down as far as ——fuckin' —the corner. An' it was brilliant. Wasn't it?

Donkey Yeah; it was brilliant.
(*After a pause.*) D'yeh know why they're called Doc Martens?

Bishop No.

Donkey Cos a fella called Doctor Marten invented them. For spas.

Bishop Really? ——Is kidnapping me a bit like robbing apples?

Ao (*not fully convinced*) Yeah. Sort of.

Donkey What's he on abou'?

Bishop One thing puzzles me. ——Why didn't you demand money, a ransom, in exchange for me?

Donkey That's a fuckin' brilliant idea!

John Jaysis, yeah! We never thought o' tha'.

Donkey Better than fuckin' jobs annyway, wha'.

Ao God, we're thick. How much d'yeh think, Your Bishop?

The **Bishop** *looks more and more like he regrets having put the idea into their heads, but tries not to.*

John Thousands.

Donkey Fifty thousand.

Ao How much is tha' each, Donkey?

Donkey Ah here! A good bit.

Ao (*going to the window*) Righ'.

Offstage, 'all hell' breaks loose: lights, sirens go on and off etc. The lads and the **Bishop** *dive to the floor, the* **Bishop** *bringing the chair down with him.*

Enter **Mr Farrell** *below, in a hurry.*

Farrell Aidan! Aidan!

Ao (*from the floor; roars*) Wha'? What's up?

Farrell You're fucked now. You're rightly fucked now. The Bishop —the Bishop's a Yank.

Ao Wha!?
(*To the lads.*) What's he on abou'?
(*To the* **Bishop.**) He says you're a Yank.

Bishop I *was* born in the New York in actual fact. Although my parents, God rest them, came back to Ireland when I was still a baby.

Farrell Are yeh listenin' to me? Aidan! He's a Yank.

Bishop But I suppose that makes me a citizen of the United States. I have a US passport.

Farrell He's a fuckin' Yank, I'm tellin' yeh.

Ao (*to the lads*) So wha'?
(*To* **Mr Farrell.**) So wha?

Farrell They want him back.

Donkey They can fuck off.

Ao (*to* **Mr Farrell**) So?

Farrell So they're after invadin' Dollymount!

The sound of an approaching helicopter is heard, and passes over the house. Two dim figures enter and pull **Mr Farrell** *offstage.*

Farrell Get your fuckin' hands off me!

Exit **Mr Farrell**. *The helicopter sound fades. Nothing is said onstage for a moment, but the fear is obvious on all faces.*

John The radio.

John *crawls to the radio and turns it on just as a rock song ends. The Dave Fanning show is on.*

Fanning That was —what was that? ——The Islamic Jihad with 'Rock Me Sideways Baby'. Right, now we're going over to Nuala in the newsroom.

Nuala Thank you, Dave. Reports are coming in that an advance force of United States Marines has occupied Bull Island in Dublin Bay. Earlier today President Reagan, speaking from the White House, said that America could not and would not stand by and watch Americans being mauled by Libyan-backed agents of terror. This is believed to have been a reference to the abduction of Bishop Fergus Treacy, Auxiliary Bishop of Dublin, this morning by three armed youths in the Barrytown area of north Dublin. Gardai at Clontarf station say that there are no reports of any casualties but sources at Raheny station admit to being worried that one of their men failed to report back after his tea. So, that headline again. Bull Island in Dublin has been occupied by a force of US Marines. We'll have a full report at nine.

Fanning Thanks, Nuala. ——Gosh! ——Here's The Corporation Workmen on demo.

John *turns off the radio as the music starts.*

Donkey Fuckin' hell.

John *(scared)* Yeh know wha' we are now, don't yis?

Bishop *(trying not to look too pleased)* Eh ——brown —bread?

The lights go down as the lads stare at the **Bishop**. *A helicopter is heard approaching.*

45

Act Two

PART ONE

The Doors play 'The End'.

It is the day after the invasion; afternoon. The **Bishop** *is standing up on the chair, arms outstretched; as much of him as possible blocking the window.* **Ao** *is standing right up against him, the gun placed firmly at the* **Bishop***'s stomach.* **Donkey** *is sitting at the bedroom door, keeping guard.* **John** *is lying on the bed. They have been like this (but swapping positions; except for the* **Bishop***) all night and day since the invasion. They are tired, very hungry, nervous, but far from ready to give up. Nothing has happened since the invasion.*

The music fades, and whirring helicopter blades and motors become the predominant sounds. The lads look up as the helicopter passes over them; then the helicopter fades, but doesn't die completely. The radio is on: Charlie Bird is describing the Marine Corps camp on Bull Island. The lads are half-listening and commenting.

Charlie Bird From my position here I can see five Sikorsky Night Hawk helicopters stationary on the fairway. And there are three, no, four more in the air. I can clearly see a large gun, possibly a Gattling or a Howitzer —

Donkey A Howitzer! Jaysis.

Charlie Bird —protruding from the side door of one of the helicopters.

Donkey (*not joking*) Fuckin' hell. The business, wha'.

Charlie Bird The helicopters are a chilling sight. So graceful yet so menacing. ——A jeep has come over the dunes to my right! And another one! They're going towards the club-house.

John So wha'!

Charlie Bird The dunes are blocking my view of a large part of the combat base but there must be at least a thousand men here.

Ao There'll be no ridin' there tonigh', wha'.

The lads laugh half-heartedly.

Charlie Bird The base is like a small busy town.

John (*scornful*) Jesus! With soldiers an' fuckin' helicopters in it!

Charlie Bird I'm now being approached by two Marines. One of them appears to be a sergeant. ——Yes, he's a sergeant.

Donkey Shoot the fuckin' eejit.

Charlie Bird Both men are armed.

Donkey Good.

Charlie They want me to turn off my —

The tape recorder is turned off.

Donkey Good.

The tape recorder is turned back on. The background noise of helicopters has been replaced by tweeting birds. **Ao** *chuckles.*

Charlie Bird I am now walking down the Causeway Road, away from the Marine combat base. I am not going to look around because I have been told that if I do, I will, quote, get a bullet in my ass.

Donkey *laughs.* **John** *goes to the back wall: he hears noises: he listens.*
Charlie Bird *is replaced by* **Pat Kenny**, *back in the studio.*

Pat Kenny Well, that report from Charlie Bird on Bull Island was recorded earlier this afternoon. Since then Maurice Murphy has been granted an interview with Lieutenant George Bukowski. Of the US Marine Corps, of course. We're going to give that to you ——Are we? —Yes, we are. Here is Maurice Murphy talking to Lieutenant Bukowski.

Enter **Lieutenant Bukowski** *and* **Maurice Murphy**, *stage left.*
Murphy *is dressed for Arctic conditions, and speaks with a strong Northern accent.* **Bukowski** *is in combat uniform, smokes a cigar and seems to be relishing the occasion, having been too young for Vietnam. His delivery is at once bland and worrying.*

Bishop (*who hasn't used his voice for a while*) This —this might be interesting.

Donkey *stares at the* **Bishop** *as if at an unfortunate but irritating eejit.*

Murphy Lieutenant Bukowski, what exactly is the US Marine Corps doing here?

John Oh, my Jaysis! Will yeh listen!

Bukowski Well, sir; Mister Murphy. We are here on the direct orders of the President of the United States of America. We are here on what I would describe as a humanitarian combat mission.

Murphy And that means *what*?

Bukowski Well, sir; this is a counter-terrorist exercise. We are here to de-abduct a citizen of the United States.

Murphy Bishop Treacy.

Ao That's you, Your Bishop.

Bukowski That is correct, sir, yes. Bishop Treacy.

Murphy You have been here a full twenty-four hours now. Why haven't you 'de-abducted' Bishop Treacy yet?

John Yeah.

Bukowski I am sorry, sir. I cannot answer that question.

Murphy How large is the force —how many men are here?

Bukowski I am sorry, sir. I cannot answer that question.

Donkey The cunt can't count.

Murphy Why have you occupied Barrytown?

Bukowski The temporary presence of our ground personnel in, as you say, Barrytown is an unforegoable part of our operation.
——I would like to stress, if I might, Mister Murphy, that our presence in Barrytown and on this beautiful nature reserve —

Murphy And golf course.

Bukowski Yes, sir, as you say. And golf course. Our presence here is very strictly unpermanent. Also; our personnel will at *no* time and in *no* way harm the indigenous population.

Murphy The people of Barrytown.

Bukowski That is correct, sir, yes. As you say; the people of Barrytown.

Ao 'Cept us, wha'.

Bukowski Sir, this is very strictly *low* intensity warfare.

Donkey Oh, good fuck!

Murphy By that do you mean that you'll try not to kill anyone?

Bukowski Aw, come on, sir. That one's booby-trapped.

Murphy (*sounding slightly given out to*) When can we expect you to withdraw?

Bukowski I am sorry, sir —

Bukowski *and* **John** I cannot answer that question.

Murphy President Reagan said this morning that he has evidence that the three youths holding Bishop Treacy have Libyan backing.

Donkey *snorts his derision.*

Murphy Are you aware of this evidence?

Bukowski I'm just a soldier, sir. I carry out my duties to the best of my ability.

Murphy Are you —?

Bukowski I will say this, sir. The American people are like the Irish. We don't like being pushed around.

Exit **Lieutenant Bukowski**.

Murphy And with that the interview was brought to an end and Lieutenant Bukowski about-turned and marched back into the famous Dollymount dunes.

Ao *laughs, a dirty laugh.*

Pat Kenny Well, we'll be keeping one ear cocked in the Dublin Bay direction. But, you know, although the eyes of the world are on us at the moment, life goes on elsewhere. Mrs Thatcher, on day two of her five-day visit to India, in Calcutta to meet Mother Teresa, tripped on the airport tarmac and fell. Ran Jan Bupta heard her screaming. He's on the phone now to tell us what exactly happened. Hello, Ran Jan —

John (*turning off the radio*) Ram Jam me bollix.

A helicopter crosses over the house. The lads brace themselves: this could be 'it'. The helicopter fades. During the following exchanges the lads should seem scared.

John They're doin' this on purpose. Yeh know. Not doin' annythin'.

Ao Yeah. ——Tryin' to scare us.

Donkey (*half to himself*) They're doin' a good fuckin' job. (*Afraid that he shouldn't have said the above.*) It was nice of your man, Gadaffi, to send us tha' message, wasn't it?

The lads grin, trying their best.

Ao I'll tell yeh one thing but. The Pope should mind his own fuckin' business.

The lads laugh. The **Bishop** *tries to bless himself but* **Ao** *sticks the gun barrel into him and his hands go back up.*

John Fuckin' sure.

Donkey *thinks he heard something on the stairs. He says nothing about it, but it worries him. They hear noises offstage, left.*

John What's tha'?

John *tries to look past the* **Bishop** *without letting himself be seen from the outside.*

Ao Don't know.

Donkey *looks over quickly, but gets back to guarding the landing and stairs.*

Donkey Is somethin' happenin'?

Ao Yeah.
  (*Listening.*) Yeah.
  (*Not convinced.*) I think so.

Nothing happens. The tension eases slightly.

John Wha' *can* they do annyway?

John *asks this question as if he's been thinking of nothing else for hours.*

Donkey They can blow us to fuck.

The lads laugh quarter-heartedly.

Ao They can't.

Donkey (*almost hurt*) I was only jokin'!

Ao I know; I know tha'. But they can't. ——Sure they can't?

No answer.

Ao They've come to rescue the Bishop. So they can't blow us up cos they'd blow him up as well.

John (*reassuring himself*) Yeah.

Ao He's no good to them dead. So as long as one of us stays like this —
  (*Meaning the way he's guarding the Bishop.*) —like this, like
  —we're alrigh'.

Bishop (*after a pause*) Ao. ——Excuse me.

Ao Yeah?

Bishop Am I expected to remain in this position indefinitely?

Ao Yeah, I think so. ——Sorry.

Bishop But it's impossible.

Donkey Tough.

Bishop I must be up here like this for at least twelve hours by now.

Donkey You're still alive, aren't yeh? So stop whingin'.

Ao Sorry, Your Bishop.

Donkey (*after a pause*) I hope they don't drop a bomb or ann'thin'. Not a nuclear one, I mean. An ordin'ry one. ——The plaster'd all come off the ceilin', yeh know. The place'd be in bits.

John It wouldn't be much of a bomb if it only took the plaster off the ceilin'.

Donkey I don't mean *on* the gaff. I mean *near* the gaff. They're not goin' to drop ann'thin' *on* the fuckin' gaff. No way. ——I think.

Ao Don't worry, for fuck sake. ——Look. Nothin's changed, I'm tellin' yis. Look. The cops wanted the Bishop alive, so they couldn't come near us. The Yanks want the same thing, so they can't come near us either. ——Except they're better at it than the cops are, that's all. ——So we have to be a bit more careful. That's all. A bit more, eh, vigilant.

Donkey (*wanting to be convinced*) Yeah. ——For ever?

Ao No!

Donkey How long?

Ao ——Fuck off, will yeh. ——A few days.

Bishop (*trying to be emphatic*) If—

Ao (*shoving the gun into the Bishop's gut*) Shut up, Your Bishop.

John Eh, ——if they, yeh know, *raid* us an' we kill the Bishop, they'll kill us. Righ'?

Ao Righ'.

John An' if they raid us an' they rescue the Bishop they'll still kill us; righ'?

Ao ——Yeah.

John An' if they raid us an' they make a bollix of it, they'll kill us all. The Bishop as well. ——So we're fucked, aren't we?

Ao Hang on. Say tha' again.

John Whatever happens we're fucked. Brown fuckin' bread.

Donkey No way. ——Are we?

Ao Don't listen to him.

John I've been thinkin' about it. They're goin' to kill us. Nothin' surer. Make an example of us. ——The Bishop's the only one tha' has a hope o' gettin' ou' alive.

Donkey He does in his arse have a hope o' gettin' ou' alive!

Ao Listen. John, listen. Look. If we can convince them tha' the Bishop's dead if they charge in here, then they won't charge in.

Donkey That's righ'.

John (*wanting to be convinced*) I suppose so ——

A helicopter approaches. The lads look up, listening; braced. The helicopter fades.

Bishop There is —

Ao Shut up.

Bishop Please, Ao, let me speak.

Donkey Go on; let him.

Bishop Thank —

Donkey Then he might shut bleedin' up.

Bishop Well ——why don't you just, simply release me?

Donkey (*contemptuous*) Will yeh listen to him! Jaysis!

The lads silently agree with **Donkey**.

Bishop If we all four of us were to walk out together they wouldn't be able to kill you. If you would just call a halt to this fiasco —

Donkey Are yeh serious, are yeh?

Bishop Yes!

Donkey Then you're an even bigger sap than I thought yeh were.

Confusion silences the **Bishop**.

Donkey (*to the lads*) Can yis imagine it!? ——Walkin' ou'. —— With our hands up, yeh know. ——The fuckin' slaggin' we'd get!!
(*Shuddering.*) Jaysis!

John Jaysis, yeah. I'd die, I would.

Ao *laughs.*

John Wha'?
(*Realising what he's just said, and laughing.*) Oh yeah.

Ao (*to the* **Bishop**) There's people round here tha' would slag yeh abou' things yeh did years ago. D'yeh know wha' I mean, Your Bishop?

Bishop Em, ——well —

The lads silently agree with **Ao**.

Ao (*very matter-of-factly*) When I was a young fella. A little young
    fella, like. I pissed in me trousers in school, yeh know.

Donkey *sniggers. He remembers that day.*

Ao I couldn't help it. I was only abou' seven.

John You were seventeen.

Donkey *laughs.*

Ao (*to* **John**) Fuck off, you.
    (*To the* **Bishop**) Annyway, there's this fella tha' used to be in
    our class. Jimmy Travers his name is.

Donkey Tha' bollix?'

Ao An' he still slags me abou' it. ——An' he wasn't even in tha'
    day.

John *and* **Donkey** *grin across at each other.*

Ao So annyway, Your Bishop, there's no way we're walkin' ou' of
    here with our hands up.

A helicopter passes over quickly.

Donkey (*to the ceiling*) Come on; come on. I dare yis.

Bishop But that's ridiculous.

The lads don't answer, silent in agreement.

Bishop You're prepared to die because you're afraid of what a few
    gurriers will say about you!?

Ao Yeah.
    (*To the lads.*) Come here; time to swap.

Bishop Have you no self —?

Ao Shut up, will yeh. ——Come on. Swap, Donkey.

Donkey (*going over to replace* **Ao**) Comin'.
    (*To* **John**.) Johnner.

John (*going to keep watch at the door; imitating* **Plain-clothes**) Okay.

Ao *jumps onto the bed, and lies back.*

Ao Ah ——. This is the life, wha'.

Donkey (*prodding the* **Bishop**'s *gut with the gun*) D'yeh drink,
    Fergus?

Bishop (*pulling in his gut*) Em ——no; not —excessively.

Donkey Yeh must eat a lot then, do yeh?

John They all do.

Ao Nothin' else to do, wha'.

The lads laugh, a dirty laugh.

Bishop Sticks and stones may break my bones.

Donkey (*looking back at the lads*) Wha' abou' bullets?

Ao Don't mind him, Your Bishop.

A helicopter approaches. The lads brace themselves. The helicopter fades.

Donkey (*relaxing*) I nearly pressed the trigger there.

John *sniggers.*

Donkey I did. ——I wonder would I really kill him if I had to.
——I'd say I would. ——Wha' d'yeh think?

Donkey *is studying his trigger hand, pressing his finger, gently squeezing the trigger. The* **Bishop** *tries to watch. He is planking, but afraid to say anything in case he annoys* **Donkey**.

Donkey Yeah; I'd say I would alrigh'. No problem. ——
Bang! ——

The **Bishop** *almost faints.*

Donkey I wonder how big a hole it'd make.
(*Laughing.*) Come here; it'd be fuckin' great to blow a big hole in him an' wave ou' at them; wouldn't it?
(*After pretending to shoot the* **Bishop**, *and waving at* **Bishop**'s *stomach.*) Howyis, Yanks! Cooee!

Ao Lay off, Donkey, will yeh. Yeh'll give him a heart attack an' then we'll be in trouble.

Donkey Ah, he's alrigh'.
(*To the* **Bishop**.) Aren't yeh alrigh', Fergus?

Bishop ——I'm very tired.

Donkey Go to sleep then. ——I wouldn't mind killin' someone, d'yeh know tha'. ——Just to see wha' it'd be like.

Ao Yeah.

John Fuckin' spacers.

Donkey *aims the gun at* **John**.

Ao Stop messin', Donkey.

John *looks around and sees the gun, and dives.* **Donkey** *puts the gun back on the* **Bishop**.

Donkey Paddy Delaney. I'd love to shoot him I would.

Ao *and* **John** *are grinning across at each other.*

Donkey I'd go up to him an' I'd say, 'Howyeh, Paddy; how's Tina?'. Then I'd blow his fuckin' head off.

Ao *and* **John** *are laughing.*

Donkey Fuck off. ——Who would youse like to kill?

John Well, I've already shot me ma.

The lads laugh.

Ao Rolf Harris.

John Ah yeah.

Donkey (*after some deliberation*) I don't think I'd shoot me ma.

A noise is heard behind the back wall.

Ao (*getting up on the bed, and listening*) There they are, the bollixes. (*Not too loud.*) Come in.

John (*hearing something downstairs*) I think they're comin' up.

Donkey Oh shite! This is it.
  (*Getting ready to shoot the* **Bishop**.) Start sayin' your Haily Marys, Fergus.

A helicopter is approaching. It hovers for a longer duration than previously. For a few seconds it seems that this is finally 'it'. The lads and the **Bishop** *are helpless, tense and very scared. The helicopter fades.*

Donkey (*letting out breath*) Oooh, Jaysis!! Fuckin' hell.

Donkey *slips to his knees. He takes the gun from his hand and massages his neck.* **John** *slumps.* **Ao** *falls back down on the bed. The* **Bishop** *begins to bend at the knees, hoping that he'll be allowed to sit down. He's exhausted, shattered etc.*

Donkey (*alert again*) Get back up there!

Bishop Please, Donkey —

Donkey Get up!

Bishop (*trying to maintain dignity, but having difficulty*) I'll collapse.

Donkey I dare yeh.

John *stands up, obviously with something on his mind. He's very agitated. He looks around, almost frantically.*

John I have to have a shite. ——I'm goin' in the corner here, Donkey; okay.

Donkey *turns. The* **Bishop** *slumps.* **Donkey** *presses the gun into the* **Bishop**'s *gut without looking back at him. The* **Bishop** *straightens up again.*

Donkey (*to* **John**) Yeh will in your shite! No way! ——Go ou' to the jacks! ——Yeh dirty bastard, yeh.

John (*desperate*) No; they're ou' there.
(*Obviously holding it in.*) Go on, Donkey. Let us. ——I'll clean it up after.

Donkey No way! ——I'll shoot yeh.

Ao (*to* **John**) I'll keep an eye ou' for yeh.

John Thanks!

Exit **John**, *dashing*.

Ao (*to* **Donkey**) Righ'. He'll be sittin' down now.
(*Roars.*) Sketch! Johnner! They're comin'. Quick!

John (*from offstage*) I don't care!

Donkey The nerve o' him! I'll clean it up after. For fuck sake! It's disgustin'.

Ao Eh, Donkey. ——I pissed in the wardrobe.

Donkey Yeh wha'!? Oh, good Jesus!

Donkey *charges over to the wardrobe and starts sniffing the clothes.* **Ao** *enjoys watching him. The* **Bishop** *sinks down and sits on the chair.*

Donkey (*into the wardrobe*) Me ma'll destroy me. ——I'll have to throw them all in the bath.
(*Copping on that he's been had; to* **Ao**.) Yeh bollix.

Donkey *sees the* **Bishop** *sitting down, and charges across to him.*

Donkey (*almost screeching*) Here! Get back up there! Quick! Quick!

The **Bishop** *jumps back up onto the chair.* **Donkey** *sticks the gun back into the* **Bishop**'s *gut.*

Enter **John**, *looking pleased. He does a ballet turn.*

John I'm a new man, lads. ——It came up ou' of the water, I'm not jokin' yis.

Bishop (*weakly*) I'm going to faint.

Donkey (*aggressively*) Are yeh? Are yeh now?

Ao Hang on. I've an idea.

Ao *takes the gun from* **Donkey**. **Donkey** *lets him because he wants to see what* **Ao**'s *going to do with it.*

Ao (*to* **Donkey**) Hold tha' sleeve there. ——Yeah; like tha'.

Donkey *holds one of the sleeves of the* **Bishop**'s *gown against the window frame, more or less in the position it would be in if the* **Bishop**'s *arm was still holding it up.*

Ao (*to* **John**) You do the same on the other side.

John (*imitating* **Plain-clothes**) Okay.

Ao Righ', Your Bishop. Climb ou'.

The lads laugh as they see **Ao**'s *plan working out. The* **Bishop** *slides out of his gown and climbs down onto the floor.* **Donkey** *and* **John** *hold the gown against the window.*

Donkey Brilliant. Fuckin' brilliant.

The **Bishop** *stands in tunic, boxer shorts, red socks, shoes and mitre.*

Bishop (*exhausted and relieved*) Many thanks.

The **Bishop** *goes to the bed.*

Ao (*pointing*) The skidmarks, wha'.

The lads roar laughing. The **Bishop** *sits on the bed, unaware of the fun.*

John Easily know yeh weren't married, Fergus.

Donkey (*unable to finish because he's laughing so much*) If the Marines charge in now —

Bishop (*beginning to stand up*) I'll have to, ——if I may —

Ao Wha'?

Bishop Visit the lavatory.

Ao Oh yeah.

Exit the **Bishop**, *trying not to walk too urgently.*

Ao I'll keep an eye on him.

Exit **Ao**.

Donkey Yeuh! Hate tha'.

John *and* **Donkey** *continue to hold the gown against the window. The novelty has worn off.*

Donkey (*after a pause*) This is stupid.

The lights over the room go down.

Enter **Lieutenant Bukowski**. *He stands down-stage, left.*

Enter **Private Crabacre**, *immediately after* **Bukowski**. **Crabacre**, *dressed for combat, is a native of Hangman's Pardon, Mississippi. He is not unlike Radar from 'M.A.S.H.', but a good deal less cuddly. He carries a field phone on his back. He is holding the receiver in one of his hands.*

Crabacre We got the Pentagon here, Sir. Lookin' for Lieutenant-Colonel Bukowski; and that's you, Sir.

Bukowski (*taking the phone*) Thank you, Private.

Crabacre Sir.

Bukowski (*waiting for the call to come through*) And, Private?

Crabacre Yes, Sir?

Bukowski (*almost absently*) Was your mother's operation a success?

Crabacre Yes, Sir.

Bukowski Good. ——That's good.

Crabacre 'Preciate it, Sir. Removed sixteen growths, Sir.

Bukowski Hmm; that's a lot of growths, I guess.

Crabacre Yes, Sir. Reckon so. Weren't but two of them nonmalignant.

Bukowski (*into the phone*) Ah, Major O'Malley!

Crabacre (*alert and listening*) Shoot!

Bukowski How are *you*, Sir?
(*after a pause*) Yes, Sir.
(*after a pause*.) Yes, Sir; Operation Eagle Beak *is* underway.
We are counting down right now, Sir.

At no time does **Bukowski** *look flustered or in need of help from* **Private Crabacre**. **Crabacre** *shows seven raised fingers to* **Bukowski**.

Crabacre Seven to go, Sir.

Bukowski (*into the phone*) Approximately seven minutes, Sir. We are going in at, eh, eighteen hundred hours and twenty-three, Sir.

Crabacre *nods.*

Bukowski (*into the phone*) Yes, Sir. And twenty-three.
(*After a pause.*) In case the enemy expects us on the hour or half hour, Sir.
(*After a pause.*) Thank you, Sir.

Crabacre *shrugs modestly.*

Bukowski (*after a pause*) Yes, Sir. We think the delaying tactic *has* worked, Sir. Our deep reconnaissance personnel have been monitoring the behavioural patterns of the enemy, Sir. And, well, Sir, they report that the terrorists have exceeded their, eh —

Crabacre Exhaustion threshold.

Bukowski —exhaustion threshold and that intercompatibility has been, eh —

Crabacre De-sustained, Sir.

Bukowski —de-sustained, Sir.
(*After a pause.*) Yes, Sir. As you say. Like rats in a trap.

Crabacre (*to himself*) An' possums up a gum tree.

Bukowski Yes, Sir. We have established moral and, Sir,
psychological ascendancy over the, eh —

Crabacre Enemy, Sir.

Bukowski —enemy, Sir.

Crabacre (*to himself*) We got those boys whooped for sure.

Bukowski Thank you, Sir.
(*After a pause.*) Yes, Sir. The assault team embussed
approximately —

Crabacre *shows him ten fingers.*

Bukowski —ten minutes ago and the, eh —

Crabacre *does a quick helicopter impression.*

Bukowski —helicraft is approaching the dropping zone. And, of
course, Sir, ground personnel are deployed and standing by.

Crabacre (*to himself*) An' the boys with the body bags too.

Bukowski No, Sir. The assault team won't be going in over the
balcony, I'm afraid. There is no balcony, Sir.
(*After a pause.*) No, Sir. It's what they call a corporation house
over here, Sir. Project housing, Sir.
(*After a pause.*) No, Sir. We've had no reports of any negroid
personnel among the indigenous population.

Crabacre Or A-rabs, Sir.

Bukowski Or middle-eastern personnel.

Crabacre The China boy, Sir.

Bukowski Although, Sir, we *did* debrief a male Asian we located at
a bus-stop, Sir.
(*After a pause.*) No, Sir. He was going to school.

Crabacre (*to himself*) Had him a reading book name of 'Peig'.

Bukowski No, Sir. You never can be too sure.

Crabacre (*to himself*) With all that Chinese writin' inside of it.

Bukowski Yes, Sir. It *is* a shame about the balcony.

Crabacre (*to himself*) Little ol' China woman on the cover.

Bukowski I agree, Sir. It would have made an awesome photo-
opportunity, as you say. But the rope ladder —

Crabacre (*to himself*) Lookin' all kind o' sinister an' Chinese.

Bukowski Yes, Sir. After the enemy has been dealt with and neutralised, Sir.
(*After a pause.*) He *is* a Catholic bishop, I know, Sir.

Crabacre (*to himself*) Ain't a real bishop.

Bukowski We *will* be careful, Sir, I assure you.

Crabacre (*to himself*) Ain't but a aux-hillary bishop.

Bukowski Thank *you* again, Sir. Goodbye, Major O'Malley.

Crabacre (*taking the phone*) I'll take this here, Sir.

Bukowski Thank you, Private. ——And your father, Private; how is he?

Crabacre Daid, Sir.

Bukowski Good. ——That's good.

Crabacre 'Preciate it, Sir.

Exit **Bukowski** *and* **Crabacre**. *The lights over the room go up.*

Donkey This is stupid.

John Yeah.

Enter **Ao** *and the* **Bishop**.

Donkey How long are we supposed to stay like this for?

Ao We'll just give the bishop a bit of a rest.

Donkey Me arms are fuckin' killin' me.

Ao I'll swap with yeh in a bit.

John Wha' abou' me?

Ao We'll take turns.

The **Bishop** *sits on the bed.* **Ao** *aims the gun at the* **Bishop** *all the time.*

Donkey I'm fuckin' starvin', d'yeh know tha'.

John Yeah.

Donkey (*to* **Ao**) Tell them we want food.

Ao No point. They won't answer again.

Donkey I'd eat a baby. I would.

Bishop (*trying to be reasonable*) If you would just call a halt —

Ao Shut up, Your Bishop.

Bishop But, ——in God's name, can you not —?

Ao I'm warnin' yeh. Shut up.

Bishop No, I will not shut up. I have tried to —

*Ao slaps the mitre off the **Bishop**'s head and puts the barrel of the gun to his neck.*

Ao (*almost polite, but menacing*) Righ'. Come on. Get up. Come on.

*The **Bishop** stands, and **Ao** pushes him towards the window.*

Ao Get back up there. Come on.

*The **Bishop** stands up on the chair and 'climbs' back into his gown.*

Donkey (*letting go of the gown*) 'Bout time.

*John goes across to guard the bedroom door. **Ao** puts the gun to the **Bishop**'s gut.*

Ao (*like a strict but fair teacher*) In future when I tell you to shut up yeh shut up. Okay?

*The **Bishop** nods.*

Ao Good lad.

Donkey (*taking over from **Ao**, in front of the **Bishop**; gun to gut*) Jaysis, I'm starvin'.

Ao Ah shut up, Donkey, will yeh.

John Maybe that's wha' they're doin': starvin' us ou'.

Donkey We can eat Fergus.

They laugh half-heartedly.

Donkey You wouldn't mind; sure yeh wouldn't, Fergus? You'd go straight up to heaven.

*Enter **Mr Farrell**. He crouches, stage-left; wearing a Marine's helmet.*

Farrell (*whisper-shouting; hissing*) Aidan! ——Aidan!!

Donkey Ao; your da's outside.

This news surprises and excites the lads.

Ao Da.

Farrell Aidan!

Ao Da. Where are yeh?

Farrell Don't shout, for fuck sake! ——I'm over here. In Smith's front.

*Ao looks carefully out the window, trying to spot **Mr Farrell**.*

Farrell (*raising himself a bit*) Here.

Ao (*half-laughing*) What're yeh wearin' the helmet for?

Farrell Camouflage.

> (*Looking over his shoulder.*) If they catch me I'm fucked. They think I'm at home.

Ao How did yeh get ou'?

Farrell I climbed ou' onto the coalshed, an' then I jumped onto Delap's shed. Then I got down into their back. Then into Gaffney's back. Then into Matthewses. No; I was in O'Driscoll's before I was in the Matthewses; isn't tha' righ'? (*Impressing himself.*) Then I went through Matthewses alley. Into their front. Then I legged it across into Prendergast's front. An' then in here.

Ao Fair play to yeh.

Donkey Ask him has he anny food.

Farrell Aidan. —They're after takin' your mammy.

Ao (*upset and confused*) Wha'!?

Farrell The Yanks. They took her in for questionin'.

Ao (*lost*) Why?

Farrell Threw her into the back o' one o' their jeeps. I s'pose she's in Dollymount by now.

Ao Why!?

Farrell Ah, they had the two of us in the kitchen, yeh know. Askin' us questions. About you an' tha'. An' then abou' politics, yeh know. An' your mammy —. Yeh know the way she is. She told them she voted for the Worker's Party. —— They think she's a fuckin' communist.

Ao Ma!?

Farrell I told them tha' she only voted for them cos she fancied tha' Pat McCartan *bastard*. But, o' course, no one ever listens to *me*. ——I hope they don't torture her.

John What's up, Ao.

Ao —— Me ma.

Donkey (*to* **John**) The Yanks have Ao's ma.

Farrell She'll be alrigh', I'd say. Yeh know *her*. She'll be ironin' their fuckin' shirts an' tellin' them all abou' her arthritis before they know wha' hit them.

Ao (*very unconvinced*) ——Yeah.

Farrell Annyway, look it; the real reason I came — (*Hearing something.*) Hang on. Somethin's up.

(*Looking offstage and seeing action.*) Somethin's up. —I'll get back to yeh.

Exit **Mr Farrell**, *crouched and in a hurry.*

Ao He says somethin's happenin'.

John (*very scared*) Oh shite!

A helicopter is heard approaching.

Donkey Here's the fuckin' Eye in the Sky again.

The helicopter becomes louder. At the point when previously the noise began to fade, it now increases. The helicopter is descending over the houses. The lads look at the ceiling, scared; sensing that this, at last, is 'it'. Gunfire and breaking glass are heard, and the **Bishop** *jumps from the chair onto the bed.* **John** *quickly turns off the light, and the lads dive to the ground.* **John***, in particular, is terrified. The gunfire continues and the helicopter comes nearer. Searchlights scan the bedroom walls and the sky above the room.* **John** *panics, and runs around the room, trying to escape from the light. He jumps onto the bed.* **Ao** *goes to pull him down. The* **Bishop** *rushes to the door, and exits.*

Ao The Bishop!

Ao *and* **Donkey** *go after him.* **John***, caught in the searchlight, covers his face and screams.*

Enter **Ao** *and* **Donkey***, hauling the* **Bishop***. The gunfire etc. continues.* **Ao** *gets up on the bed to pull* **John** *to safety.* **Donkey** *and the* **Bishop** *fight on the floor.* **Ao** *and* **John** *fight on the bed.*

The drone of the helicopter wavers, then stops. The lads and the **Bishop** *stop fighting, and listen. The screech of the helicopter falling from a height is heard, followed by an almighty explosion. Shimmering, vivid red light is seen downstage, left. The helicopter has crashed. Sirens are heard. The lads and the* **Bishop** *stay still for a while. They don't understand what has happened.*

Donkey (*looking around*) It missed.

Sirens and minor explosions are still heard. The red light becomes less vivid, but remains for the rest of the scene.

John Somethin's after happenin'.

Ao (*sarcastically*) Go 'way!

Donkey Wha' happened!?

John They should be chargin' in now!

Enter **Mr Farrell**, *in a hurry.*

Farrell Aidan! Aidan!!

The lads dash to the window. The **Bishop** *remains on the floor, looking dazed.*

Ao Wha' happened, Da?

Farrell Their helicopter's after crashin' into the Community Centre!

Mr Farrell *laughs, and dashes downstage to look at the blaze.*

Donkey Jaysis!

The sirens etc. are still heard.

Farrell (*dashing forward again; thrilled and important*) I seen it. —— Straight into it. I never seen annythin' like it in me life. (*Matter-of-factly*) The caretaker's fucked.

John Is he brownbread, Mister Farrell?

Farrell Wha'? Not at all. He wasn't there. An' he should've been. He was at home watchin' 'My Favourite Martian' on the Super channel.

Mr Farrell *dashes back to look, and forward again. The lads half-enjoyed listening to Mr Farrell, but they're eager to know what exactly happened and if they're now safe.*

Farrell He'll be sacked now. Father Molloy'll sack him. Molloy might play the guitar an' tha' but he's a terrible hard man if yeh start actin' the prick with him. ——Did yis see wha' happened, did yis?

Lads No!

Farrell The hellier got caught in Flannigan's aerial. It hit the wall o' the Centre like a ton o' bricks. (*Reconstructing the explosion.*) PAA-DOOM!

Exit **Mr Farrell**.

Enter **Bukowski** *and* **Crabacre** *from stage right. Both are carrying field phones. As they talk they walk across the stage,* **Crabacre**, *in particular, on the lookout for snipers.*

Bukowski (*into the phone*) Major O'Malley. How are *you*, Sir?

Crabacre (*into his phone*) Speak up there, Nelson. I might could hear you better if you was to speak into that thang you got there for speakin' into.

Bukowski (*into the phone*) I'm afraid, Sir, that the news from the operational area seems to be unpositive.

Crabacre (*to* **Bukowski**) It's a A-bort, Sir.

Bukowski (*into the phone*) Sir, I have to report an abort on Operation Eagle Beak.

Crabacre (*into his phone*) That's bad to hear, Nelson.

Bukowski (*into the phone*) Yes, Sir; an abort. I'm afraid so.

Crabacre (*into his phone*) Slow down some, Nelson.

Bukowski (*into the phone*) Well Sir, it would appear that —

Crabacre (*to* **Bukowski**) Blade failure again, Sir.

Bukowski (*into the phone*) The helicraft suffered blade failure over the dropping zone during air insertion, Sir.

Crabacre (*into his phone*) Must've singed your eyebrows some, Nelson.

Bukowski (*into the phone*) The craft couldn't maintain its hover and it banked to left and, well —

Crabacre (*to* **Bukowski**) Made uncontrolled contact with an indigenous leisure module, Sir.

Exit **Crabacre**.

Bukowski (*into the phone*) Made uncontrolled contact with an indigenous leisure, eh —

Crabacre (*from offstage*) Module, Sir!

Bukowski (*into the phone*) —module, Sir.

Exit **Bukowski**.

Enter **Mr Farrell**, *still in a hurry but more relaxed*.

Farrell An' I always thought Larry Flannigan was a mean ol' cunt for not gettin' the piped in.

Donkey (*looking across at Flannigan's roof*) Jaysis, yeah; look it.

Farrell He'll have to get it now though, wha'. An' a new chimley.
——Lucky there was no one in the Centre.

John Is there no one brownbread, Mister Farrell?

Farrell Will yeh stop! It's like the fuckin' Alamo!
(*Going back a few steps and looking at the blaze.*) They're all dead. Every one o' them. Splattered. There's half a Marine stuck to the door o' the hairdresser's. ——Chuck Norris, wha'.
(*Dashing downstage again.*) Yeh can smell it from here. It's fuckin' terrible.

Donkey Aah, Mister Farrell!

Exit **Mr Farrell**.

Enter **Bukowski** *and* **Crabacre**.

Bukowski (*into the phone*) Yes, Sir. I'm afraid so, Sir.

Crabacre (*into his phone*) Gotcha, Nelson.
(*To* **Bukowski**.) No indigenous casualties so far, Sir. Try that
one on him.

Bukowski (*into the phone*) There are no indigenous casualties, Sir.

Crabacre (*into his phone*) That's fearful to hear, Nelson.
(*To* **Bukowski**.) Seventeen inoperative personnel, Sir.

Bukowski (*into the phone*) There was an ammunition cook-off, Sir.
Sir, we have seventeen inoperative personnel, I'm afraid.

Crabacre (*into his phone*) One o' those boys owed me five dollars.

Bukowski (*into the phone*) Yes, Sir. And, as you say, one dead
helicopter.

Crabacre (*into his phone*) Word I'd pick to describe what you're
seein' there is the word 'Apocalyptic', Nelson.

Bukowski (*exiting; overhearing* **Crabacre**; *into the phone*) Sir? Sir,
it's apocalyptic down here, Sir.

Crabacre (*overhearing* **Bukowski**; *running after him*) Shoot!

Exit **Bukowski** *and* **Crabacre**.

Enter **Mr Farrell**, *strolling, eating a bag of chips*.

Farrell I'll tell yeh one thing. It's lucky it's not the bingo nigh'.
——Half the women in Barrytown would've been dead by
now. ——Yeh wouldn't be able to get *near* the chipper if tha'
happened, wha'.

John *and* **Donkey** *enjoy that comment*. **Ao** *is a bit distant; thinking*.
Mr Farrell *strolls downstage, to get a better view of the action*.

Enter **Bukowski** *and* **Crabacre**.

Bukowski (*into the phone*) Sir; Sir, I think ——. Sir? ——General
Mahoney!

Crabacre (*hearing* **Bukowski**) Shoot a hog!

Bukowski (*into the phone*) How are *you*, Sir?

Crabacre (*into his phone*) Stop cryin' there, Nelson. It ain't
dignified for you to be cryin'.

Bukowski (*into the phone*) Yes, Sir. I'm afraid so, Sir.

Crabacre (*into his phone*) Nelson, listen up, boy. Would Ollie
North be cryin', Nelson?

Bukowski (*into the phone*) Yes, Sir. It *is* a black eye for the Corps, Sir, as you say.

Crabacre (*into his phone*) I don't think he would be neither, Nelson.

Bukowski (*into the phone*) Yes, Sir. It *is* an unacceptable kill ratio.

Crabacre (*into his phone*) Got to leave you there, Nelson. Pentagon's all riled up on line two. Take care, boy.

Bukowski (*into the phone; exiting*) No, Sir, I'm not a Catholic myself but my wife once dated, eh —

Crabacre Teddy Kennedy, Sir!

Bukowski —Teddy Kennedy, Sir.

Exit **Bukowski** *and* **Crabacre**.

Mr Farrell *strolls forward. He squashes the chip bag into a ball and throws it away.*

Farrell (*looking away from the blaze*) Well, we've no Community Centre now. Were yis ever in it?

Donkey and John No.

Farrell No. Neither was I.

Mr Farrell *walks downstage, getting up on his toes to see better.*

Enter **Bukowski** *and* **Crabacre**. **Bukowski** *looks worried, and* **Crabacre** *is stuck to his side, listening to every word.*

Bukowski (*into the phone*) No, Sir. I'm not Jewish.

Crabacre (*to himself*) Ain't no call for that.

Bukowski (*into the phone*) Well, Sir, I think I *do* appreciate the gravity of the situation, Sir.

Crabacre (*to* **Bukowski**) Seventeen inoperative personnel, Sir.

Bukowski (*into the phone*) Sir, I have seventeen inoperative personnel down here —

Crabacre (*to* **Bukowski**) Mechanical failure to blame, Sir.

Bukowski (*into the phone*) Well, Sir, I don't think it would be right for me to refer to my men as dead meat, Sir.

Crabacre Daid meat!

Bukowski (*just before the General hangs up*) Yes, Sir. I'll do my —

Farrell (*strolling forward*) There's all sorts o' people in uniforms runnin' round over there.

Crabacre *takes the phone from* **Bukowski**, *who looks stunned.*

Bukowski Thank you, Private.

Farrell Billy Delap's over there in his Civil Defence gear; the fuckin' eejit.

Crabacre Sir, you all look like death jawin' a week-old ham bone.

Farrell (*musing*) It's gas.

Bukowski Are you a Catholic, Private?

Crabacre No, Sir. I'm a Christian.

Bukowski Good. ——That's good.

Exit **Bukowski** *and* **Crabacre**.

Farrell Gas. They can invade annywhere they want but they can't break into a fuckin' house.

Donkey *and* **John** *are looking as if they feel that their troubles are over. The* **Bishop** *is still sitting, head down, on the floor.*

Ao (*as if it's only really occurring to him now*) They were goin' to fuckin' kill us there.

A single shot is heard from offstage.

Farrell Oh fuck! See yis.

Exit **Mr Farrell**, *dashing and ducking.*

The lads duck, scared again. They see the **Bishop**.

John The Bishop.

Ao (*pointing the gun*) Here, Your Bishop. Back up on the chair.

The **Bishop** *stands up and starts to move towards the window; then stops.*

Bishop (*simply, decisively, impressively*) No.

The **Bishop** *moves towards the door.* **Ao**, *genuinely furious, shoots between the* **Bishop's** *feet. The* **Bishop's** *resistance collapses.*

Ao (*shaking in anger; grabbing the* **Bishop** *and pushing him over to the chair*) Listen, you; I don't like yeh, righ'. ——They were goin' to kill us there so we might as well kill you. It makes no difference.

The **Bishop** *climbs onto the chair.* **John** *and* **Donkey** *are impressed with* **Ao**, *but disturbed too.*

Ao I'd kill yeh now only we need yeh for the window. But just once more. ——Once more!

Donkey (*to* **Ao**) He's a cheeky bollix, so he is.

Ao *is beginning to calm down.*

Donkey (*after a pause*) I'm fuckin' starvin'.

Ao (*angry again*) Righ'. This is it.

Ao *pulls the* **Bishop** *from the chair.*

Ao Get down. Come on. They give us food *now* or that's it. They're not goin' to starve me; no fuckin' way.

Ao *puts the* **Bishop** *in front of the window, holding his head down roughly, and puts the gun to the* **Bishop**'s *temple.*

Ao (*roars*) Hey! ——Hey! Are yis lookin!?

Donkey *and* **John** *crouch.*

Bishop (*whispering; praying*) No, no, no, ——no —

Ao Are yis lookin'!? ——We want food now. Now, righ'! —— Now!!

Ao *is on the verge of pulling the trigger, and the* **Bishop** *knows this.* **John** *and* **Donkey** *watch, expecting* **Ao** *to shoot; bracing themselves.*

The lights go down.

Eddie Cochran sings 'Three Steps To Heaven'.

PART TWO

It is the morning after Operation Eagle Beak and the destruction of the Barrytown Community Centre. **Ao** *is asleep on the bed, lying against the wall, his legs apart. The* **Bishop** *is also asleep, lying back against* **Ao**'s *chest. He is wearing* **Donkey**'s *mother's dressing-gown.* **Ao** *is holding the gun to the* **Bishop**'s *head.* **Donkey** *is standing on the chair at the window, wearing the* **Bishop**'s *gown and mitre.* **John** *is moseying around the room, eating a bowl of cornflakes, now and again peeping out the window. There is a large box of groceries on the floor, and some items lying on the floor around the box.*

Donkey (*looking down at* **Ao** *and the* **Bishop**) Yeh'd love a camera, wouldn't yeh?

John (*stopping and looking*) Yeah.

Donkey Just slap a bit o' lipstick on Fergus.

John Take it easy, will yeh. I'm eatin' me breakfast.
(*Looking out the window.*) ——Nothin'.

Donkey (*squirming*) I never knew yeh had so much sweat in your back, d'yeh know tha'.

John (*still looking out, and searching*) Where are they? ——There's no helicopters either.

Donkey Maybe they're run ou' of them.

John *sniggers.*

Donkey I know where they are. They've all gone to the funeral.

John (*mock-serious*) Oh, yeah. That's it.

Donkey *blows 'The Last Post' through a bugle made from his fist.*

John Not so loud, for fuck sake. They'll hear yeh.

Donkey Fuck them.
(*after a pause.*) Seventeen dead.

John (*looking out the window; preoccupied*) Yeah.

Donkey That's five an' a half each.

John Wha'? ——Oh, yeah. Yeah.

71

Donkey (*giving a clenched fist salute*) Yeow!

Donkey's *raised arm leaves part of the window exposed, and* **John** *jumps for cover.*

Donkey They were lookin' for it. Yeh can't expect to come helicopterin' into Barrytown an' think you're goin' to get ou' alive.
(*After they laugh.*) Still. I'm sure it'll be very sad.

Donkey *starts to do 'The Last Post' again. It isn't a pleasant sound.*

John Jaysis, Donkey, don't do the bugle again. ——Talkin' abou' bugles, I wonder wha' Ao's dreamin' abou'.

Donkey *thinks that this is one of the funniest things he has ever heard. The* **Bishop** *snaps awake, grunting.*

Donkey Howyeh, Fergus.

John (*to the* **Bishop***; urgently*) Don't move! ——If yeh wake Ao up too quickly he'll probably shoot yeh in the head.

The **Bishop** *freezes. He tries to see the gun without moving his head.*

John (*creeping towards* **Ao**) How are we goin' to get Ao to wake up without him shootin' Fergus?

Donkey Shout at him an' hope for the best.

John (*whispering into* **Ao**'s *ear*) Wakey, wakey!

Ao I am awake, yeh spoon.

The relief shows on the **Bishop**'s *face.*

John Mornin'.

Ao (*pushing the* **Bishop**) Get up off me there!

Ao *and the* **Bishop** *look a bit embarrassed as they get off the bed.* **Ao** *looks very bad-humoured.*

Ao (*to the* **Bishop**) I'm first.

Ao *takes a roll of toilet paper from the grocery box, and exits.*

Donkey He's still in his moods.

John I'd say it's because of his ma.

Donkey Yeah.

John Or maybe he's just havin' his period.

They laugh slyly.

John (*to the* **Bishop***; pointing at the box*) There's cornflakes there.

Bishop Em, ——no, thank you. I don't think so.

Donkey Wha' d'yeh usually have for your brekker, Fergus?

Bishop Well, I would normally start with half a grapefruit —

Donkey Yeuh! Jaysis, stop!

John Wha' d'yeh do with the other half?

Donkey *and* **John** *roar laughing.*

Enter **Ao**. *He turns on the radio.*

John Good idea.

Charlie Bird ——on what promises to be a beautiful Spring day.
Despite the deaths yesterday evening of seventeen of the
Marine Corps, there has been a very definite relaxation of
security here. Local people and onlookers are strolling around
the base, mixing freely with the military.

Donkey The military wha'!?

Behind **Charlie Bird**'s *voice can be heard the sound of happy people
mingling and, perhaps, a Mister Whippy van. The voices of two women
hawkers become more prominent.*

Charlie Bird There is an almost carnival atmosphere today. An
atmosphere more fitting, perhaps, to the weather and
surroundings.

Hawker One Get your Mars Bar an' chocolate now.

Hawker Two Last o' the Mars Bars an' the Twixes.

Hawker One Your Mars Bars an' chocolate now.

Hawker Two The last o' the Mars Bars an' the Twixes.

The lads laugh, but they're confused.

Ao (*holding the radio*) What's the fuckin' story?

Charlie Bird Excuse me, ladies.

Hawker One Yes, love?

Hawker Two Are you from 'Gay Byrne', are yeh?

Charlie Bird No, no.

Hawker Two D'yeh want us to kill a sheep for yeh?

Both women laugh.

Charlie Bird Is business booming this morning?

Hawker One Oh, God, it is, yeah. Very good.

Hawker Two Look it. I've only got three Dairy Milks left an' it's
not even nine o'clock yet.

Charlie Bird How does it compare to, say, a rugby international?

Hawker One Ah, the rugby crowd are no good.

73

Hawker Two Useless.

Hawker One They're too well fed.

Hawker Two The soccer's much better.

Hawker One Much better, yeah. But the Gaelic's the best. Even the hurlin'.

Hawker Two They'd eat ann'thin'. They don't even take them ou' o' the wrappers.

Both women laugh.

Hawker Two Bruce Springsteen was the best ever though.

Hawker One *He* paid for me sun bed.

Both women laugh.

The lads are still confused, and worried. Without saying anything, **John** *goes to guard the door and* **Ao** *aims the gun at the* **Bishop**.

Charlie Bird Are the Marines buying much?

Hawker One Oh they are, yeah. They're buyin' the most of it.

Hawker Two They're starvin', sure. They only have canned stuff to eat.

Donkey What's wrong with tha'?

Ao Shut up a minute.

Hawker One They're very nice.

Hawker Two Yeah, they are. Very polite. One o' them called me 'baby'.

Both women laugh.

Hawker Two Your man over there. D'yeh see him? The black fella.

Hawker One The skinny one.

Hawker Two Look. He has 'Hell Sucks' written on his ha'. D'yeh see him?

Charlie Bird Yes.

Hawker Two His name's T-Bone Doolightly. He's from Memphis.

Hawker One In America.

Hawker Two His daddy used to cut Elvis's grass for him. He said he'd've been able to get Elvis's autograph for us, only he's dead.

The lads try to laugh properly.

Donkey What's goin' on, Ao?

Ao *doesn't answer.*

Charlie Bird Here's a young man who seems to be enjoying himself. What is your name?

Boy I'm not tellin' yeh.

Charlie Bird Why not?

Boy Cos I'm mitchin'.

The lads laugh.

Charlie Bird And you wish to remain anonymous?

Boy Yeah.

Charlie Bird What's that you have with you?

Boy A grenade.

Charlie Bird Where did you get that?

Boy Over there.

Charlie Bird You stole it!

Boy I did not! ——It's mine.

Charlie Bird And what are you going to do with it?

Boy Kill me da.

Charlie Bird Well, I can only advise parents to frisk their children when they come home from school this afternoon. ——So. Bull Island is a very different place indeed this morning. —— Half an hour ago I asked a young Marine Corps sergeant what he thought his superiors' next move would be. And he said, 'We'll see after we've had our breakfast'. And I couldn't help thinking that, like another wave of invaders before them, the US Marines are becoming more Irish than the Irish themselves.

John I smell a rat, d'yis know tha'?

Ao It's the Bishop.

This comment marks the return of **Ao**'*s good humour, and* **John** *and* **Donkey** *laugh. On the radio,* **Pat Kenny** *is holding the fort back in the studio.*

Pat Kenny That was Charlie Bird reporting from Marine Corps Camp Navaho on Bull Island. And that softening of attitude so evident in Charlie's report seems to extend to Washington itself. At a specially covened press conference in the early hours of this morning President Reagan had this to say:

Donkey Who cares wha' ——?

Ao, John and Bishop SHHH!

Reagan And ——on behalf of the American people, I would ——
like to apologise ——to the ——members of the Royal Dublin
——Golf Club ——for the surface damage our ——boys did to
the fifteenth green. ——And to Christy O'Connor, that great
——golfer, democrat and Irishman. ——Christy, ——from
one old timer ——to another: Give 'em hell, Christy.

Ao Good Jesus! He's a fuckin' looper.

Pat Kenny Mister Reagan was no longer referring to the 'Three
Dublin Libyans' or 'The Trinity of Terror'. He was now
talking about 'those misguided young men'.

Donkey I'll misguide him.

Pat Kenny He pleaded directly to 'The Barrytown Three'.

Ao Fuckin' hell! He's talkin' to us.

John (*joking*) Jesus, I'm scarleh!

Reagan To those three —

Donkey Bollixes.

Reagan —misguided young men I say ——this:

Ao (*contemptuous*) Young men!

Reagan Let Bishop Treacy go home ——to his flock. Please, let
the Bishop go.

Donkey (*to the* **Bishop**) Does he know you or somethin'?

Bishop No, ——no.

Pat Kenny The President concluded the conference stating that, if
necessary, he was prepared to talk to The Barrytown Three
himself. ——I'm joined on the phone now by George
Llewellyn, Professor of American Studies at the University of
Scunthorpe. Doctor Llewellyn, is this a climb-down by
President Reagan?

Enter **Mr** *and* **Mrs Farrell** *while* **Pat Kenny** *is speaking.* **Mr Farrell**
is 'looking after' **Mrs Farrell**, *although* **Mrs Farrell** *doesn't need to be
looked after.* **Mr Farrell** *likes to think that his wife is helpless and
hopeless, but she isn't: she couldn't be: she's been married to* **Mr Farrell**
for twenty-two years.

Farrell Aidan! Aidan!!

Ao (*turning off the radio*) Da!?
(*Looking out the window.*) Da.

Farrell I have your mammy here with me.

Ao Ma!

Mrs Farrell Hello, Aidan, love.

Ao Are yeh alrigh'?

Farrell (*his arm around* **Mrs Farrell**'s *shoulders; sounding like a Samaritan*) She'll be grand. ——Give her time.

Mrs Farrell I'm grand, love. ——I'm a little tired, that's all.

Farrell Fatigue. ——Shock, maybe as well.

Ao Did they hurt yeh, Ma?

Mrs Farrell Ah, no. —

Farrell It's a bit early to say as yet.

Mrs Farrell (*to* **Mr Farrell**) They *didn't* hurt me.

Farrell Just cos you're not gushin' blood doesn't mean they didn't hurt yeh. It mightn't show from the outside.

Mrs Farrell I don't know wha' you're talkin' about, Edward.

Farrell (*whispering; hissing: looking around to make sure no one's listening*) The fuckin' compensation! That's wha' I'm talkin' abou'.

Mrs Farrell I never thought of that.

Farrell That's why you stay at home an' I go ou' —

Mrs Farrell An' deliver vegetables to shops in your van.

Farrell Fuck off.

Mr Farrell *grins.* **Mr** *and* **Mrs Farrell** *understand each other.*

Mrs Farrell (*to* **Ao**) I'm sure I'll recover. ——With the help o' God.

Farrell (*quietly*) Good girl.

Mrs Farrell (*to* **Ao**) Is the Bishop there with yeh?

Ao Yeah, he is.

Mrs Farrell Hello, Your Grace.

Bishop Good —

Donkey Shut up, yeh thick! They'll know I'm not you.

Mrs Farrell Aidan's a terrible boy for kidnappin' you. I don't know where he got the idea from but he certainly didn't get it from his mammy or his daddy.

Farrell (*agreeing*) No way.

Donkey Me back's sweatin' again.

Ao Sorry, Ma. Jaysis, if I'd known they were goin' to interrogate yeh I prob'ly wouldn't've done it.

Mrs Farrell Ah, they didn't really interr —

Farrell Shhh!

Mrs Farrell (*joking*) Sure, I hadn't been in Dollymount in years.

John (*dirtily*) I wonder wha' she did the last time she —

Ao Don't fuckin' start, you, righ'!

Donkey Ask them are the Yanks still after us.

Ao What's happenin' an'annyway?

Farrell That's why we're here. The Yanks sent us. Their main fella. I forget his name. Ski somethin'. He's hidin' behind the chipper. He told us to tell yis there's been a bit of a backlash in America. The Irish over there are goin' spare. The city o' Boston is givin' us a new Community Centre.
(*Sarcastically.*) A bigger one, o' course. The State o' New Jersey is givin' us a new Community Centre as well. Twenty-seven Community Centres we're gettin'. They'll have to knock down half the fuckin' houses!

Mrs Farrell Don't listen to him, lads. He's messin'. We're only gettin' the two.

Farrell Annyway. ——Your man says they now know they, eh, went for the wrong strategic option. I think that's American for sayin' they made fuckin' eejits ou' o' themselves.

The lads grin at each other: this sounds good.

Farrell So annyway; he says they can't just pack up an' go home just like tha' cos they're the world's greatest democracy, d'yeh see, an' it wouldn't look good. An', to be honest with yis, I can see his point.

Mrs Farrell (*sardonically*) Can yeh?

Farrell Don't start. ——Yeh see, they can't have it lookin' like they've been beaten by three snotty-nosed gets from Dublin.

Bishop (*annoyed*) *My* well-being no longer seems to be of paramount importance.

Ao Ah now, Your Bishop. *We* hope yeh get ou' okay, don't we, lads?

Donkey (*sweetly*) Ah, yeah.

Farrell So ——.

(*Chuckling.*) Now, yis needn't believe this if yis don't want to. ——Are yis listenin'?

Mrs Farrell Of course they're listenin', Eddie.

Farrell Annyway: this is the plan. Yis aren't goin' to believe this; it's fuckin' gas. They've rigged up one o' their satellites an' what's goin' to happen is: Ronnie Reagan's goin' to talk to yis.

Mr Farrell *laughs.*

Donkey Jaysis, wha'!

John Deadly!

Ao Hang on. Go on, Da.

Farrell Well, like ——He talks to yis. I don't know wha' abou'. Exactly. He asks yis to let the Bishop go. You let the Bishop go. An' then you're let go. ——An' then I beat the shite ou' o' yeh when I get yeh home.

Mrs Farrell He won't touch yeh, Aidan. He's messin' again. You'll do it, won't yeh?

Farrell It's very clever really. Youse go free, the Bishop goes free, an' Ronnie Reagan only looks like a regular gobshite instead of a king-size one. ——Will yis talk to him? Yeh may as well, wha'. They're puttin' the best bits on the telly.

Ao (*to the lads*) Okay?

John (*imitating* **Plain-clothes**) Okay.

Donkey Ah, def'ny.

Ao (*out the window*) Righ'. Okay.

Farrell Good man.

Mrs Farrell Good boy, Aidan.

Exit **Mr** *and* **Mrs Farrell.**

Farrell (*roaring to the wing as he exits*) They'll do it!

Ao (*to the lads; worrying*) Come here but; we're still in trouble. We have to be. ——The Yanks might let us off but our cops won't. No way. Not after all tha'.

The lads look despondent.

John (*inspired; only realises it as he speaks*) We'd be alrigh' if the Bishop said we never kidnapped him.

Donkey (*after a pause; impressed*) Brilliant.

Ao Wha' d'yeh say, Your Bishop?

Bishop (*coldly*) As you would quite succinctly put it yourself: No way.

Ao Ah; Your Bishop.

John (*to* **Donkey**) Fergus is bein' sarcastic.

Donkey (*getting down off the chair*) He'll be dead in a minute if he doesn't change his mind.

Ao Go on, Your Bishop. It won't kill yeh.

Bishop (*furious*) Won't kill me! For the past two days you have done little else but threaten to kill me.

Ao Ah now, Your Bishop, don't exagger —

Bishop Shut up! You beat me; you humiliated me — (*Beginning to sense that he's in charge.*) Or attempted to humiliate me. You shot at me and you —you think this is all some sort of a game! ——Well, let me tell you —

Donkey No!
(*Pushing the* **Bishop** *before him, and onto the bed.*) You shut your mouth! ——You're wastin' your time givin' us your sermon. We don't want to hear it. ——You just do wha' Ao says or I'll kick the livin' crap ou' of yeh.
(*Stepping back.*) Ask him again, Ao.

Ao Will yeh tell them we didn't kidnap yeh, please, Your Bishop?

Bishop (*after glancing at* **Donkey**) Oh, what difference does it make! Alright, alright; I'll tell them.

Donkey Good.

Ao Thanks.

Bishop At least I have one reason to be grateful to you: I now realise just what a sick society it is I live in!

John (*to the* **Bishop**) Good man. Get it out o' your system.

Donkey *pretends to puke; his answer to the* **Bishop**'s *insult. He climbs onto the chair.*

Ao What'll I say to Ronnie, lads?

John (*joking*) Tell him we're very sorry an' we'll never do it again.

Ao *and* **John** *look out the window, into the wing, at the preparations being made for the broadcast.*

Enter **Mr** *and* **Mrs Farrell**, *dressed up for the broadcast. They have a picnic and pope chairs with them.* **Mrs Farrell** *is doing most of the carrying. They are followed by* **Lieutenant Bukowski**.

Bukowski Thank you, Mister Farrell. Missis Farrell.

Mrs Farrell Ah, hello.

Bukowski Hello again, Missis Farrell.

Farrell Can we stay an' watch?

Bukowski I guess that would be alright, Mister Farrell.

Farrell Thanks very much.

John (*looking out*) There's a camera, look.

Ao Oh, yeah.

Donkey (*turning on the chair*) Let's see.

Ao No; better not.

Donkey (*disappointed*) Aaah.

Ao Come here. Will we do a mooner at them?

The lads laugh. They're getting excited. The **Bishop** *pours himself a bowl of cornflakes. He sits on the bed, slowly chewing them, looking miserable.*

John Look it; they're puttin' up speakers, look.

Ao They're very quick. They weren't there a minute ago. An' look it. There's a fella with one o' them furry yokes.

John Wha'!? ——That's a microphone, yeh spoon.

Ao (*laughing*) I was wonderin' wha' it was.

Donkey Ah, let's see, will yis.

Ao (*strict*) No.

Enter **Private Crabacre**, *holding the field phone receiver.*

Crabacre Lieutenant Bukowski. Sir, I got General Ma*hon*ey here. But it ain't me he's lookin' to communicate with.

Bukowski Thank you, Private.
(*into the phone.*) General Ma*hon*ey. How are *you*, Sir?

Farrell (*earwigging*) Jaysis! A general!

Mrs Farrell (*to* **Crabacre**) Oh, hello, John Wesley.

Bukowski (*into the phone*) Yes, General. We *have* completed disengagement and evacuation is ongoing, Sir.

Crabacre Mornin', Mam.

Bukowski Yes, Sir. The fifteenth green is being reinstated, Sir.

Mrs Farrell Eddie, this is John Wesley I was tellin' yeh about.

Bukowski (*into the phone*) I'll do that now, Sir.

Farrell (*shaking hands*) Eddie Farrell. Howyeh.

Crabacre Honoured, Sir.

Bukowski (*into the phone*) Yes, Sir.

Farrell (*to* **Mrs Farrell***; sticking out his chest and strutting*) 'Sir', wha'.

Mrs Farrell (*laughing*) Sir Eddie Farrell.

Farrell An' Lady Veronica.

Crabacre *takes the phone from* **Bukowski**.

Bukowski Excuse me, Mister Farrell.

Farrell Yes, son?

Bukowski Would you introduce me to your son, please?

Farrell Introduce yeh? ——Ah, I'm no good at tha' sort o' thing. Veronica here'll do it for yeh.

Bukowski You would, Missis Farrell?

Mrs Farrell Ah, yeah.

Bukowski Thank you.

Mrs Farrell (*after clearing her throat*) Aidan?

Ao Ma.

Mrs Farrell Aidan, I'd like you to meet Lieutenant —— Bukowski?

Farrell That's righ', yeah.

Mrs Farrell And, Lieutenant Bukowski, this is my son, Aidan Farrell.

Ao Howyeh.

Bukowski How are *you*?

Ao Not too bad. An' yourself?

Bukowski I'm fine, I guess. ——I want to go up there and talk with you. Is that alright with you, Ai*dan*?

John Ai*dan*!?

Ao Shut up, Jon-*athan*.

John Fuck off.

Ao Wha' d'yeh want to talk abou'?

Bukowski Well, I want to run through the broadcast procedure with you and, eh, that's it, I guess.

Ao (*to the lads*) Okay?

John (*imitating* **Plain-clothes**) Okay.

Donkey May as well.

Ao (to **Bukowski**) Okay. ——No guns, righ'.

Bukowski Absolutely not.

Ao Righ'. Come on up.

Bukowski Private.

Crabacre (*roars*) Sir!?

Mr *and* **Mrs Farrell** *jump*.

Bukowski (*exiting*) This way.

Private (*following; not too enthusiastically*) Shoot.

Exit **Bukowski** *and* **Crabacre**.

Mrs Farrell Aidan.

Ao Howyeh, Ma.

Mrs Farrell Your hair, Aidan.

Ao (*leaving the window*) Ah, it's alrigh', Ma.

The **Bishop** *is still eating slowly, and looking miserable; sulking.* **Ao** *rushes to the door with the gun, to meet the Marines.*

Ao (*as he goes*) Yeh righ', John?

John *follows* **Ao**. **Donkey** *stays on the chair.* **Ao** *and* **John** *stand against the wall, hidden by the door as it opens in, braced.*

Bukowski (*from the landing*) Hi?

Enter **Bukowski**. **Ao** *is behind him and pushes him to the wall beside the window and* **Donkey**.

Ao Righ'. Hands on the wall. Come on. Legs apart. Come on.

Bukowski *obeys* **Ao**, *and* **Ao** *frisks him.*

Enter **Crabacre**. **John** *puts him to the wall and frisks him.*

John (*as he frisks*) Book him, Danno! Hands against the wall,
    motherfucker.

John *puts the phone receiver to the back of* **Crabacre**'s *neck and kicks his feet wide apart.*

Bukowski I'm Lieut—

John (*like a Nazi*) Silence!

The **Bishop** *is still eating.*

John (*having a ball; into* **Crabacre**'s *ear as he frisks him*) Go ahead,
    asshole. Make my day.
    (*Into the phone; sings.*) Car 54, where are youuu?
    (*Into the phone.*) Ten four, Rubber Duck.

Ao *puts the gun to the back of* **Bukowski's** *neck.*

Bukowski (*nicely*) Hey, this isn't necessary, you know.

Ao Righ'; turn slowly.

The first thing **Bukowski** *sees as he turns is* **Donkey.**

Donkey Ha ha! You thought I was the Bishop, an' I'm not.

John He isn't even a priest.

Bukowski (*to* **Donkey**) How are *you*?

Donkey Who's askin'?

Bukowski *is bemused: was he just asked a question?*

Bukowski Bishop Treacy?

Bishop (*looking up from his cornflakes; surly*) Good morning.

The **Bishop** *closes the dressing-gown over so the American soldiers won't be able to see his legs.*

Bukowski (*to the* **Bishop**) How are *you*, Sir?

Ao He's grand.

Bukowski (*to the* **Bishop**) It's good to see that you're still able for a hearty breakfast, Sir.

Bishop (*looking at the cornflakes, and hating them*) It's hardly what you would call a *hearty* breakfast.

John (*to* **Bukowski**) Yeah don't have half a grapefruit on yeh, do yeh?

Donkey *roars laughing.*

Bukowski I guess not.

Donkey *gets down off the chair and goes to shake hands with* **Bukowski.**

Donkey Howyeh.

When **Bukowski** *puts his hand out to grip* **Donkey's,** **Donkey** *takes his hand away and scratches his head, and walks past* **Bukowski.**

Donkey (*into* **Crabacre's** *ear; shouts*) Howyeh!

Crabacre Honoured!

Ao *sits on the bed beside the* **Bishop** *and casually aims the gun at him.*
John *takes a Twix from the grocery box and hands it to the* **Bishop.**
The **Bishop** *eats, and enjoys the Twix; and reads the wrapper, paying no attention to what is going on.*

Donkey What's tha' you're eatin', Fergus?

The **Bishop** *hides the Twix and won't let* **Donkey** *see.*

Ao (*to* **Bukowski**) What's the story?

Bukowski Have you elected a representative to speak to the President?

Ao Yeah. Me.

Bukowski And were you democratically elected?

Ao Eh, ——yeah.

Bukowski Good. Ai*dan*. I'm going to explain the procedure to you now. It's pretty straightforward.

Donkey It'd want to be.

Bukowski Why is that, Sir?

Donkey (*about* **Ao**) Cos he's as thick as shite.

Bukowski Is that right? ——Well, that shouldn't be too big a problem, Ai*dan*. You won't have to say much, I guess. The President will handle most of the talking side of the operation. The President will say 'Good morning' to you and, well, we think it would be kind o' nice if you were to say 'Good morning' to the President. How would you feel about that, Ai*dan*?

Ao Okay. No problem.

Bukowski Could you say that now, please?

Ao Wha'? Good mornin'?

Bukowski Yes.

Ao Eh ——Good —

Bukowski At the window, please. For the TV people.

Ao Ah now.
  (*After thinking.*) Donkey.

Donkey Yeah?

Ao Take the gun here and put it to the Bishop —. No. Hang on. (*Standing up; to* **Bukowski**.) Sit down there.

Bukowski *sits beside the* **Bishop**. *The* **Bishop** *ignores him*. **Ao** *gives the gun to* **Donkey**, *and* **Donkey** *climbs onto the bed and stands behind* **Bukowski**. *He puts the barrel to the top of* **Bukowski**'s *skull*.

Ao (*to* **Donkey**) Now, if annythin' happens to me while I'm over here at the window would you mind puttin' a bullet in tha' man's head.

Donkey Certainly. No problem. ——I might do it annyway, cos

I've never seen it done this way before an' I'd be very
interested to see if his brains go up, or down.

Bukowski Hey, it's cool. ——No tricks.

Donkey If it's *cool* why are yeh shakin' so much, *man*?

John (*imitating* **Plain-clothes**) Okay, man.

Ao *goes to the window.* **Mr** *and* **Mrs Farrell** *are having their picnic.*

Farrell There's Aidan.

Ao (*to* **Bukowski**) Just 'Good mornin''?

Bukowski Yes.

Ao (*out the window*) Eh ——Good mornin'. —Tha' alrigh'?

Mrs Farrell That was lovely, Aidan.

Farrell Very clear. Like Alistair Burnett.

Bukowski (*'sincere'*) That was very good.

Farrell Only he wouldn't be sayin' 'Good mornin'' on the 'News
At Ten'. Unless he was scuttered.

Bukowski So that's how the operation will commence. It's nice.
Breaks the ice, I guess.

Donkey (*absently*) Breaks your head, I guess.

Donkey puts the gun to different parts of **Bukowski**'*s head, trying to
judge where the bullet would come out.*

Bukowski After the exchange of greetings the President will give
us a short statement on yesterday's tragedy. Brief. Some nice
words for the bereaved personnel at home, I guess. ——At the
conclusion of which the President will ask you to release the
Bishop. And, then, Ai*dan*; it'd be neat if you could say
something along the lines of, say, 'We will release the Bishop
immediately, Mister President'. I think that would be good.
What do you think about that?

Donkey It's thick.

Ao Okay.

John (*imitating* **Plain-clothes**) Okay.

Bukowski Or, if you prefer, something less formal like, say,
'Okay; here he is' will be fine.

Ao No; the first one's better.

Bukowski Good. I think so too. Could you say that, please?

Ao (*going to the window*) Okay. ——Wha' is it again?

Bukowski We will release the Bishop immediately, Mister President.

Donkey He'll never remember tha'.

Ao (*out the window*) Eh, we will release the Bishop immediately, Mister President.
(*To* **Donkey**.) There, bollix.

Farrell I never knew he had it in him.

Mrs Farrell Aidan, love. Pat down your hair. It's standing up.

Ao *pats his hair, a bit embarrassed.*

Bukowski Good. Very good. I like that. —— And, well, I guess that's it.

Ao Is tha' all?

Bukowski Yes.

Donkey Hey, Mister. There's somethin' after movin' in your hair.

Bukowski (*nervous; diplomatic*) Is that —right?

Donkey Yeah. Do yeh want me to shoot it for yeh?

Bukowski I —guess not.

John Does it have wings, Donkey?

Donkey I'm after losin' it. ——Come ou' with your wings up.

Ao D'yeh want me to say 'God bless America' or somethin' like tha'? It'd be no problem.

Bukowski No, I guess not, Ai*dan*. I think the President plans on using that one himself after the Bishop has been re-instated into a, eh —

Crabacre (*still against the wall*) Nonrestrictive environment, Sir.

Bukowski —nonrestrictive environment.

Ao Ah well, fair enough then.

John Tell him all his films are poxy.

Bukowski I don't think that would be advisable.

Donkey He's only messin'.
(*Looking into* **Bukowski**'s *hair*.) Do they have Head an' Shoulders in America?

Bukowski (*bemused*) ——Yes. ——Well. —Thank you all for your cooperation. I guess I can stand up now?

Ao Yeah. Donkey, guard the Bishop.

Bukowski *stands up carefully.* **Donkey** *sits on the bed, beside the* **Bishop**.

Donkey Howyeh, Fergus. Did yeh miss me?

Bishop I have got nothing to say to you.

Donkey Ah, Fergus. ——Have yeh anny tickles?

Donkey *starts tickling the* **Bishop**, *and the* **Bishop** *squirms.*

Bukowski Bishop Treacy? Sir?

Bishop *(stops squirming)* Yes!?

Bukowski Goodbye, Sir.

Bishop *(gruff)* Goodbye.

Bukowski *(to all; exiting)* Goodbye. And thank you again.

Crabacre 'Preciate it.

Exit **Bukowski**. **Crabacre** *remains, unable to move.*

John Cheerio.

Donkey Seeyis.

Crabacre Lieutenant!

Bukowski *(entering)* Private?

Crabacre I'm kinda stuck here, Sir.

John *and* **Bukowski** *help* **Crabacre** *to the door.*

Crabacre *(exiting; in pain)* 'Preciate it.

Donkey *(looking in the box)* D'yeh want a banana, Fergus?

Bishop No, thank you.

John You can eat them, yeh know.

The lads laugh, excited.

John Are yeh goin' to say wha' they want yeh to?

Ao Ah, yeah. I'd better.

John Yeah.

Donkey Chicken.

Ao Fuck off.

Enter **Bukowski** *and* **Crabacre** *from the left wing.* **Crabacre** *is having problems walking.* **Bukowski** *is talking into the field phone.*

Bukowski *(into the phone)* Is that right, Sir? That is good news.
      (To **Mr Farrell**.) Budweiser are sponsoring the broadcast.

Farrell Go 'way.

Mr Farrell *raises his eyes to heaven.*

Bukowski (*into the phone*) I'll do that now, General.

Crabacre (*taking the phone*) Sir!

Bukowski I have to liaise with TV personnel, Private. You entertain these good people while I'm gone.

Crabacre Yes, Sir!

Exit **Bukowski**. *The* **Bishop** *is dozing*.

Ao (*at the window*) Hey, Da. Is it on live?

Farrell Yeah. But come here. It's on at the same time as 'Neighbours' so there mightn't be annyone watchin' it.

Mrs Farrell (*remembering; then disappointed to miss it*) Oh! 'Neighbours'.

Crabacre That your boy, Mam?

Mrs Farrell That's right. Aidan.

Crabacre (*giving out to* **Ao**) You all might should be ashamed of yourselves abductin' the aux-hillary Bishop an' cahootin' with them A-rabs an' leavin' your mamas frettin' an' beatin' their breasts in anguish.

Ao What's he sayin'?

Mrs Farrell (*explaining*) His mammy had an operation.

Crabacre That's right, Mam.

John She needed one after him. The head on him.

Crabacre Sixteen growths removed.

Farrell Where are the other fifteen?

Mrs Farrell Eddie; stop that. Leave him alone.

Enter **Bukowski**.

Bukowski The link-up is operational, Private.

Crabacre That's good news to hear, Sir.

Bukowski (*to the lads*) One minute. ——This is live TV, right?

The lads put on serious television faces. **John** *and* **Donkey** *push each other for better position.*

Farrell (*indignant, to* **Bukowski**) We're washed, ready an' waitin'.

Bukowski Is that right? ——So, well, thank you for your cooperation.

Farrell (*dismissive*) Ah, no problem.

Crabacre 'Preciate it.

Bukowski So, well ——. Stand by.

Farrell (*rubbing his hands*) Here we go.

Donkey Fergus.

The **Bishop** *snaps awake and sits up, alert.*

Mrs Farrell (*as the Marines exit*) Bye bye now.

Bukowski Goodbye, Missis Farrell.

Exit **Bukowski**.

Mrs Farrell John Wesley?

Crabacre Mam?

Mrs Farrell You'll be able to get those vests I was tellin' you about in Guiney's on Talbot Street, if you're not goin' straight back to America.

Crabacre 'Preciate it, Mam.

Mrs Farrell Bye bye.

Crabacre (*saluting*) Mam.

Exit **Crabacre**.

Mrs Farrell He has a bad chest.

Farrell Fuck'm.

Ao (*to the* **Bishop**) Remember now, Your Bishop. We didn't kidnap yeh.

Bishop (*still sulking*) Yes. I know.

Donkey Good man, Fergus.

There is a short pause. The lads stare out the window, braced and excited; pushing a bit.

Reagan's Voice Hello, Iceland-Ireland. ——Good morning, boys.

Ao Good mornin', Mister President.

Reagan You're the one they call Ai*dan*?

Ao Yeah. ——Yes, Mister President. That's righ'.

Mrs Farrell *grabs* **Mr Farrell**'*s arm.*

Donkey I'm the one they call Donkey.

Reagan Good morning to you, Donk, em, Donkey.

Donkey How's it goin'.

Reagan Boys, I'm sure you know why we are talking to each other like this across the mighty Atlantic Ocean. There is no death more tragic or more wasteful than the death of youth. Without youth to follow in our steps our dreams, our goals, our achievements mean nothing.

The lads begin to look bored; stifle yawns etc.

Reagan Our efforts to protect and preserve freedom with peace are empty if there are no young people to flourish in that freedom. A nation is only as alive and as vigorous and as essential as that nation's young citizens. Boys, yesterday our nation, the United States of America, lost seventeen young men she could not afford to lose.

Donkey (*quietly*) Aw!

Reagan (*on the verge of tears*) Boys, I'm asking you now this morning, so the loss of those seventeen young lives might in *one* way become meaningful. I'm asking you now. Let Bishop Treacy go home.

Farrell I thought we'd be here for the rest o' the fuckin' day.

Mrs Farrell Shhh, you.

Ao (*nervous but determined*) Mister President. I've got three words to say to you.

John Not 'God bless America'!?

Ao The first one is 'Fuck'. An' the second one is 'Off'. An' the third one is 'Pal'.

The lads are shocked, but delighted: they're definitely on the map now.

Mrs Farrell Aidan! Oh, my God almighty!

Mr Farrell *looks around for Marines and bullets, and then starts laughing.*

Reagan ——I —

Ao Now I think the Bishop wants to say a few words to yeh. —— Your Bishop.

*The **Bishop** goes to the window. He stands there, erect and dignified in underpants and lady's dressing-gown.*

Donkey (*warning the **Bishop***) Hey.

*The **Bishop** ignores him.*

Bishop Mister Reagan, —

Reagan Your Grace, I'm glad to see —

Bishop I was not kidnapped.

Reagan (*after a pause*) Oh.

Bishop (*getting into his stride*) I have been incarcerated in this house with these ——*boys* for the last two days because if we had attempted to step outside we would without doubt have been shot and killed. By your *boys*.

Ao (*quietly*) Good man, Your Bishop.

Bishop (*after glaring at* **Ao**) Your pretext for this fiasco, Mister Reagan, was my *American* citizenship. Well, let me tell you: when I get home — *If* I manage to make it all that way without being shot or bombarded by your *boys* —I will immediately locate my *precious* American passport and burn the wretched thing. ——My regard for you, Mister Reagan, has never been high. As of today it isn't even low!

The **Bishop** *about-turns and strides grimly and manfully out of the room.*

Donkey Good luck, Fergus!

Enter the **Bishop**.

Bishop (*pointing to* **Donkey**) You go and shite!!

Exit the **Bishop**.

Donkey (*a bit hurt*) Ah, there was no need for tha'.

Ao (*out the window*) We will release the Bishop immediately, Mister President.

Farrell (*the proud father*) There now. Follow tha'!

He hugs **Mrs Farrell**.

The lads celebrate, and sing 'Here we go, here we go, here we go'.

Donkey *exits*.

Farrell Tha' was gas.

Mrs Farrell (*collecting the picnic things*) Aidan was very rude.

Farrell He was dead righ'. If he hadn't o' sayin' it, I would've.

Mrs Farrell He could've said it nicer.

Farrell We might as well go home.

Mrs Farrell Yeah. I'm jaded.

Farrell I don't think we'll get anny compensation ou' o' the Yanks now.

Mrs Farrell Ah well.

Farrell I got some rashers an' sausages in.

Mrs Farrell Wha'? All by yourself?

Farrell I'll tell yeh one thing. They're an awful fuckin' price.

Mrs Farrell Are yeh goin' to give me more money?

Farrell Oh, I am, yeah. ——In my arse.

Exit **Mr** *and* **Mrs Farrell**.

Ao *and* **John** *are sitting on the bed. Enter* **Donkey** *with a hoover, singing 'Here we go' quietly.*

Donkey Oh fuck. Fergus is after goin' off with me ma's dressin'-gown.

Ao Don't worry. We'll get a new one an' rip some o' the threads ou' of it.

The three lads are sitting on the bed, facing the audience.

John (*after a pause*) Tha' was brilliant crack, wasn't it?

Ao Yeah; brilliant.

Donkey Brilliant.
(*After a pause.*) What'll we do now?

John *searches in the grocery box and takes out the gun. They look at it, and then at the audience.*

As the lights go down Sam the Sham and The Pharaohs play 'I'm In With The Out Crowd'.

War

Dedicated
to Belinda

CHARACTERS

The Finnegans	**George**	Early 40s.
	Briget	40.
	Yvonne	20.
The Pub	**Leo**	The barman; late 30s.
	Denis	The quizmaster; late 40s.
	Sandra	The Lounge Girl; 16.
George's Team	**Martin**	Early 40s.
	Features	Early 40s.
	Gary	Early 20s.
Bertie's Team	**Bertie**	Early 40s.
	Tommy	Mid 30s.
	Angela	Mid 30s.
	Noel	Early 40s.
Yvonne's Team	**Lorraine**	20.
	Niamh	20.
	Dermot	22.

The Quiz scenes all take place on a Monday night. The Kitchen scenes take place on different occasions before the quiz.

War was first staged at the SFX Centre, Dublin, in September 1989.

Director	Paul Mercier
Producer	John Sutton
Designer	Anne Gately
Lighting	Tony Wakefield
Briget	Caroline Rothwell
Leo	Éamonn Hunt⋆
Tommy	Robert English
Noel	Donagh Deeney
Lorraine	Sharon Murphy
Yvonne	Aoife Lawless
Martin	Mick Nolan
Features	Gerard Byrne
Gary	Stephen Dunne
Denis	Gerry Walsh
Bertie	Paul Raynor
Sandra	Susan Church
Niamh	Sharon Coade
Angela	Susie Kennedy
Dermot	Andrew Connolly
George	Brendan Gleeson

⋆ Mick Egan replaced Éamonn Hunt during the play's run.

Act One

The set is in two parts; the Pub Lounge and the Kitchen. The Lounge, stage-right, is a newish suburban lounge; large, gaudy and colourful. It is beginning to show signs of wear. It is known as The Gaza Strip by the people of Barrytown, but the owner insists on calling it The Hiker's Rest. There are posters on the walls: 'Sunday 15th—Barrytown Utd V. Raheny Boys—3.00 pm—Support and lifts welcome'; 'Larry O'Rourke—Barrytown's Elvis—Sings for the Third World—Here— Sat. 14th—Tickets £2—Great Cause'. The pitch 'n' putt club's fixture list, a complicated-looking chart, is also tacked to a wall. Only a corner of the total Lounge is seen onstage. There are three tables and sets of chairs and stools, and a leatherette couch. Behind the bar there are rows of bottles, optics, a cocktail shaker, a glass full of little paper umbrellas. There are sports trophies and tacked-up postcards. There are some collection boxes on the counter, and some of **Denis***'s reference books.* **Denis***'s homemade scoreboard is on the ground, leaning against the counter. The toilet doors are at the end of the bar, towards centre back-stage.*

The Kitchen, stage-left, is in a corporation house and is small, bright and modern, but not cluttered with gadgets: the **Finnegans** *are comfortable but not well off. There are some cupboards and a worktop, and an old fridge. There is a well pawed kettle-jug on the worktop, and some old biscuit and tea tins. There is a Whitney Houston calendar on the wall, and a teenager's heavy-metal-inspired drawing attached to the fridge door by a magnet. Two of* **Briget***'s completed jigsaws, framed, are also on the wall. There is a biscuit-tin lid full of sand in a corner, and a saucer of milk.*

Groucho Marx sings 'Lydia The Tattooed Lady'. It is 7.45 pm. The Quiz is due to start in fifteen minutes, at 8.00 pm.

Briget *is in the Kitchen. She turns on the kettle. She takes dirty plates off the table and brings them to the sink, perhaps offstage. When the kettle boils she makes a cup of tea. Then she sits at the table and does the Evening Herald crosswords. She does all this while the action in the Lounge takes place. Towards the end of Scene One* **Briget** *gets up and makes a second cup of tea, for* **George***. The Lounge seems empty.*

There are two half-drunk pints on one of the tables. They are **Noel**'s *and* **Tommy**'s.

Enter **Leo**, *the perfect barman, from stage-right as the music fades.* **Leo** *is in his late thirties, is from Dundalk, and was once called the Red Adair of the Lounge-bar world. He is carrying a pile of glass ashtrays. He quickly, but without rushing, lets an ashtray drop, spinning, onto each table.*

Leo (*at each drop*) Now.

Tommy (*unseen; from behind the couch; seriously*) You'd never know wha' yeh'd put your hand on under here.

Leo (*only slightly puzzled*) Now ——?

Tommy Glass or ——. Here it is. ——No. ——Got it!

Tommy *appears head-first from behind the couch, looking quietly triumphant. He is in his thirties, and was once described as being 'a bit, —yeh know; unfortunate'. He sees that* **Noel** *isn't there and looks puzzled; then let down. As* **Leo** *goes behind the Bar* **Noel** *comes out of the Gents.* **Noel** *is in his early forties and was once in a band that played Mud, Sweet and Smokie hits at weddings and dinner dances. He puts a hand through his hair and roughs it up. He slips his comb into his back pocket. He is quite happy with his appearance, and everything else about himself.*

Tommy I found it, Noel.

Noel (*a bit absently*) Wha'?

Tommy The tenpence.

Tommy Oh, righ'. Good man.

As **Noel** *turns to the Bar his expression changes to one of bewildered, superior amusement.*

Noel Have yeh got those pints for me, L ——?

Before **Noel** *finishes speaking* **Leo** *places two pints of Guinness on the counter in front of him.*

Leo Now.

Noel Wha' kept yeh?

Leo *takes £4 from* **Noel** *and exits, stage-right, to the till. We hear 'Now', and then the till opening. As* **Leo** *exits,* **Yvonne** *and* **Lorraine** *enter and* **Martin** *comes out of the Gents.* **Yvonne** *is* **George** *and* **Briget**'s *twenty-year-old daughter. She is charmingly aggressive, and less charming when she doesn't get her way.* **Lorraine** *is Tonto to*

Yvonne's *Lone Ranger*. **Martin** *is in his early forties and, although there are lines on his face, it wasn't worry that put them there. Tonight, though,* **Martin** *looks miserable; really miserable. He automatically checks that his fly is closed as he goes to the Bar.*

Lorraine Over here?

Yvonne (*on the way to their table*) Yeah. ——Anyway, I said to him; you're not my boss, you. You're only a shelf stacker in a suit. Like the rest of us.

Noel *deliberately gets in their way on his way from the Bar to his table.*

Noel Howyis, girls.

Yvonne Ah, howyeh, Mr McGrath.
(*To* **Lorraine**; *mouthing secretly.*) He fancies me.

Lorraine (*mouthing*) Jesus.
(*Back to normal.*) An' wha' did he do?

Yvonne He told the manager; the spa.

Lorraine Jesus.

Yvonne An' he said I had to do it.

Lorraine An' did yeh?

Yvonne Yeah. ——But I made a mess of it.

Noel *puts the new pints on the table, in front of* **Tommy**.

Tommy (*giving* **Noel** *the tenpence and looking seriously pleased*) There.

Noel Eh, good man, Tommy.

As **Leo** *comes back with* **Noel**'s *change,* **Features** *and* **Gary** *enter.* **Features** *is in his early forties, and is a very nice man: even his wife and kids like him.* **Gary**, **Features**'s *brother-in-law, is in his early twenties. He's a student. His father thinks that a couple of years in the army would sort him out.*

Features (*greeting all; rubbing hands*) Ha Ha —Ha Ha —Ha Ha.

Noel's *hostility and* **Tommy**'s *uncertainty are clear.* **Tommy** *doesn't know if he should say 'Howyeh' to* **Features**.

Lorraine Oh Jesus, there's a fuckin' quiz on.

Yvonne Come on.

Yvonne *and* **Lorraine** *get up and exit, watched by* **Noel** *and* **Gary**, *who looks at once impressed and disdainful.*

Features Not stayin' for the oul' quiz, Yvonne?

Yvonne (*scornful, but friendly*) No way.

Leo (*holding up change over the collection boxes*) Lifeboat, the missions or yourself?

Noel (*very emphatically*) Meself.

Noel *goes over for his change.* **Leo** *puts the change on the counter ('Now') and puts a pint in front of* **Martin**.

Martin (*heart-broken and hostile*) I don't want tha'.

Leo (*a bit surprised*) Now?

Features Leo, can I've a —

Leo *puts the pint in front of* **Features**.

Leo Now.

Features Lovely.
    (*Greeting.*) Martin.

Martin *grunts.*

Noel (*noticing* **Gary**; *suspicious*) Hey Features, are yis playin' a banger?

Features (*friendly but emphatic*) We are not. This is Gary. He's Trudy's little brother.

Noel (*aggressively, to* **Gary**) Who wrote 'Elmer Gantry'?

Gary (*reluctant to admit it and a bit overpowered*) I —eh —can't remember.

Noel Useless.
    (*To* **Tommy**) He doesn't know who wrote 'Elmer Gantry'.

Tommy (*to please* **Noel**; *doesn't like saying 'fuck'*) Fuckin' eejit.

They laugh, including **Features**. **Martin** *doesn't laugh.* **Gary** *is humiliated and furious but tries not to look it.* **Martin** *leans over the counter and whispers his order ('Ballygowan') to* **Leo**, *who bends to get it.*

Features What'll yeh have, Gary?

Gary Eh, —a bottle of Heinek —No, a pint of Bud.

Leo *changes direction as* **Gary** *changes his mind. By the time* **Features** *orders the Budweiser the glass is under the tap, and filling.*

Features A pint of ——Bud there, Leo, please.

Leo (*to* **Martin**) Now.

Martin (*almost viciously*) Thanks.

Martin *pours the Ballygowan with his back turned to the rest; then puts the bottle over the counter. He heads for his table, with* **Features** *and* **Gary**.

Features All set, Martin?

Martin ——Yeah.

Features This is Gary I was tellin' yeh about.

Noel He doesn't know who wrote 'Elmer Gantry'.

Martin *ignores* **Noel**. *He nods at* **Gary** *who nods back.*

Features He'll be great for the science ones. An' the oul' pop, wha'.

Gary *squirms at the mention of 'pop'. As* **Features** *speaks* **Denis** *enters, carrying more of his reference books.* **Denis**, *in his late forties, devotes hours and hours of his time to planning the quizzes, yet detests the contestants; every one of them. He was the only person in Barrytown to vote for the Progressive Democrats in the last election, although he accidentally spoiled his ballot paper.*

He puts the books beside the other pile, straightens them up, then turns to exit; a man with a mission.

Features Hey, Denis. Give us a few hints, wha'.

Denis (*stopping for a second; very earnest*) Never.

Features, Noel *and* **Tommy** *grin across at each other, sharing their opinion of* **Denis**. *This unity lasts only a second. As* **Denis** *exits* **Bertie** *enters.* **Bertie** *is in his early forties. He is liked, respected and feared by those who know him, and just feared by those who don't know him. He regularly breaks into 'High Chaparral' Spanish, a habit he picked up after being slagged about going to Benidorm on his honeymoon.* **Bertie** *draws an imaginary gun and holds it at the ready until* **Denis** *goes around and past him. Then he puts his gun back into its holster.*

Bertie (*to all, and loud*) Compadres!

Sandra *enters; runs past* **Bertie**, *trying to get her jacket off and keep her handbag on her shoulder at the same time. She is sixteen, and very self-conscious. She is in her uniform; black skirt and white blouse. She isn't very confident on her high heels.* **Leo** *enters from the till.*

Leo (*accusingly*) Now.

Sandra (*aggressive*) I had to go on a message.
    (*As she bursts into the Ladies.*) It's not my fault.

Bertie (*starting again*) Compadres!

Tommy *in particular is happy to see* **Bertie**.

Features There y'are, Bertie.

Bertie *hisses at* **Features**.

Bertie (*indicating the right wing*) Big fuckin' crowd inside.
    (*Pointing at* **Gary**.) A gringo.

Noel (*scornfully*) Don't worry 'bout *him*, Bertie.

Features (*defensively, but not cowering*) He's Trudy's little brother.

Bertie (*pretending to spit on the floor, and staring at* **Gary**) I speet on
    Trudy's leetle brother.
    (*Sits down beside* **Noel** *and* **Tommy**, **Tommy** *in the
    middle*.) That'll shut the little cunt up for the first couple o'
    rounds.

Tommy *chuckles conspiratorially.*

Features Don't mind him, Gary. He's only messin'.
    (*To* **Martin**.) Isn't he?

Martin Yeah. Usually.

Bertie (*to* **Features**, *re* **Gary**) He looks a bit thick, Features.

Features (*a bit chuffed*) He goes to N.I.H.E.

Bertie Oh, F.U.C.K.; does he? Hey, compadres, they might
    actually win this time, wha'.

Noel *and* **Tommy** *scoff.*

Denis *enters, with a Bewley's tin. He is very business-like and urgent.
They all dig into their pockets for the admittance money.*

Denis (*officially*) It's ten pounds per table.

Noel Any reduction for mentlers?

Denis *ignores him.*

Bertie (*giving* **Denis** *his money*) There's the pesos, Signor Denis.

When they hand over their money **Denis** *gives each team some sheets of
paper, stapled together, on which to write the answers. Each team also
gets a cardboard team number card, made and hand-printed by* **Denis**.
Bertie's *team is Number 36;* **George**'s *team Number 37;* **Yvonne**'s
team Number 38.

Bertie Leo, uno pint of the Guinneese, like a good man.

As **Bertie** *orders,* **Leo** *puts a pint on a tray.* **Sandra** *comes out of the
Ladies and takes the tray.*

Leo Mr Gillespie.

Sandra I know!

The tray wobbles as **Sandra** *puts it down on* **Bertie**'s *table.* **Noel** *and*
Tommy *grip their pints in case of an accident.*

Bertie (*refusing the change* **Sandra** *hands him*) No, you're alrigh'. Buy yourself a hat.

Sandra (*going away; to herself, but loud*) Buy yourself a bar o' soap.

Features (*giving* **Denis** *£7.50*) George'll be here in a minute.

Noel He's swottin' at home.

Denis It's ten pounds per table irregardless of the number of contestants.

Martin He'll be here in a minute.

Denis (*insistent*) It's ten pounds.

While **Features** *digs into his pocket for the extra money,* **Yvonne,** **Lorraine** *and* **Niamh** *enter.* **Niamh** *was in the same class as* **Yvonne** *and* **Lorraine,** *but they don't often meet these days.* **Niamh** *feels that she has grown up faster than* **Yvonne** *and* **Lorraine.** *After all, she's nearly engaged to* **Dermot**; *although* **Dermot** *doesn't know this.* **Sandra** *follows them to their table.* **Noel** *gives them a hungry look.*

Yvonne (*not enthusiastic*) Can we not just go downstairs? I fuckin' hate quizzes.

Niamh Ah, come on, Yvonne. It'll be a bit o' buzz.

Lorraine (*more enthusiastic*) Jesus, I'll be useless. I don't even know why men can't help actin' on Impulse.

Niamh Come on, Yvonne. I haven't seen yis in ages. Dermot can answer the questions.

Yvonne *and* **Lorraine** *glance at each other, amused and contemptuous.*

Denis (*to the girls*) It's ten pounds.

Noel Jaysis, Denis, yeh sound like a brasser on Mount Street.

Denis *ignores him.*

Lorraine (*complaining to* **Denis**) It's very dear.

Sandra (*impatient*) Are yis ready to order your drinks yet?

Yvonne No, we're not actually, Sandra.

Sandra *moves away.*

Niamh Little bitch. ——I'll pay for Dermot.

Lorraine (*mock-admiring* **Denis**'*s team card*) Oh, isn't tha' lovely!

Yvonne (*looking to right wing*) Which one's Dermot?

Niamh (*indignant*) He's not one of them, Yvonne! He's not here yet. He has classes on Mondays.

Yvonne (*very slightly bitchy*) Why? Did he fail his Leaving?

They laugh, after a short hesitation.

Lorraine (*after they laugh*) Don't mind tha' wagon, Niamh. Come here, is he good lookin'?

Yvonne Sandra. Over here, please.

The girls continue to talk quietly, and regularly laugh.

Features *is fighting a losing battle, trying to inject a bit of good humour and excitement at his table. He rubs his hands, winks at* **Gary**, *nudges* **Martin**. *He regularly stands up and looks out at the rest of the Lounge, judging the amount of teams inside. He enjoys the crack at* **Bertie**'s *table, although* **Bertie**'s *team ignores him.* **Martin** *stares at his Ballygowan, detesting it. He tries to smile, but he's feeling too sorry for himself.* **Gary** *wears a smug, amused expression, except when* **Bertie** *looks at him.*

Features (*standing up; to* **Martin**) No sign o' George.

Noel Thank Jaysis.

Bertie Maybe George, he has copped on at last.

Features Oh, he'll be here alrigh'. Don't worry.

Bertie Righ', Tommy, compadre mio. Biggest earthquake?

Tommy (*serious and pleased*) China, 1556.

Bertie Good man. Worst volcano?

Tommy Krakatoa, 1883.

Noel Longest langer?

Tommy Bertie Gillespie, 1989.

Bertie Fuckin' sure. An' that's inches he's talkin' about there. Not millimetres now. I speet on your millimetres.

Yvonne (*quietly to the girls*) That's fuckin' disgustin'.

Features (*looking into right wing; standing up*) It must be the biggest crowd yet.
(*Beginning to worry.*) Still no sign o' George but.

Martin *tries to share* **Features**'s *concern, but his heart isn't in it.*

Gary Can we not do without him?

Features Are yeh jokin' me, Gary!? ——He'll be here. He'll be here.

Denis *is now sitting on a stool at the Bar, erect and self-important. He taps his microphone.*

Denis Testing one —testing testing. Can yis all hear me?

Nearly All No!

106

Denis Righ'. ——On behalf of the Barrytown Wheelies Cycling Club I would like to thank yis all for comin' out tonight for the quiz.

As **Denis** *speaks* **Dermot** *enters, looking confident but lost. He is in his early twenties. He's a grand, popular lad, but a bit dull. He stands at the Bar.* **Angela** *enters, sees* **Bertie**'s *team, and goes over to them. They're happy to see her.* **Angela**, *in her mid thirties, is a hard, good-humoured woman. Her husband sneaked out on her a while ago and, after a few bad months of grief and shame, she's beginning to enjoy life again.*

Denis Tonight's prizes are a bit special. Four Kenwood kettle-jugs.

Niamh (*enthusiastically*) Oh that's very good, isn't it?

Yvonne *and* **Lorraine** *aren't as impressed.*

Noel Wha'; each?

Denis *ignores him.*

Niamh (*getting up and going to the Bar*) There he is.

Denis The runners up prizes are four vouchers for the Barrytown Stay Hard Fitness Centre.

The **lads** *laugh scornfully.* **Yvonne** *and* **Lorraine** *look a bit impressed. Then ——*

Yvonne (*looking at* **Dermot** *and* **Niamh**) Jesus, it's him!

Lorraine Wha'?

Yvonne It's him.

Lorraine (*unsure*) Yeah.

Yvonne No, it's *him*. Remember I told yeh?

Lorraine (*lost at first; then ——*) Oh Jesus! It isn't.

Yvonne It is, I'm tellin' yeh.

Lorraine That's Dermot but. ——Oh, fuckin' Jesus. I'm scarlet, I must be. Am I? I'm goin' to the tylet.

Yvonne Don't fuckin' budge, you.

We see **Dermot** *ordering a drink from* **Sandra**, *who is on her way to give a pint of Guinness to* **Angela**.

Angela Thanks very much, love. I'm tellin' yeh now, I need it. How's your mammy?

Sandra (*friendly for the first time*) She's grand, thanks, Mrs. O'Leary.

Noel *leers at* **Sandra** *as she goes back to the Bar.*

Angela (*taking a sip; loud*) Ah Jaysis, Leo, you're a fuckin' genius.

Leo (*offstage; modestly*) Ah now.

Denis (*checking his index cards; into the microphone; trying not to get flustered*) Righ'.

Angela I'm tellin' yis, tha' little bastard, David; he always knows when I'm goin' out. Always. He does now. Yeh can't get the little fucker into his bed when I'm goin' out. He tried to climb into the fridge tonight, he did. ——Ah, he's lovely though.

Bertie Si.

Tommy I'll tell yeh one thing, Angela. He's goin' to be a great little footballer.

Bertie Oh si.

Dermot *is being introduced to* **Lorraine** *and* **Yvonne.** **Lorraine** *won't look at him.*

Lorraine Hiyeh.

Yvonne Hiyeh, —Dermot.

Niamh (*introducing him again*) This is Dermot. Sit here, Dermot.

Dermot *sees* **Yvonne** *properly for the first time. He looks stunned for a second, then panicky; but seems to recover.* **Yvonne** *looks at him reluctantly, then definitely; then away from him; then back, defiantly.* **Dermot** *and* **Niamh** *sit down.*

Niamh How did your class go tonight, Dermot?

Dermot (*through a dry mouth*) Eh, —fine. Great.

Lorraine Did yeh get anny eccer?

She looks stern, then giggles; then looks stern again. **Yvonne** *tries not to laugh. The Quiz is about to start.* **Denis** *reads the questions and the teams confer, and write their answers on their sheets. The sheets are collected at the end of each round, and* **Denis** *gives them the answers. Because the teams are positioned very close to one another they have to confer very carefully and quietly.*

Denis Righ'. Make sure your table numbers are —. Are yis listenin'? —Make sure your table numbers are on the top righ' hand corner of your page. Now, yeh won't get any marks if the number is missin', so ——just make sure.

Leo (*getting at* **Denis**) Better safe than sorry, Denis. Isn't tha' it?

Bertie Oh si.

Denis (*ignoring them*) There are ten rounds, with five questions in each of them. ——Righ'. We'll commence —now. Round One.

There is silence. Pens are held, at the ready. **Bertie**'s *team hunches over the table, ready to confer.* **Features** *looks into the right wing, worried.* **Niamh**, *in charge of her team's answers, is happily writing the table number on all the sheets. She sits close to* **Dermot.** **Yvonne** *and* **Lorraine** *sit as far from* **Dermot** *as they can.* **Yvonne** *and* **Dermot** *seem determined not to look at each other.*

Denis Question Number —One.

Features Hang on, Denis. Here's George.

Noel (*quietly*) Fuck.

Bertie *hisses. His team's hostility and scorn are good-humouredly obvious.*

Denis (*determined*) Question Number One.

George *enters, charging, holding his jacket close at his stomach.* **George**, *in his early forties, is the obvious captain of his team.* **George** *plays to win. He is the quiz's John McEnroe although, unlike McEnroe, he hasn't won anything yet.*

George Hold your horses, Denis!

There is mock-cheering. **Features** *is delighted to see* **George**. **George** *goes behind* **Bertie**'s *table on the way to his own. He glares down at them very quickly, without stopping.*

George (*grudgingly*) Howyis.

Bertie *hisses.*

Yvonne Hurry up, Daddy.

George *grins, pleased and surprised to see her.*

Denis I said, Question Number One!

George An' I said, hold your fuckin' horses, righ'!
    (*To the rest, as he sits down.*) Fuckin' little virgin mary.
    (*To* **Sandra**.) A pint, Sandra, please.

Sandra (*who doesn't dislike* **George** *too much*) Okay.

George *takes the answer sheet from* **Features**, *and takes his biro from his jacket pocket.*

George Righ'.
    (*To* **Gary**.) Howyeh.

Gary (*looking, warily amused, at* **George** *braced for action*) Hi.

In the Kitchen, **Briget** *gets up from the table and makes* **George**'s *cup of tea.*

Denis What was —Wha' was Fred Flintstone's wife called?

George Ah, give us a challenge, will yeh.

George *and* **Bertie***'s teams have no difficulty with the answer.*

Noel (*loud enough for* **George***'s team to hear*) Trudy.

George (*to* **Features**) Don't mind him.

Gary *looks a bit embarrassed.* **Yvonne***'s team confers, but* **Niamh** *is the only one enthusiastic.*

Yvonne (*quietly but snottily; responding to* **Niamh***'s whispered question*) I don't know!

Noel (*watching* **Bertie** *write the answer; aping Fred Flintstone*) Will—ma!

Lorraine (*hearing* **Noel**) Jesus, yeah!

Angela Yeh thick fuckin' eejit, Noel.

Niamh *writes the answer.* **Bertie***'s team is not impressed with* **Noel**.

George (*annoyed*) I'm lodgin' a complaint here, Denis.

Noel Lodge it up your arse.

George (*pointing at* **Noel***; threatening*) Don't fuckin' —

Bertie (*pointing at* **George***; more threatening*) Hey! —— Compadre —.

George *looks less aggressive, and avoids* **Bertie***'s stare.*

Denis Are yis listenin'!?
(*Staring at them.*) ——No shoutin' the answers. It spoils everythin'. ——Question Number Two.

George Good man, Denis.

The teams glance aggressively across at each other as they wait for the next question. **George***'s team's aggression melts a bit when* **Bertie** *looks at them. He looks amused.* **Leo** *looks over* **Denis***'s shoulder at the index card, and is pleased to see that he knew the answer; ('Now').* **Sandra** *eats a packet of crisps.*

Denis (*after staring at* **Noel**) How many Number One hits —

Some of the older men groan. **Noel** *sits up.*

Noel Here we go.

Denis How many Number One hits did the pop grouuup, the Thompson Twins, have?

Noel English or Irish charts?

George (*quietly*) Will yeh listen to Larry fuckin' Gogan.

Denis (*very definitely*) English.

Bertie *looks at* **Noel**, *waiting for the answer.* **Denis** *checks one of his reference books to make sure that he is right about the English charts; and he is.*

Noel (*chancing his arm; backing out*) If it was the Irish ones ——.

They confer.

Angela None.

Noel *disagrees.* **Lorraine** *knows the answer.* **Yvonne** *remains distant.* **Dermot** *wants to take control of the team, but he's almost afraid to move, and keeps glancing worriedly at* **Yvonne**.

George (*to* **Gary**; *expecting the answer*) Well?

Gary I don't ——. I'm not really into commercial groups —.

George (*before* **Gary** *has finished; dismissive; annoyed*) Two.

He looks to **Features** *and* **Martin** *for confirmation.* **Features** *nods, and looks to* **Gary**. **Martin** *and* **Gary** *shrug.* **George** *looks briefly and very contemptuously at* **Gary**. **Bertie**'s *team quickly, but not unanimously, agrees on an answer while* **Denis** *asks the next question.*

Denis Question Number Three. What player —Wha' player
    scored for both teams in the 1981 FA cup final?

George (*quietly pleased*) I knew it!

He whispers the answer to **Features**. *As* **George** *writes the answer he laughs quietly to himself; remembering something.*

Features That's the man. Very good.

We see **Bertie**'s *team with the answer on the tip of their tongues.* **George** *and* **Features** *look over at them, quietly delighted and triumphant.* **Features** *nudges* **Martin**, *to show him the opposition's plight.* **Martin** *looks as if the nudge causes him agony, but bears it manfully.* **Dermot** *knows the answer.*

Niamh Dermot knows the answer.

Lorraine *and* **Yvonne** *glance at each other, mock-impressed.*

Dermot *sees this.*

George (*quietly; to* **Yvonne**) Hey, Yvonne, how many Number
    Ones did the Thompson Twins have?

Angela Here, none o' tha'!

George *looks defiantly caught.*

Angela Denis!

George *grins guiltily and defiantly, and looks at his answer sheet when* **Bertie** *looks across at him.*

Yvonne He didn't do annythin'.

Denis *breathes deeply, controlling his indignation.*

Denis Question ——Number ——Four.
(*More relaxed.*) Where would ——Where would yeh find the Walloons?

Noel Drimnagh.

This comment doesn't get the laughs **Noel** *expected.*

Angela (*under her breath*) Eejit.

Niamh Oh, I know this one.

Yvonne ('*so what*' *style*) So do I.

George *shows his team the answer he's written, but he takes the page back before* **Gary** *has a chance to see it. He looks across to see if the others know it.* **Martin** *winces and* **Features** *notices.* **Noel** *wordlessly and secretly demonstrates to* **Bertie's** *team that the Walloons are in the back of your mouth.* **Tommy** *disagrees. He knows the answer. He whispers it to* **Bertie.**

Denis And Question Number Five. Who said —

Noel *is annoyed when he sees* **Bertie** *writing down* **Tommy's** *answer.*

Denis Who said: "Romantic Ireland's dead and gone. It's with O'Leary in the grave"?

Lorraine (*recognising the quote*) Jesus!

All of **Yvonne's** *team know the answer, and are pleased; difficulties temporarily forgotten.* **Gary,** *looking a bit smug, leans over and whispers the answer to* **George.**

Bertie Jack Charlton.

Angela (*doubtful*) Are yeh sure?

Bertie (*remembering*) After one o' the matches. He said it to Jimmy Magee.

Tommy (*almost apologetic, but definite*) No. —It was George Hamilton. I remember it.

Bertie (*writing the answer*) Big —Jack —Charl —ton.

Denis Righ'. Sandra here will collect your answers from yis.

Sandra (*indignant, outraged*) I will not, you!

Leo (*warningly*) Now.

Sandra, *furious, drops her tray onto the counter and goes to collect the answer sheets.*

Denis (*as* **Sandra** *passes; a bit contrite*) Thank you very much, Sandra.
(*To the teams.*) Make sure now your number is on the top or yis won't get any points.

Noel (*sarcastic*) Oooh!

Angela (*to* **Noel**) Cop on, will yeh.

The teams relax, although **Yvonne** *and* **Dermot** *are still tense, and don't look at each other.* **Sandra,** *furious, collects* **Niamh**'*s answer sheet.*

Features (*wanting to order drink*) Sandra.

Sandra I'm busy.

Yvonne (*as* **Sandra** *moves away*) Your zip's open, Sandra.

They watch **Sandra** *trying to check that her skirt is done up.*

Martin *picks his glass up and stares into it, still looking miserable.* **George** *and* **Features** *exchange looks, nodding at* **Martin**: *they don't know what's wrong with him.* **George** *and* **Tommy** *stand up.* **Leo** *whispers something to* **Denis.** **Denis** *starts to exit, looking righteous. He comes back for his index cards, and exits, looking even more righteous.*

George The jacks.

He deliberately barges past **Tommy** *on his way to the Gents.*

Yvonne (*to* **George**) Hey, Daddy. They didn't have any.

George *turns to go back and change his answer.* **Angela** *lunges, grabs the answer sheet from* **Features,** *and hands it to* **Sandra.** **George** *turns back to the Gents, furious.*

George (*from inside the Gents*) Mind your own fuckin' business!

Bertie'*s team grin and chuckle.* **Denis** *enters, looking grimly triumphant, brandishing a copy of the Guinness Book of Records. He grabs the microphone.*

Denis (*holding up the book*) Team number 13 have been disqualified for havin' this book under their table. Open! ——I don't care who it is.
(*From the heart.*) I'm not havin' it!

There is cheering and clapping, most of it ironic.

Bertie (*looking into the right wing*) Caramba! D'yeh see who it is? It's Father Molloy's team!

This news is greeted with a mixture of delight and horror. All look offstage.

Lorraine Jesus!

Features There now, Gary. Didn't I tell yeh it was a great night out?

Lights fade.

SCENE TWO — THE KITCHEN

Groucho sings the 'La la laa —La la laa' part of 'Lydia The Tattooed Lady'. It is 7.30 pm; half an hour before the quiz is due to commence; a quarter of an hour before the start of Scene One.

Briget *brings* **George**'s *cup of tea to the table.* **Briget**, *forty, is a good-humoured, intelligent woman. She's not exactly unhappily married: she still sees in* **George** *a lot of what she saw when they first started going with each other twenty-two years ago, but there are times when she can't stand the sight of him. She's bored but she's never said it to anyone, or herself.* **George** *enters from the left wing, carrying his jacket, one arm in a sleeve. He is dressed as in Scene One. He carries a few sheets of paper; lists of capital cities, mountain ranges, presidents, cabinet ministers etc.* **Briget** *sits down, to resume her crossword.*

George (*spotting the tea*) Sound.

He puts the sheets of paper in front of **Briget**, *on top of the crossword, and then puts sugar and milk into the cup.*

George Ask us a few, will yeh.

Briget (*dismissive*) You know them off by heart.

George Go on; a few only.
  (*Testing the tea.*) A.1. ——Go on. You're doin' nothin' else.

Briget (*not too indignant*) Excuse me, George! I'm doin' me crossword.

George Nothin' important.

As **Briget** *asks the questions below* **George** *looks in some tins and shelves, searching for something.*

Briget (*scanning the sheets indifferently*) An' this is important, is it?
  (*Before* **George** *can answer.*) Alabama?

George No, not from the top. Go into the middle.

Briget (*as if she's done this before*) ——Florida?

George Tallahassee.

Briget (*gently mocking*) Correct. New Mexico?

115

George Santa Fe.
  (*Giving up the search; slightly irritated.*) Where are they?

Briget (*looking for a hard one*) I had to hide them again. Nev —?

George Carson City.

Briget (*throwing the sheet onto the table*) Yeh know them backwards, George.

George (*looking in one more tin*) Yeh'd never know. We were badly caught the last time. ——One more, go on. A hard one.

Briget (*knowing there's no point*) Wyoming.

George (*doing a John Wayne impression*) Cheyenne. ——I give up. Where are they?

Briget (*enjoying teasing him*) I had to hide them.

George Yeah yeah. Where but?

Briget *nods to the door and* **George** *looks out, making sure that the kids aren't coming.* **Briget** *stretches under the table and pulls out a box of Jaffa Cakes that has been taped to the table, like a bomb under a car.*

George Coast's clear.
  (*Seeing the hiding place.*) Jaysis.

Briget (*cheerfully*) I'm running out o' places.

George (*admiring her ingenuity*) You'll never run out o' places, Briget.

He sits down, looking at his watch: he doesn't have much time.

He takes a sheet of paper from the bottom and puts it on the top of the pile.

George Ask us some o' them.

Briget Ah, no.

George (*daring her to refuse*) Please.

Briget (*reading the sheet*) Yeh know all these ones as well. You've got more useless information inside in your head than annyone I know. 'Cept your mother.
  (*Before* **George** *can object.*) Energy?

George Bobby Molloy.
  (*Looking at his Jaffa Cake.*) These aren't as nice as they used to be, sure they're not?

Briget Yeh don't have to eat them if yeh don't like them.

George I didn't say I didn't like them. I said they're not —

116

Briget Health?

George Doctor Rory O'Hanlon.

Briget Education?

George Eh, —Mrs. Mary O'Rourke.

Briget Social Welfare?

George (*venomously*) Woods.

Briget Correct correct correct.
    (*Gently sardonic.*) You're a genius, George. I've always said it.

George So have I. You're no thick yourself, missis.

Briget I know.
    (*Indicating the sheets.*) I know all those as well.

George (*defensively*) They're only easy ones.

Briget Then why don't yeh have a list of the hard ones?

George (*good-humoured, but with an edge*) Do I ask you how yeh
    cook the dinner, do I? ——Or how yeh do your crosswards, do
    I?
    (*Grabbing the paper.*) Stupid fuckin' things.

Briget (*almost hiding her annoyance*) Give it back here, you.

George What's this supposed to mean, look it? 'How you were
    caught with your paw in the paint pot'.

Briget (*as if it's obvious*) Red-handed.

George Wha?

Briget Red-handed. That's the answer. *Caught* red-handed. With
    your —(*Showing her hand.*) *Paw* in the paint pot. D'yeh see?
    It's —

George (*before* **Briget** *can explain; throwing the paper onto the
    table*) Load o' shite.

Briget *decides to let* **George** *get away with this.*

Briget (*indicating the sheets*) Ask me a hard one; go on.

George (*putting her back in her box; thinking of a very hard
    one*) Righ'. ——Who —? Who scored two goals in the FA
    Cup Final: one for each team?

Briget Tommy Hutchinson.

George How did yeh fuckin' know tha'?

Briget Cos you kicked the cat after he scored the second one;
    remember? An' I had to bring the poor little thing to the vets,
    remember. An' I had to bring Yvonne to the doctors because

she kept havin' nightmares about flyin' cats. Oh, I remember Tommy bloody Hutchinson alright. An' so does the cat.

George (*looking briefly at the cat's tray; guiltily*) I bought him a ball with a bell in it.

Briget (*re the quiz*) I'd be as good as you are.

George (*scornful*) Would yeh ever —. Righ'; who wrote 'Elmer Gantry'? The buke.

Briget ——I don't know. Who did?

George (*not giving away the secret*) Ah, now.
(*Standing up; lifting the cup.*) See now. ——Will I wash this?

Briget (*a little vindictively*) Yeah.

George *exits, annoyed, to wash the cup. There is slight malice in* **Briget**'s *expression when she speaks.*

Briget Hope yeh win this time.

George (*entering; sounding a bit worried*) So do I.
(*Picking up the sheets; trying to remember.*) Wha' was the name o' tha' square in China where the students all —

Briget Tiananmen Square.

George That's righ'; yeah.

Briget Everyone knows tha'.
(*Enjoying pronouncing it.*) In Beijing.

George (*as if afraid he'll forget*) That's righ'.
(*Re the sheets.*) I don't really need these.
(*Changing his mind; putting them in his pocket.*) —Still.
(*Checking that he has money; half to himself.*) Fuckin' ——
Paddy can't make it tonight. Olive's mother's after havin' a bypass or —fuckin' —a zebra crossing or somethin'.
(*As if it's a feeble excuse.*) So he can't make it.

During the above **Briget**'s *face lights up. She's on the verge of suggesting herself as a replacement.* **George** *doesn't notice this.*

George Features is bringin' Trudy's brother instead. He'd better be good. He's a fuckin' student, ——but —.

Briget's *disappointment is not too obvious.*

George Paddy could go on 'Mastermind'. Only he'd keep slidin' off the chair.
(*Heading for the door.*) Good luck so, love. I'll bring yeh home a few chips, will I?

Briget You're off tomorrow, aren't yeh?

George (*stopping; a bit cagey*) Yeah.

Briget (*determined*) You can come to the parent-teacher meetin' with me, so.

George I can in me hole.

Briget (*exasperated*) Ah —?

George I've a match tomorrow. Pitch 'n' putt.

Briget It'll only be for —

George Against Sinbad McCabe. He bet Features on Saturday, so I'll have to have a practise in the mornin'. I can't stand the cunt.

Briget (*getting a bit angry*) So I have to go on me own while you enjoy yourself, is that it?

George (*surly and defiant*) No.

Briget Well, then? The kids, George. Jesus, they're your responsibility as well, yeh know.

George What d'yeh mean!? Listen, you. Where did the turkey come from tha' we had at Christmas? Well?

Briget This is stupid.

George Where!?

During the following **Briget** *realises the futility of arguing with* **George**: *he must win.*

Briget Pitch an' putt, George.

George That's righ'. An' your mother's turkey, remember. An' your sister's. An' if I hadn't o' won it playin' pitch 'n' putt she'd've been havin' easy slices sandwiches for her Christmas dinner, knowin' tha' fuckin' waster she got herself lumped with. So don't talk to me about responsibilities, righ'.

By now **Briget** *is shaking her head, marvelling at* **George**'s *neck.*

George (*reasonably*) Sure Jaysis, yeh don't have to go at all, Briget. Which one o' them is it for annyway?

Briget Gavin.

George Listen, they're always the same. The nice ones will tell yeh he's makin' good progress an' the bollixes will tell yeh he isn't. So yeh might as well stay at home an' watch a Doris Day picture on the telly. ——Good luck.

Briget *grins, resignedly.*

George (*on his way out*) Oh, come here; I forgot this ——.

He takes a small Toblerone from his jacket pocket and puts it in front of
Briget.

Briget (*a bit pleased*) Aah.

George (*exiting*) See yeh later, righ'.

Exit **George**.

Briget Right, love.
>(*Picking up the Toblerone and her biro.*) Where's 'Red-handed'
>before I forget it?

Lights fade.

SCENE THREE — THE QUIZ

Groucho sings 'La la laa —La la laa'.

It is about 8.45 pm. The third round of the quiz is over and the teams are waiting as **Denis** *adds up the scores.*

During Scene Three **Briget** *does some quiet work around the Kitchen. She then leaves the stage for a while. She comes back, dressed differently, towards the end of the scene, with a jigsaw and a large piece of board. She starts to put the jigsaw together, and glues the pieces onto the board.*

At the start of the scene **Lorraine** *and* **Yvonne** *are at their table;* **Niamh** *is offstage, in the Ladies;* **Dermot** *is at the bar, and staying there until* **Niamh** *gets back from the Ladies.* **Noel** *and* **Tommy** *are at the bar, annoying* **Denis;** **Angela** *is in the Ladies;* **Bertie** *is in the Gents.* **Gary** *is at the bar;* **Features** *and* **Martin** *are at their table;* **George** *is offstage.* **Leo** *is filling glasses, opening bottles, quietly going 'Now, Now, Now . . .'.* **Sandra** *is loading four pints of Guinness onto her tray. She picks up the tray a few times before she's happy that she's holding it properly. She also has difficulty taking her eyes off* **Dermot.**

Noel D'yeh not think that's a reasonable question, Denis?

Enter **George** *from the wing.*

George (*to* **Noel;** *as he goes to his seat*) Sit down ou' o' tha'.

Noel *ignores him but* **Tommy** *gives him a quick glance.* **Denis** *ignores* **Noel,** *and continues to correct the answers and bring the scores up to date on the scoreboard. Totting up the scores is not* **Denis**'s *strongpoint.* **Noel** *nudges* **Tommy,** *who grins conspiratorially, but uneasily.*

Noel Denis?

Features (*to* **Martin**) Ah, that's shockin', Martin. I wouldn't want one o' them.
   (*To* **George,** *as he sits down.*) Poor Martin has an ulcer, George.

Martin *winces; then puts on what he hopes is a brave face.*

George Wha'? ——A real one?

Features (*emphatically*) Oh yeah. Shockin', isn't it?
(*Harmlessly; sympathetically.*) Rather you than me, Martin.

George How did yeh get tha'?

Martin (*after coughing*) He ——He said it might have somethin' to
do with stress.

George Stress!?

Martin *nods. So does* **Features**.

George What stress? You never gave a fuck about annythin' in
your life.

Martin (*heart-broken*) I know.

Yvonne *and* **Lorraine** *are whispering about* **Niamh** *and* **Dermot**.
Lorraine *bursts out laughing.*

Lorraine Yeh dirty bitch, yeh, Yvonne.

*She then realises how loudly she's spoken, and looks around to see if
anyone heard her.* **George***'s table did, but they hardly notice.*

Lorraine (*laughing; embarrassed*) Oh Jesus, I'm scarlet.

Noel I'm waitin' for an answer, Denis.

Tommy Yeah.

George (*over his shoulder*) Sit down. ——Don't mind him, Denis.

Noel (*to* **Dermot**) Fuckin' desperate, isn't it?

Dermot (*not wanting to offend*) Eh, yeah. ——Sure is.

Denis *studiously ignores them.* **Dermot** *looks a bit lost and
uncomfortable, and smiles at anyone who looks his way.*

Sandra *carries the tray very, very carefully to* **Bertie***'s table.* **Noel**
gawks at her as she passes, then back at **Denis***. We hear her
whimpering slightly as she lowers the tray onto the table.* **Dermot**
watches **Sandra** *until he notices* **Yvonne** *and* **Lorraine** *looking at him,
and he turns back to the bar.*

Martin (*sighing*) That's what he said annyway. The doctor.

George What the fuck would he know about it?

Martin An' he said as well —

Gary (*from the bar*) Sorry, eh, Martin? They've no Ballygowan left.
Will Tipperary do instead?

Martin (*letting go; not loudly*) Fuck the poxy Tipperary —!!

Features (*patting* **Martin***'s shoulder*) Ah now.
(*To* **Gary**.) That'll be grand, Gary. Good man.

122

Martin *has his head down; breathing deeply.* **George** *looks around, a bit embarrassed.* **Features** *searches for his handkerchief, to give to* **Martin**. **Sandra** *is now beside* **Tommy**.

Sandra Six pounds an' twenty.

Noel Bring them over here, will yeh.

Sandra Bring them yourself.

Leo (*warningly*) Now.

Sandra (*quietly aping* **Leo** *as she gets* **Noel** *and* **Tommy**'s *pints*) 'Now'. Fuckin' spa.

Yvonne She's a snobby bitch.

Lorraine Shhh! He'll hear yeh.

Yvonne I don't care. She is.
(*Aping* **Niamh**.) 'Dermot has classes on Mondays'. D'you remember when she used to go with Ju Ju Lips Redmond?

Lorraine Jesus!

Lorraine *and* **Yvonne** *laugh, trying not to be too loud.* **Features** *offers* **Martin** *his handkerchief.* **Angela** *comes out of the Ladies.*

Angela (*to* **Noel** *and* **Tommy**) Anny luck?

Noel *raises his eyes to heaven. He's not as good-humoured as he was at the beginning of the scene.*

Tommy (*to* **Denis**) Fair's fair, Denis.

Angela (*about* **Denis**) Ah, tha' poor eejit needs a good ride, so he does.
(*Sees her pint; sitting down.*) An' I need this. Thank you, Sandra, love.

Denis *is hurt and disgusted by* **Angela**'s *remark, but he still says nothing.* **Sandra** *is with* **Lorraine** *and* **Yvonne**. **Lorraine** *is whispering something to her. They laugh.* **Angela** *looks around as if she'd like someone to talk to. She watches what's going on at* **George**'s *table.*

Martin (*pushing the handkerchief away*) No. No, thanks. I wasn't cryin'.

Features Oh, we know tha'.

Angela (*curious*) Is he alrigh'?

George (*curtly*) Yeah.

Features (*more considerate*) Yeah.

Gary *is bringing the drinks to the table.* **George** *picks up the Tipperary bottle and reads the label.* **Tommy** *goes to the Gents.*

George (*while reading the label*) Go to another doctor. Yeh'd never know.
(*Picking up his pint; to* **Gary**.) That answer, the one about the ozone layer. Brilliant.

Gary (*pleased, despite himself*) Eh, thanks.
(*Modestly explaining.*) I just saw it on —

George (*interrupting him; insistent*) No, praise where praise is due.

George *looks around to see what's keeping* **Denis**. **Gary** *feels more like one of the lads.* **Features** *is the proud brother-in-law.*

Features (*praising* **George**) I'd never have been able to remember tha' place, eh —

George (*perfect pronunciation*) Tiananmen Square; yeah. In Beijing.

Features Ah, very good.

Martin I knew tha' one.

Gary It used to be called Peke —

George We know.

Features (*explaining*) George is our places an' politics specialist, Gary.

George (*sounding a tiny bit worried*) Three rounds over annyway, wha'.
(*Wishing it.*) I reckon we're ahead, d'yeh know tha'.
(*Looking over at* **Denis**.) What's keepin' tha' cunt? —Fuck Rosemary annyway.

Noel (*angry, but with a sing-songy delivery*) Den—nis, I'm waitin' for an ans—wer.

Denis (*holding up his black marker*) If you don't stop trying to *influence* me I'll deduct three points from your overall score.

Leo (*quietly backing up* **Denis**; *as he works*) Now.

George Good man, Denis.
(*To his team; amused.*) D'yis hear him?

Denis *holds the marker over the scoreboard, waiting for* **Noel** *to go away.*

Noel (*across to* **George**'s *table*) Hey; spell 'Gadaffi'.

George No!

Noel (*giving up; to* **Denis**'s *back*) It's not supposed to be a fuckin' spellin' test.

Denis (*muttering*) It's not my fault if some people don't know how to read or write.

Angela (*to* **Noel**) Ah, leave it. We'll catch up.

George (*quietly*) Yeh will in your arses.

Noel *sits down.* **Bertie** *comes out of the Gents, followed by* **Tommy**. **Tommy**'s *hands are still wet.* **Dermot** *is looking over* **Denis**'s *shoulder.* **Sandra** *is back at the bar, loading cocktails with little umbrellas in them onto the tray.*

Bertie Hey, Leo, the smell in the jacks is Paraic Pearse. It's mucho fuckin' terrible.

Leo *takes a bottle of Domestos from under the bar and offers it to* **Bertie**.

Leo Now.

Bertie (*laughs; then picks up the bottle*) Care to name it for us? (*Dr. Neil Butler impression.*) It's Vortex. (*As* **Sandra** *goes by with the tray of cocktails.*) Here, Signorita, stick some of this in them.

Sandra *whines, afraid that she's going to drop the tray; and exits, dashing.*

Denis (*to* **Dermot**) Have you got a query?

Dermot No.

Denis Tha' makes a nice change.

Tommy (*sitting down; to* **Noel** *and* **Angela**) The smell in the jacks is Paraic.

Noel (*sardonically*) Go 'way!

Angela Men's piss is always smellier.

Martin (*under his breath*) She should know, wha'.

George *has been testing* **Martin**'s *water.*

George It's very watery.

Martin It's fuckin' water!

George I know tha' but ——it's more water than normal water —eh —

Martin It's piss. I'm tellin' yis, lads. If annyone ever offers yeh an ulcer don't take it.

They laugh, and **Martin** *tries to.*

Gary (*to* **Martin**) Is it duodenal?

Martin ——I think so, yeah.

George *stares at* **Gary. Features**, *rubbing his hands, looks at* **George**.

Features (*pleased and proud*) I told yeh.

Dermot (*to* **Denis***; pointing*) That should be twelve.

Denis, *changing the score, says a silent prayer. He then gets off his stool and heads for the Gents; stops, goes back and takes the question index cards, giving* **Dermot** *a suspicious glance. Then he goes into the Gents.*

George Where's he goin' now? ——Jesus, tonigh'.
(*To* **Features**.) 'Of Mice An' —'?

Features (*answering quickly*) John Steinbeck.

George (*to* **Martin**) FA Cup, nineteen fifty —

Martin Newcastle.

George (*finishing the question*) Eight.

Martin Eh, fuck ——Bolton Wanderers.

George Yeh sure?

Martin (*indignant*) Yeah, I am. ——Seventh President of America?

George (*as if the question is beneath him*) Andrew Jackson.
(*Looking anxiously at the Gents door.*) Come on, come on, Denis.
(*Contemptuous.*) He's prob'ly washin' his hands.

Niamh *enters, and sees* **Dermot** *alone at the bar.*

Niamh (*affectionately*) What're you doing here? All on your own-io.

Dermot I couldn't remember what you wanted, so I —

Niamh Vodka, Dermot! Jesus, you can answer all those questions but yeh can't remember what I drink.

Niamh *goes to their table.*

Yvonne She's put on weight, hasn't she?

Lorraine If you say so, Yvonne.

Yvonne Fuck off, Lorraine.

Niamh (*coming towards them*) Hiyis.

Yvonne Hiyeh, Niamh.

Lorraine *sniggers.* **Yvonne** *kicks her.* **Leo** *enters, picking up empty glasses.* **Angela** *gives him a hand when he arrives at* **Bertie's** *table.*

Angela (*while she helps* **Leo**) She nearly ran over me with her fuckin' shoppin' trolley. Rosemary. She did; an' she never even said sorry. In her tracksuit. Squashed into it, she was.

126

Bertie Si.

Angela I'm tellin' yeh now, if she ever does it again I'll make her wobble, so I will.

Bertie Oh, si.

Angela (*admiring* **Leo***'s perfectly ironed shirt*) D'yeh iron your own shirts, Leo?

Leo Oh, I do ——Now.

Leo *goes up to the girls' table.* **Denis** *comes out of the Gents.* **Sandra** *rushes onstage, grabs a cloth from the bar, and rushes offstage; looking hassled and furious.* **Dermot** *goes up to the girls' table.* **Yvonne** *stares boldly at him when* **Niamh** *isn't looking.* **Dermot** *tries to pretend that she doesn't.*

Angela (*about* **Leo**) God, I think he's great.

Bertie Jaysis, Conchita, I'd buy an iron tomorrow meself if I thought it was worth me while.

Angela It's a car-wash you need; the state of yeh.

They laugh.

Bertie (*jokingly offering himself to* **Angela**) I would give meself a good wash though. And iron me poncho.

Angela (*good humouredly*) Get lost, amigo.

Denis *is a bit flustered; not convinced that he's done his addition correctly.*

Denis Right —eh —.

Noel (*fancying his chances; to* **Angela**) I iron me own stuff.

Angela (*coldly*) Do yeh?

Tommy *has been rolling up his trouser leg. He points to a mark.*

Denis Righ' —.

Tommy See tha', Bertie?

Bertie Si.

Tommy An iron did tha'.

Bertie Si?

Denis I am now ——in a position to bring yis up to date with the overall scores after Round —Three.

George 'Bout fuckin' time.

Noel Fix.

Denis (*trying to ignore them*) An' again, I'm sorry about the delay.

127

But, like I said, I'm on me own tonight because Rosemary had to ——eh —.

Bertie (*to his team*) I speet on Rosemary!

Denis Righ'. There are forty-six teams contestin' so I won't go through them all.
(*Attempting geniality.*) We'd only be here all night. ——I'll just give yis the leaders. There are six teams with twelve points out of fifteen. They are ——as follows: Table numbers 7, 23, 24, 31, 36 and 43.

Angela *checks their team number on the table.*

Noel (*to* **Bertie**) We should be fuckin' thirteen.

Bertie Ees no problem, compadre.

Niamh One of them is Philo's team.

Lorraine (*peering out into the wing*) Fuck off; are yeh serious? She was in the happy class; remember?

Denis There are four teams with thirteen points: Table numbers 1, 17, 29 and 37.

George Yeow.
(*Chants.*) G—A
G—A—D
A—F—F—I

George *and* **Features** Gadaffi!

Bertie *hisses.* **Gary** *is embarrassed.*

Angela (*sardonically*) Ha fuckin' ha.

Denis One team is leadin' by themselves at this point in the quiz. With fourteen points. An' that's very good. Table number 11.

George Cunts.

There is general agreement about **George**'s *verdict.* **Bertie** *and* **George**'s *team look scornfully offstage, at Table 11.*

Features It's some goin', all the same.

George (*getting up*) Ah, don't start bein' nice, for fuck sake.
(*Looking into the wing.*) Fuckin' Sinbad.

Sandra *runs onstage, throws her tray onto the bar, and charges into the* **Ladies**. *When* **George** *sees her he tries to attract her attention.*

George (*seeing* **Sandra**) Here —!
(*Standing up.*) I'll give Leo the shout before Denis starts.

Denis Righ'. ——Round Four.

Bertie Quick, Tommy, get us a few crisps.

Tommy *gets up and collides with* **George** *on their way to the bar.*

George (*grabbing* **Tommy**'s *jumper*) Here! I'm sick o' you fuckin' gettin' in me way!

Bertie (*out of his seat very quickly*) Leave him alone, compadre.

The girls scream very briefly. **Leo** *is quickly on the scene. He pulls* **George**'s *hand away from* **Tommy**, *slapping it twice until* **George** *releases his grip. The others half-stand, unsure; unwilling to get too involved.* **Yvonne** *stands up, ready to throw her coke bottle at anyone who touches* **George**.

Leo (*slapping* **George**'s *hand*) Now —Now —.

In the Kitchen, **Briget** *enters and starts to do the jigsaw.*

Bertie (*gently, but threatening*) Sit down, George.

George (*pointing at* **Tommy**) He —

Bertie (*exactly as before*) Sit down, George.

George (*hiding the fact that he is conceding defeat*) I'm orderin' me round, righ'.

Noel *does a not-too-loud chicken impression.* **Angela** *shushes him.*

Bertie Leo.

Leo Now, George?

George ——A pint o' Budweiser, two pints an' a water.

George *sits down, after trying to stare* **Tommy** *out of it without including* **Bertie** *in his stare.* **Bertie** *and* **Tommy** *sit down.*

Features *tries to get a look of reconciliation across to* **Bertie**'s *table but* **George** *stops him.*

Denis (*snottily*) I think we're ready to resume, ladies and gentlemen. Question Number One.

There is silence; all eyes down waiting for the question. **Denis** *realises that he's left his index cards in the Gents, and dashes off to get them; trying not to dash.*

Noel Fuckin' eejit.

The teams sit back a bit. Again **Features** *tries to look across, but* **George** *won't let him.*

George 'Satanic Verses'?

Features (*reassuring* **George**) Salman Ruuushdie, George.

They look at the Gents door, waiting for **Denis** *to come out.*

Noel (*to* **Tommy**, *re* **George**) You could have him ou' anny day.

Tommy *doesn't look convinced.* **Bertie** *glares across at* **George**'s *team, through half-open eyelids.*

George (*quietly*) Don't mind him.

Yvonne (*getting her bag and standing up*) The tylet. ——I never asked yeh, Dermot. Did yeh enjoy the party?

Dermot (*aghast, but hiding it*) ——Yeah.

Yvonne *goes to the Ladies.* **Denis** *comes out of the Gents.* **Lorraine** *is torn between wanting to follow* **Yvonne** *and wanting to stay, to hear what happens next. She picks up her bag and half-stands, but sits down again and drops the bag.*

Niamh (*nicely*) Wha' party?

Denis Righ'. Sorry about tha'.

Bertie No problem, Signor Deniiis.

Dermot That party I was tellin' you about. At —
(*Pretending he's trying to remember.*) when you were in Blackpool. I can't —

Denis How many —

Dermot (*to* **Niamh**; *bracing himself for the answer*) Hang on.

Denis How many sons did Adam and Eve have?

Bertie *and* **George**'s *teams confer quietly and intensely. Only snatches can be heard.*

George It can't be. Too easy.

Noel Was Abel not a young one?

Niamh An' was Yvonne at the party?

Dermot (*busy counting Adam and Eve's offspring*) ——Wha'? —Oh, yeah.
(*To* **Lorraine**; *whispering.*) Two?

Lorraine *shrugs, embarrassed.*

Niamh Were yeh talkin' to Yvonne at the party, Dermot?

Dermot (*showing three fingers; whispering*) Three?

Lights fade.

SCENE FOUR — THE KITCHEN

Groucho goes 'La la laa —La la laa'.

It is evening, a week or so before the quiz.

Yvonne, *not dressed exactly as in Scenes One and Three, is sitting at the table with* **Briget.** *Her jacket is hanging over the back of her chair. Her handbag is on the floor, under the table. As she speaks she is absently playing with one of the jigsaw pieces.* **Briget** *works at the jigsaw as she talks and listens. She glues the pieces to the board when she's sure they're in the right place.*

Briget (*amused*) Gordon?

Yvonne Yeah.
(*Mock-posh.*) Gordon.

Briget An' did yeh meet him below in the pub?

Yvonne Are yeh jokin' me, Mammy? Tha' place!? I hate it there. Darts an' quizzes. An' oul' creeps starin' at yeh an' droolin'.

Briget Ah, Yvonne now. It's not tha' bad.

Yvonne Well, I think it is. ——No; Howth, I met him in. Saints.

Briget (*re what* **Yvonne** *told her before the start of the scene*) ——I'd love to have seen his face.

Yvonne Ah, yeh should've seen it, Mammy, I'm not jokin' yeh. You know when yeh see some fellas the first time an' they look really good lookin'?

Yvonne *looks for an answer, then remembers that it's her mother she's talking to. They laugh a little, slightly embarrassed.*

Yvonne You know. They look gorgeous. But when yeh look at them for a while they don't look as gorgeous as yeh thought they did, an' yeh start noticin' their spots an' tha'.

They laugh again.

Briget That's just like the young lads that are in those videos.

Yvonne (*agreeing*) Yeah.

131

Briget Sometimes I flick onto them durin' the ads an' I see this young lad singin', in a denim jacket an' a tee shirt, yeh know. Walking' through the desert or somethin', an' I say to myself. —My God ——. So I watch the rest of it. An' by the end of it I'm sayin' to myself tha' George was as good lookin' as him when he was his age.

Yvonne Daddy! Can't yeh just picture him in a group!

Briget Can't you just now. In a pair of leather trousers.

George *enters while they're laughing.*

George (*grumpy, for entertainment's sake*) What're youse two laughin' at?

Yvonne (*good-humouredly aggressive*) Nothin'.

Briget (*secretly to* **Yvonne**; *re* **George**) Jason Donovan.

George *opens the fridge and bends down to have a good look inside. We hear him as he roots around in the fridge.*

George Nothin' me arse. Nothin' important maybe. I've been watchin' the news there. My Jaysis. Earthquakes. Child abuse. RUC men bein' blown to shite, up there.

George *closes the fridge door. He has a chicken leg. As he speaks below, he takes the salt cellar from the table and shakes some salt on the chicken. Salt falls on the jigsaw.* **Briget** *gives him an annoyed look, but says nothing.*

George I don't know wha' yis have to be laughin' abou'. But fire away. Don't let me stop yis.

As he exits, he fills his mouth with chicken.

Briget (*with slight contempt*) Did it have annythin' abou' starvation?

George (*not realising that he's being slagged*) No.

Exit **George**.

George (*offstage*) Put it back onto The News there. ——Go on!

Briget (*re* **George**; *quietly; to herself*) Eejit.
(*Fitting a piece.*) Got yeh. ——Wha' were we talkin' about? Before Vere Wynne-Jones interrupted us.

Yvonne Daddy bein' in a video.

Briget (*chuckling*) Oh yes.

Yvonne Annyway, he —Gordon —he looked gorgeous when I saw him the first time. Really now. A ride.

Briget (*with half-hearted disapproval*) Yvonne!

132

Yvonne Sorry. He was though. An' then when he came over an' started talkin' to me; Jesus! Lorraine couldn't take her eyes off him. But, Jesus Mammy, he kept goin' on an' on, about himself. Even Lorraine got sick of him. Then he said he was goin' to Australia, because this country had no future as far as he could see.
(*After raising her eyes to heaven.*) Annyway, he had a voice like Bugs Bunny. An' he had loads of blackheads here –.
(*Indicates the side of her nose, and then the corners of her mouth.*) —An' his skin was all dry an' cracked here, yeh know, so I told him to fuck off to Australia.

Briget (*trying not to laugh too much*) Could yeh not just have sat somewhere else, to get rid of him?

Yvonne Ah, he got on my wick, Mammy. He was so full of himself, yeh know.

The doorbell rings.

Yvonne (*as* **Briget** *starts to get up*) Let someone else.

Briget (*sitting back down*) Yeah.

She takes the jigsaw piece from **Yvonne**, *and tries it. It fits.*

Briget I've been lookin' for that bit for ages.

Yvonne Sorry.

Briget I'll say tha' much for your daddy when we were goin' out with each other. He was never boring. He was sometimes drunk. An' usually disgustin', but he was never boring.

Yvonne Ah, Daddy's great. All my friends think he's great.

Briget's *look is very sceptical, but not too seriously so.*

Yvonne They do. When we're down there; when we go down there —We don't go there much. We don't really like it, —I hate it —but —

George (*from offstage; cheerful*) Will yis be makin' tea in there?

Briget You'd never know.

George Well, we want some of it, righ'.

Briget (*sardonic*) Yes, Your Majesty.

George (*gruff, for entertainment's sake*) Don't start.

Features *and* **Martin** *can be heard laughing, offstage.*

Yvonne Annyway, when we hear people laughin' an' we turn round to see who it is it's always Daddy tha' made them laugh. Always, it is.

(*Re the jigsaw piece in* **Briget**'s *hand*.) Look it, it goes there.

Briget Get away! ——He's a great sense of humour alrigh'. I'll never forget it; did I ever tell yeh? The first time he came to your nan's and grandad's for his tea. We were sittin' there an' he picked up one of your nan's sandwiches, yeh know, an' he tapped it on the table. ——Like that. An' he asked her had she been hangin' onto them since the last time I brought a fella home with me. He was only jokin'; but your nan! An' then when I told her I was marryin' him, a few weeks later only! Your grandad liked him though. He still does.

Yvonne Philo thinks he's gorgeous.

Briget Jesus; God help her. ——He was a fine thing though. Always very smart.

Yvonne Yeah, she thinks he's lovely. She says tha' if you ever die —

Briget Jesus, Yvonne!! ——Tell Philo to feck off. Whoever she is.

Yvonne Yeh know her. Yeh do. Kavanagh.

Briget Oh. ——Well, if she's annythin' like her mother I'd better keep a close eye on George. She won't wait till I die.

Yvonne Did yeh ever see the gear on Mrs. Kavanagh?

They laugh, bitchily; enjoying themselves.

Yvonne (*standing up and putting on her jacket*) Philo's not like tha'; not really. She might be when she gets older though.

Yvonne *picks up a stainless-steel pot from the worktop and looks at its side, trying to check her make-up.*

Briget Are yeh goin' to Saints tonight again?

Yvonne Ah yeah. It was gas the last time. A great bit o' buzz. Come here, Mammy, you should come with us the next time. It'd be brilliant.

For a horrible second **Yvonne** *thinks that* **Briget** *is going to accept the offer.*

Briget ——Ah, no.

Yvonne Ah; okay.
(*Bending to get her handbag*.) Me bag.

George *enters; followed, a little bit sheepishly, by* **Features** *and* **Martin**. *It is pre-ulcer* **Martin**, *a more cheerful version.*

George (*just before the lads enter*) Where's the tea?

Briget (*a bit curtly*) That's the kettle over there.

George *glares at* **Briget**. *She deliberately doesn't look at him.*

George (*in great public form; going to the kettle*) Come on on on on in, lads. ——Goin' ou', Yvonne?

Yvonne Yeah.

Martin There's Briget.

Briget Ah, Martin. An' Features; howyeh.

George (*to* **Yvonne**) Good girl. D'yeh need a few bob?

Yvonne Ah no. Thanks.

George (*digging into his pocket for money; determined to be generous*) Here. ——Here.

Features Grand ol' evenin', Briget.

George (*holding out a fiver*) Just in case, wha'. You'd never know; yeh might meet a dark, handsome prince who'll ask yeh for a lend of his bus fare home.

Yvonne (*taking the fiver*) He can walk. ——Ah thanks.

Features Yvonne, you're nearly lookin' as nice as your mother.

Yvonne *grins at* **Briget**, *then raises her eyes to heaven.*

George (*turning from the kettle*) Hey, Features; I only said yeh could have a cup o' tea.

They laugh, **Briget** *a bit begrudgingly.* **George** *is making tea for them all.*

Yvonne (*exiting*) See yis.

Briget Bye bye, love. Enjoy yourself.

George Bring us back a stick o' rock, Yvonne.
(*To* **Martin** *and* **Features**.) She's a good looker though, isn't she?

They readily agree.

Martin (*agreeing; nodding his head*) Ah, now.

George She got your looks there, Briget. An' mine. An exotic blend of the east and west.

Briget (*who's heard it many times before*) Because I came from Finglas East an' you came from Cabra West.

George That's righ'.

Martin *and* **Features** *laugh, and* **George** *laughs with them.* **Martin** *looks at* **Briget**'s *jigsaw work, and then at the jigsaw on the wall. During the short exchange below about* **Yvonne** *and money* **Martin** *and*

135

Features *laugh where they think they should, but at times look a bit embarrassed, as if they shouldn't be listening.*

Briget Have yeh anny more fivers to give away?

George Are yeh joking me!?

Briget You're not to be givin' her money, George. She earns good money herself.

George (*beginning to get rattled, but aware of the lads*) Ah Jaysis, Briget.

Briget Martin an' Features must think we're loaded. ——You know; we were just talkin' about it. I was married to you when I was her age.

George Well, she can't marry me, so don't begrudge the poor young one the odd fiver.
(*To* **Martin** *and* **Features**.) Wha'.

They laugh, led by **George**.

Briget (*mimicking* **George**; *just about hiding her annoyance*) Wha'. ——Wha'.
(*To* **Features**.) How's Trudy, Features?

Features Tip-top, Briget. She's in grand ol' form. She —

George (*good humoured, but insistent*) Never mind abou' Trudy. You're here to talk tactics.

Briget *is annoyed at the rudeness of the interruption, but becomes interested.*

Martin (*to* **Briget**; *nodding at* **George**) NATO, wha'.

George (*re the tea*) Nearly ready here.
We're gettin' snared too often.
(*After they agree with him.*) Goin' grand up to the last couple o' rounds; sometimes leadin': usually. Then —.

Words aren't necessary.

Features (*quite formally*) Why do yeh think that is?

Martin We're thick.

Only **Martin** *and* **Briget** *laugh.* **Features** *smiles.*

George How many sugars d'yeh want, Briget?

Briget (*grinning sardonically*) Guess.

She tries to share the humour of the situation with **Martin** *but he looks away.*

George (*handing* **Briget** *a mug; re the sugar dispensing*) Here sure.
Yis can do it yourselves, can't yis.
(*Handing mugs to* **Martin** *and* **Features**.) I think maybe we
drink too much in the first half.

Martin That's me arse, George. Listen; it's because the questions
get harder.

George Then our heads should be clearer for them.

Martin I think better with a few pints inside me.

Features I think ——. This sounds stupid now. ——In the last
rounds 'specially, I just don't know the answers.

George *and* **Martin** *look at each other*. **George** *looks impatient*.

Features (*before* **George** *can interrupt; getting into his stride*) An'
what's more, I'll never know them. There's too much.

George *and* **Martin** *concede agreement*.

Features I watch The News, *all* o' them, an' 'Today Tonight' and
——I get the ol' 'Radio Times' an' that an' I try to remember
who plays who in 'Neighbours' an' 'Home and Away', and —.
I even went into Easons there an' spent about an hour lookin'
at the names of who wrote the books.
(*Shaking his head*.) But —.

Briget You should specialise.
(*Almost apologetic*.) Shouldn't yeh?

George (*after killing the urge to tell her to mind her own
business*) Wha' d'yeh mean —, Briget?

Briget You should divide the things, the categories, out among yis
an' concentrate on them; each.

Martin (*tentatively*) Tha' sounds —the business.

Features You mean, like Martin would be Sport an' I'd be Books
an' —

Briget (*joking*) Literature.

Martin Yeow, Features. Literature, wha'.

Martin *and* **Features** *like the idea*.

George (*unwilling to be too enthusiastic*) It might work alrigh'.

Briget Course it'll work.

Features Fair play to yeh, Briget.

Briget (*modestly, but pleased*) Ah —.

George (*taking over the idea*) Righ'; I'll be, eh Places an' (*Getting excited.*) We'll knock the shite ou' o' them this time, wha'.

The doorbell rings. **George** *stays put.*

Briget (*getting up and exiting*) I'll go.

The men are looking well pleased.

Martin (*as* **Briget** *exits*) Shite; fuck, I forgot. ——Paddy said to get someone else for Monday.

George Wha!?

Martin The mammy-in-law's gettin' somethin' done to her.

George Shite on it annyway!

Martin —In Beaumont.

Features (*remembering*) Oh that's right. She was on the waitin' list for —

George (*interrupting him*) Well, we're fucked now annyway. (*Stressing the importance of* **Paddy**.) Paddy ——.

Features ——I'd say Briget'd be good —

Martin *begins to agree.*

George (*very deliberately ignoring and interrupting* **Features**) Trudy's brother, you were talkin' abou'.

Features Gary.

George Get him.

Features Okay. Righto. I just thought —

George Gary. That's his name?

Features Yes; Gary.

George An' he has it between the ears?

Features Oh, he does alrigh'.

George He'll do us.
(*To* **Martin**; *good-humouredly insisting on his agreement.*) Wha'.

Martin Ah yeah. Young blood.

George Fuck Paddy though.

Enter **Briget**.

George (*cheerful again*) Here, Briget. Look it. (*Taking a fiver from his pocket.*) Righ', lads. This fiver, righ', to the first one o' yis tha' can find ou' where Briget's hid the Jaffa Cakes.

George *and* **Briget** *roar laughing.* **Martin** *and* **Features** *laugh, but they don't really know why.*

Lights fade.

SCENE FIVE — THE QUIZ

Groucho goes 'La la laa —La la laa'.

It is about 9.00 pm; the middle of Round Four.

The teams are at their tables, conferring; huddled, running out of time.
Yvonne's team isn't as huddled as the other two. Niamh is trying to be
engrossed in the quiz, but she can't help looking at Dermot and
Yvonne. She's worried, unsure. So is Dermot. Yvonne is a vision of
innocence; with the odd glance to Lorraine. Lorraine is loving it. At
some early stage Dermot puts his arm around Niamh: she lets him.
Niamh gives Yvonne a look that could be described as modestly
triumphant. Yvonne and Lorraine look at each other. While the teams
confer, Leo puts a bottle of coke with a straw and a paper umbrella in
it in front of Sandra, who is leaning against the counter, looking
miserable.

Sandra (*suspecting something at first*) ——Thanks.

Leo (*very quietly*) Ah, now.

Angela Silver.

Noel (*contemptuously*) No!

Angela (*equally contemptuously*) Wha' then?

George Trigger?

Lorraine (*remembering the answer*) Aah! Jesus!

Gary (*leaning over to George*) Black Bess.

George (*quietly elated*) Ah, yes!
(*As he writes.*) No ——sweat.

Denis Question Number Four —.

Angela Put down Champion.

Bertie (*not really convinced*) That sounds righ'.

Bertie *and* **George**'s *teams are still huddled.* **Bertie**'s *team looks*
doubtful; unhappy with their last answer.

Tommy It's not Champion.

Angela (*irritated*) Wha' is it then!?

Bertie It'll do, it'll do.
   (*Calling for reconciliation.*) Compadres.

Yvonne smiles at **Niamh,** *and* **Niamh** *smiles back.* **Lorraine** *watches the other three.* **Features** *gives* **Gary** *the thumbs-up.* **Gary** *is pleased.* **Martin** *leans over, pats* **Gary**'s *shoulder; then winces.* **Features** *looks at* **Martin,** *concerned.*

Martin (*courageously*) I'm alrigh'.

Denis Who played —?

Tommy (*quietly; regarding the last question*) Maybe it was —

Angela Shh!

Denis Who played Miss Jones in the long runnin', popular comedy
   series, 'Rising Damp'?

Angela Thank you, Denis!

She takes the sheet from **Bertie** *and the others watch her writing the answer.* **George**'s *team looks lost; although* **Features** *is sure the answer is in his head somewhere.* **Yvonne** *whispers the answer to* **Niamh.**

Niamh Are yeh sure, Yvonne?

Yvonne (*a bit put out*) Yeah. I am.

Yvonne raises her eyes to heaven, looking at **Dermot**; *conspiring against* **Niamh** *as she writes the answer.* **Dermot** *looks away from* **Yvonne,** *and watches* **Niamh** *writing.* **Bertie** *hisses at* **George**'s *team, trying to put them off.*

George (*ignoring* **Bertie**; *to* **Features**; *expecting the answer*) Well?

Features (*especially to* **Gary**) Trudy'd know this one.

George That's a great fuckin' help, isn't it!?
   (*Closing his eyes; putting his fingers to his temples.*) Are you
   there, Trudy? Can you hear me, Trudy?

Then he glares at **Features**. *The team thinks hard,* **Gary** *doing his bit with the rest of them.* **Sandra** *is collecting empty glasses from the tables.* **Noel** *makes a leering noise from the side of his mouth as she bends down at his table.* **Angela** *gives* **Noel** *a good dig.*

Sandra (*To* **Angela**) The state of'm.

Leo goes into the Gents.

Denis Question Number Five.

Martin (*giving up*) Haven't a fuckin' breeze.

George Fuck yeh; I had it there.

Features (*not really believing his answer*) Wendy Craig.

Denis Who is —?

George (*getting desperate*) No! The skinny one —.

Denis Who is the singer —

Noel (*sitting up*) Here we go.

Denis —with the internationally successful Norwegian Grouuup, A-ha?

Bertie Ah here!

Angela Ah Jaysis.

George *refuses to be amused.* **Sandra** *is taking up glasses at his table.*

George (*wanting her to tell him the answer*) Sandra?

Sandra Wha'?

George (*looking around furtively*) Who —?
(*Deciding not to ask her.*) You're alrigh'. Go on.

Sandra Please yourself.

Lorraine (*good-humouredly annoyed*) I do not like them, Yvonne; fuck off.

Niamh *joins in the fun, and* **Dermot.**

Noel (*clicking his fingers*) ——It begins with a —

Tommy Morton.

Bertie (*beginning to write*) Si!

George (*to* **Gary**, *sneering*) Are A-ha a commercial group?

Gary Eh, yeah —.
(*Almost ashamed; leaning closer to* **George**.) But I know the answer.

George Good man. Ha ha!

George (*giving* **Features** *and* **Martin** *an order*) Your woman from 'Rising Damp', righ'.

Denis I require the surname *and* the christian name there.

Noel Do yeh want his address an' his fuckin' phone number as well!

George (*objecting; to* **Denis**) He's Norwegian, for Jaysis sake!

Denis I am sorry. I must have both names.

Sandra, *on her way back to the bar, laughs.*

Sandra (*quietly*) Yeh saps.

Features That's fair enough, really.

142

George *looks at him, but says nothing.*

Features (*sort of defending himself*) They don't know it either.

Martin Felicity somethin'.

George Felicity Morton!?

Martin No, yeh gobshite. 'Risin' Damp'.

Denis (*looking almost nervously at* **Sandra**) Sandra will now collect your answers.

George (*getting desperate*) Felicity wha'?
(*To* **Gary**.) Morton wha'?

Denis Remember to write your table numbers on the top. That's very important.

Sandra *collects the answers very promptly.*

Bertie I'll put Anderson; si?

Noel (*tortured*) I know it!

Angela (*half under her breath*) You know fuck all.

Features Kendal?

Martin De La Tour.

George (*relieved*) Good man!

He scribbles the answer.

Sandra (*to* **George**) Give us your answers.

George (*to his team*) Morton wha'?; come on; quick.
(*When no answer is forthcoming.*) Fuck yis; you're useless.

Sandra *grabs his sheet before he has time to fold it properly. She exits, to collect the answers from teams offstage.* **Leo** *comes out of the Gents, his face momentarily grim.*

Dermot Eh, we did well there.

Niamh Yeah.

Yvonne (*enthusiastically agreeing; mocking*) Yeah.

Martin Fuck it.

Features Wha' —?

Martin Felicity De La Tour was in 'The fuckin' Good Life'.

Features No. Tha' was —

George (*hoping to God*) She might've been in the both o' them. She'd better've been.

Tommy (*very earnest*) I'd say we got four there anyway.

Noel (*furious; thumping his knee*) Morton, Morton, Morton, Noel!

Angela My God almighty.

Denis (*to* **Sandra**, *offstage; through the mike*) Sandra; have you collected all the answers yet?

Sandra (*offstage*) Nearly. ——Give us it! ——Yeah.

Denis (*attempting cheerfulness*) Righ'. I'll put yis ou' of your misery —.

Noel Wha'? Are yeh goin' to kill yourself?

Denis (*back to his normal self*) Adam an' Eve had three sons.

All three teams look pleased, and relieved.

Features I knew it couldn't only've been two.

Niamh (*pointing at* **Dermot**; *chuffed*) Dermot.

Yvonne *and* **Lorraine** *nod at each other, mock-gravely.* **Dermot** *tries to smile modestly, but then sees* **Yvonne**'s *expression.*

Denis The capital of Burma is Rangoon.

George (*to his team*) Thank you, thank you.

All three teams still look pleased. **Sandra** *enters, stage-right, from behind the bar, with a pile of answer sheets which she throws in front of* **Denis**.

Sandra There.

Denis Dick Turpin's faithful horse was called ——Black Bess.

Noel Shite!

George *sneers across at* **Bertie**'s *table.* **Bertie** *hisses; takes out his 'gun' to see if it's loaded and cocked.*

Denis Miss Jones was, of course, played by Frances De La Tour.

George (*to* **Martin**) Yeh fuckin' eejit, yeh.

Martin Fuck off, you.

Bertie's *team sneers across at* **George**.

George (*to* **Denis**; *chancing his arm*) De La Tour, Denis. De La Tour.

Angela No way.

Denis Frances De La Tour, George.

George (*turning away*) Fuck yeh, Denis.

Denis And A-ha's singer is, of course, Morten —Harken.

Bertie *and* **George**'s *teams no longer look pleased. The girls are delighted. They cheer, and* **Dermot** *looks more relaxed.*

Yvonne Hey, Daddy. We got five ou' of five.

It takes **George** *a second to force himself to be pleased for* **Yvonne**.

George Did yis? ——Fair play to yis.
(*To his team; accusingly*.) They got five.

Denis (*to* **Leo***; indicating the answer sheets; happily disgruntled*) Will you look at this lot!

Leo (*sympathising*) Oh, now.

Noel (*standing up; indicating the wing*) There's Sinbad over there. ——With his sister. I'm impressed.

Noel *exits*.

Angela I don't think she'll be impressed. Unless she's only ou' for the day.

George (*to* **Features***; accusingly*) 'Risin' Damp'. That's your department.

Features No, George, no. It's not a soap.

George Well, it's a series.

Martin (*defending* **Features**, *and explaining*) Situation comedy. ——Paddy.

George Fuck Paddy annyway. The sooner tha' oul' bitch snuffs it the better.
(*To* **Gary**.) No offence, son. You're doin' great.

Lorraine Sandra.

Sandra *unhappily goes to* **Lorraine***'s table*.

Martin Sandra.

Sandra Wait.

Martin *gets up, delicately;* **Features** *ready to assist*.

Martin (*miserably*) I can't wait. I'm gummin' for a Ballier. Same again, lads?

Features (*standing up*) I'll come with yeh.

Bertie (*giving* **Tommy** *money*) Up yeh go, Tommy.

Sandra (*to* **Leo***;* **Lorraine***'s order*) Pint o' Heineken, three vodkas an' only two cokes, an' four packages of crisps.

Niamh (*very 'cheerful'*) Annyway, was it a good party?

Yvonne (*before* **Dermot** *can answer*) Ah yeah, it was great. Wasn't it, Dermot?

Dermot (*trying to make the answer sound acceptable to both women*) Yeah, it was alright alrigh'.

Niamh Were you at it as well, Lorraine?

Lorraine No. ——I heard it was *brilliant* though.

Lorraine *kicks* **Yvonne**.

Niamh (*'just' curious*) An' were yis talkin' to each other at it?

Dermot Yeah, we —

Yvonne Hardly. Just Howyeh and Seeyeh really, yeh know.

She looks to **Dermot** *for confirmation.*

Dermot (*relieved, but trying not to look and sound it*) Yeah.

Niamh (*also relieved*) Oh. Ah yeah; sure yis hardly know —

Yvonne An' we had a dance.

Dermot *nearly passes out.*

Yvonne ——A whole gang of us, yeh know. It was gas, wasn't it?

Dermot (*noncommittal*) Yeah. ——I don't really like dancing —that
   much.

Niamh (*agreeing*) No.

Yvonne (*innocently surprised*) Oh, do yeh not!?

Sandra *arrives with the tray. At the bar* **Martin** *and* **Features** *are
watching* **Denis** *flying through the scores.*

Features Your hand's a blur, Denis.

Denis (*responding to the praise; not looking up*) When you've been in
   this game as long as I have —

He looks up, sees **Martin**'s *expression, and looks down.*

Gary (*to* **George**; *drink is loosening him*) I didn't really have to
   repeat. I just ——I don't know —. I got six honours when I
   repeated and it was —
   (*Clenching his fist to express his elation, drive and ambition;
   attempting modesty.*) Cos it's quite an achievement when you
   think about it.

George (*trying to shake off his stunned expression*) Fuck, yeah.

George *looks around for distraction.* **Gary** *is getting drunk.*

Gary (*one of the lads*) Hey, Martin. Are yeh brewin' the fuckin'
   stuff yourself?

Martin (*after a long stare*) No.

Features (*to* **Martin**) He's a good bit younger than Trudy.
   (*To* **Tommy**.) How did yis do in tha' one, Tommy?

Tommy (*looking around; uncomfortable*) ——Alrigh'.

Features We could only manage three.

Martin *nudges him.*

Denis (*appalled at the stupidity of one team's answer; to himself*) My God.

Martin *tries to read what appalled* **Denis**, *but* **Denis** *won't let him.*
Sandra *puts more glasses and bottles on her tray and carries them offstage, concentrating on not dropping anything.* **Tommy** *studies the pitch 'n' putt fixtures board.* **Leo**, *seeing that* **Sandra** *isn't there, comes out from the bar, to bring* **Angela** *and* **Bertie** *their pints.* **Angela** *and* **Bertie** *have been talking about* **Angela***'s husband.*

Angela I wouldn't have him back now. Not if he got down an' kissed me feet I wouldn't.

Bertie Si.

Angela I would've. Even a couple of months ago I would've.

Leo *delivers their pints, and immediately heads back to the bar.*
Sandra *runs back onstage.*

Angela (*affectionately; grateful*) Ah, Leo.

Leo Ah now.

Sandra (*trying hard to remember the orders; to* **Leo**) Two pints o' Guinness, a gin an' a tonic an' a Britvic 55; three pints o' Guinness an' a Crested: a pint o' Guinness, two pints o' Carlsberg an' a West Coast Cooler.

Tommy (*turning from the fixtures list*) Hey, Bertie —.

Bertie *indicates wordlessly that he'll be with* **Tommy** *in a minute.*
George *has turned away from* **Gary** *and is chatting quietly to*
Yvonne*'s team. They burst out laughing.* **Gary** *plays the drums on the table.*

Angela Yeah. I hadn't liked him for —oh, years really. But if he'd o' come back I'd ——I'd've let him hit me nearly. ——Not now but. ——Fuck'm.

Bertie I never liked him.

Angela (*quite surprised*) Did yeh not?

Bertie No.

Angela I thought ——. I wouldn't want anyone now. At home, yeh know.

Bertie 'Cept Leo maybe, wha'.

Angela (*fondly and humorously*) Ah, yeah. He'd be grand.

Bertie Yeh really like him, don't yeh?

Angela I do, yeah. I think he's fuckin' lovely.

Bertie *looks as if he wants a more detailed explanation.* **Sandra** *exits, with a tray-load.*

Angela I don't know. He's just —. He's so —; he's always ——. Reliable; that's what he is. Workin' away there, never whingin'. He'd make yeh feel secure, yeh know. ——He irons his own shirts, for fuck sake.

Bertie *seems happy with that answer.*

Angela An' if he ever tried to hit me I'd be able to beat the livin' shite ou' of him.

They laugh. **Sandra** *enters in a hurry, her tray empty. She starts piling more orders onto it.*

Sandra (*calling out*) A pint o' Guinness an' three Harvey Wallbangers.

Features Some poor chap got stung there.

He heads over to **Tommy** *at the pitch 'n' putt fixtures board. At first* **Tommy** *looks as if he wants to escape.*

Martin (*bringing* **George** *and* **Gary** *their drinks*) Serves him righ' for bringin' his mot ou' midweek.

George *gets up as* **Martin** *arrives. He raises his eyes to heaven, indicating* **Gary**.

Denis (*still adding*) Nearly there now.
(*Into the mike.*) Sorry abou' the delay, ladies an' gentlemen. But I'm on me own tonight, so I'm having to do everything here. We'll be commencing again in a minute.

Features Take your time, Denis.

Gary (*to* **Martin**) Yoh, Martin. My main man.

Martin (*indicating pint of Budweiser he puts on the table*) There. That's yours.

Martin *goes back to the bar, getting away from* **Gary**.

Bertie George.

George (*coldly and cagily*) —Wha'?

Niamh (*as* **George** *goes*) Ah, he's gas, isn't he?

Yvonne Yeah.
(*To* **Dermot**.) Isn't he, Dermot?

Dermot (*trying to be carelessly cheerful*) Yeah. ——I —eh, think I'd better get another pint, before the next round.

Bertie (*indicating the seat beside him*) Come on; sit down, compadre. Come on.

148

Dermot *gets up and goes to the bar.* **Sandra** *exits, with a full tray.* **Dermot** *gets in her way.*

Sandra Watch it, will yeh!
   (*Noticing that it is* **Dermot**, *who she likes.*) Sorry.

Gary *softly sings a song from the indie charts, accompanying himself by drumming the table.* **Tommy** *and* **Features** *are engrossed in the fixtures board, arguing happily ('He will not', 'He will so' etc.).*

Tommy An' come here, look who I'm playing the week after the week after next.

George *reluctantly sits down beside* **Bertie.**

George Wha'?

Niamh *gets up and goes to* **Dermot.** **Lorraine** *nudges* **Yvonne.** **Martin** *watches* **Denis** *at work.*

Lorraine She has put on weight.
   (*After they snigger.*) You're a terrible cunt but, Yvonne.

Bertie (*after drinking a mouthful; keeping* **George** *waiting*) Did youse get Black Bess?

George (*unwilling to give away information but afraid to cross* **Bertie**) —Yeah.

Bertie Fair play. Wha' abou' A-ha?

George No.

Bertie No, neither did we.
   (*To* **Angela**.) Sure we didn't? ——Three?

George Yeah.

Bertie Same here. You're still ahead. ——But not for long, compadre.

George (*trying to be at ease*) We'll fuckin' see abou' tha', —— compadre.

Bertie (*gently*) Lay off Tommy, George, will yeh.

George Ah now, listen —

Bertie Shut up a minute. I'm askin' yeh, righ'. Leave him alone.

George (*carefully*) This has nothing to do with you, Bertie.

Bertie (*a little bit threatening*) It does. He's a friend o' mine.

George ——It's not me. He's the one that keeps —

Bertie He's harmless, for fuck sake.

Angela Course he is. He's like a child.

Bertie Si. ——It's not a fair fight, George.

George (*annoyed, worried; but flattered*) Ah, I know. It's just —. You'd be the same, Bertie, if you —

Bertie How long have we been compadres, George?

George *is about to say 'Years'.*

Bertie Many moons, righ'. Many fuckin' moons.

George Yeah.

Bertie When this place was a field.

George Yeah.

Bertie (*a nod indicating* **Yvonne**) When young Yvonne there was still lodgin' in Briget.

George (*smiling*) Yeah. That's goin' back a bit.

Bertie It fuckin' is. I remember the day yis moved in.

Angela Was tha' before or after The Famine?

Bertie Rev up, you. ——We're not going to let —fuckin' this come between us now, are we? Not after all these years, are we?

George No.

Bertie Good man.

George (*an excuse to get away*) ——Eh, the jacks.

Bertie Off yeh go.

George *gets up and goes to the Gents.* **Bertie** *raises his eyes to heaven, to* **Briget.** **Sandra** *enters.* **Lorraine** *looks around. She sees* **Gary.** **Gary** *sees her, and salutes her, John Wayne-style.* **Lorraine** *turns away from him quickly.*

Lorraine Jesus!
Yvonne Wha'?
(*Sees* **Gary** *looking.*) Jesus.

Lorraine *and* **Yvonne** *laugh.*

Denis Righ'. We've a few changes at the top at this point, I think. ——Yeah; hang on.

Sandra *puts a pint of Guinness and two of the Harvey Wallbangers on her tray.* **George** *comes out of the Gents.*

Sandra (*holding up the third Harvey W.*) She's changed her mind. She says can she have a Persian Sunset instead.

Denis ——Yeah. ——Sorry 'bout this.

Leo *pours some blackcurrant cordial into the Harvey Wallbanger and replaces the little umbrella with a bigger one.*

Leo Now.

Sandra exits. **George** *leans over and says something softly to* **Leo**.

Niamh (*slightly desperate*) It's good enough fun, isn't it?

Dermot Yeah.
(*Indicating the scoreboard.*) We're doin' well.

Denis Yeah; right ——.

Niamh The girls are great, aren't they?

Dermot Yeah, yeah.
(*Embarrassed; after glancing around.*) Not a patch on you
though.

Niamh (*loving it*) Ah, feck off.

The team members drift back to their places.

In the Kitchen **Briget** *clears the jigsaw from the table, and exits.*

Denis I'm really sorry about all the time it's taking to ——but
Rosemary —

Angela We know!

Denis (*after sniffing his contempt*) After Round Four there's ——
five teams in third place neck and neck. Table numbers 1, 29,
31, 37 —

Gary Yes!

Denis —and 38.

Lorraine Jesus!

Yvonne's *team is very pleased.* **Sandra** *enters, and puts four pints of
Guinness on her tray.*

George Well done, Yvonne.

Features Very good, yeah.

Denis One team is in second by themselves, one point ahead.
Table number 17. An' Table number 11 are still leadin', but
only by one an' that's not what you'd call a commanding lead
so there's still everything to play for.

Martin (*wincing*) Will yeh listen to that gobshite.

Denis Righ'; back to the part of the quiz I'm good at —(*waits to be
insulted.*) —the questions.

Denis *waits to be insulted again.* **Noel** *enters, looking happy with
himself. He winks at* **Tommy** *and* **Bertie**. **Dermot** *and* **Niamh** *head
back to their table.* **Briget** *enters the Kitchen. She is wearing a dressing-*

151

gown over a nightie, and slippers. She wipes the table, and does a bit of tidying.

Niamh (*enthusiastic; as they reach their seats*) Did you see wha' the prizes are; kettle-jugs.

Dermot (*humorously scornful*) Oh brilliant!

Niamh *looks a little hurt, and lost. She looks to see if* **Yvonne** *noticed.*

Yvonne (*sweetly*) Hiyis. Were yis off dancin'?

. **Dermot** *stares her out of it. She stares back.*

George (*to his team*) Righ', come on. There wasn't too much damage done there.

Bertie (*to his team*) Heads down, compadres.

Denis Round Five. Table numbers on your answer sheets, please.

George (*to his team*) No fuckin' around this round, righ'.

Sandra (*putting the pints on* **Bertie**'*s table*) They're from Mr Finnegan.

George'*s team looks as shocked as* **Bertie**'*s.* **Noel** *studies the pint, for poison.*

Angela Thanks very much.

Bertie Si, George! Mucho.

George No problem.

Denis Question Number One —

George (*quietly, to his team*) I'm lullin' the cunts into a false sense of security.

Denis (*as the lights go down*) Wha' well known singer —

The teams huddle.

Noel This is me.

Angela *scoffs.*

Denis Wha' well known singer and accordion player —

Noel (*disappointed and frustrated*) Ah, Jaysis.

Lights fade.

SCENE SIX — THE KITCHEN

Groucho goes 'La la laa —La la laa'.

It is morning, just after breakfast; a few days before the quiz. The radio is on, softly. **Briget** *has cleared and wiped the table, leaving only* **George**'s *mug. There is a milk bottle on the worktop. She puts on the kettle. She sniffs, bends down and picks up the cat's biscuit tin; and carries it offstage. She re-enters quickly, takes the milk bottle from the worktop and tops up the cat's milk.*

Briget (*to herself*) Doesn't deserve it, the dirty so an' so.

George *enters, from stage-left, dressed for work. There is a piece of paper covering a cut on his chin. He touches it carefully now and again to make sure that it's still there. He's in a mean mood, and he's annoyed to see that the table has been cleared.*

George Where's me plate?

Briget *straightens up.*

George There was a good bit o' rasher still —

Briget (*taking no nonsense*) There was not.

George *sits down at the table and takes out a sheet of paper and a biro.* **Briget** *takes a letter from her dressing-gown pocket, and re-reads it. It is a reminder from the school that the children's registration fee is due.*

George (*to offstage*) Yvonne!

Briget You shouldn't wait for her.

George (*unwilling to discuss*) Ah.
   (*Muttering loudly; looking at the list.*) I'm not goin' to bother with the Lebanon annymore; fuck it.

Briget *wants to talk to* **George** *about the letter.*

Briget (*as if for the third or fourth time*) What abou' this?

George Yeh only have them learnt when one o' them gets shot or blown up.

Briget George?

George (*whispering*) Sunni Moslems, Shia Muslims, Druze.

153

(*To* **Briget**.) Wha'?
(*Before she can speak*.) Is your man, Wally Jumblatt still alive?

Briget Wha'? Oh, I don't know.

George (*before* **Briget** *can say more*) Haven't heard of him in a good
while. I'd say he's dead; wha' d'yeh think?

Briget *says nothing*.

George Great fuckin' help you are.
(*Crossing Jumblatt's name off, and standing*.) Dead. Pity.
Yvonne!! ——He was the easiest one to remember.

Briget Never mind abou' Wally Jumblatt.
(*Re the letter*.) What'll we do about this?

George *goes to the fridge*.

George (*dismissive*) I don't know!

He opens the fridge and takes out his tinfoiled sandwiches.

George (*warily; re the sandwiches*) What are they?

Briget Ham.

George (*relaxing*) Don't worry about it.

Briget It's thirty-five pound!

George We haven't got it.

Briget I know, but —.

George Not for tha' annyway.

Briget (*not too ready to agree*) —Yeah.

George Well then, what's your problem?

Briget We still have to —
(*Turns off the radio*.) We have to pay it.

George We didn't pay it the last time.

Briget Cos you weren't workin'. I went up an' —

George Go up again.

Briget You're workin' now.

George They don't know tha', do they?

Briget Now, look —

George Don't fuckin' 'Now look' me.

Briget (*determined to finish*) ——I'm not havin' Gavin an' Joanne
an' Derek tellin' their teachers tha' they can't pay their
registration money cos their daddy's on the labour. Because
you're not.

154

George (*exasperated*) Ah.
   (*Unwilling to concede defeat.*) It's supposed to be free fuckin'
   education.

Briget That's not the point.

George (*saying this to kill the discussion*) It is the fuckin' point. It is
   the fuckin' point! ——Yvonne!!

Briget You're just bein' ——.
   (*Giving up; resigned.*) Will I tell Gavin to say tha' we'll pay it
   in instalments?

George (*interrupting* **Briget**; *unwilling to agree to anything*) Tell him
   what yeh want.
   (*Less aggressive; handing over the responsibility.*) Do what's best.

Briget *stands there, and 'gathers' herself.*

Briget (*shrugging; unhappy*) ——Okay.

George Look it; sorry, righ'. —I've —

Briget (*sardonic*) The situation in the Lebanon's gettin' yeh down,
   is it?

George (*pointing at* **Briget**) Don't start your fuckin' —.

Yvonne *enters, and* **George** *stops pointing.*

Yvonne Hiyis.

She opens the fridge, takes out a carrot, and puts it in her handbag.

George Good girl.
   (*Grimly cheerful.*) 'Bout bleedin' time.

Yvonne (*to* **Briget**) Gavin's still in bed.

George Is he?; by Jaysis.
   (*Exiting; doing his bit.*) Stay where y'are, Briget. I'll get him
   up for yeh.
   (*Offstage.*) Here; Gavin —!

Briget (*remembering*) It's a holy day.
   (*Running after* **George**.) Yeh bitch yeh, Yvonne. It's a holy
   day.
   (*Offstage.*) It's alrigh', George.

Yvonne (*indignant; self-pitying*) I didn't do ann'thin'.

Lights fade.

SCENE SEVEN — THE QUIZ

Groucho goes 'La la laa —La la laa'.

It is nearly 10.00 pm; during Round Six.

George *and* **Yvonne** *are back at their tables.* **Gary** *is drunk.*
Yvonne's *team are going to be drunk.* **Leo** *and* **Sandra** *are offstage.*

Bertie (*aloud, for all to hear*) Cliff Richard.

All laugh, except **Denis***;* **George** *reluctantly, and* **Martin** *with*
difficulty. **Sandra** *enters in a hurry. The teams onstage huddle together*
and try to think of the answer.

Sandra (*indicating a far corner, offstage*) They can't hear yeh.

Denis (*annoyed at first*) Some people didn't hear me properly there
so I'll have to give yis tha' question again in its entirety.

Yvonne's *team think they're near the answer.*

Yvonne (*agreeing; recognising*) Oh yeah.

Niamh She was in tha' Dusty Springfield song.

Denis Christine Keeler was one of the women involved in the
notorious Profumo Scandal. Who was the other one?

The teams laugh softly again, **Gary** *louder than the rest; remembering*
Bertie's *answer.* **Leo** *enters, takes some pints from under the taps,*
bends down, holds some packets of crisps in his mouth, and exits with
the pints and crisps.

Angela Your woman with the ha' like a bathing cap. Ah, wha' was
her fuckin' name!

Martin *whispers the answer to* **George***, who writes it down.*

George Good man.
(*Looking across at* **Bertie**'s *team as he writes.*) Sound.

Features (*looking around, pleased*) None o' the others know it.

Noel Mandy somethin'.

Bertie Si!

Angela (*at the same time as* **Bertie**) Yes!

156

Bertie's *team are pleased that they're close, but annoyed that they haven't the full answer yet.*

Dermot (*close to the answer*) Hang on ——.

Niamh *watches him, confident that he'll produce the answer; willing him to.* **George** *is on the verge of saying something across to* **Bertie**'s *team when* **Gary** *speaks.*

Gary (*looking at* **George**'s *answer; too loud*) Mandy Rice Krispies!

He laughs. **George** *and* **Martin** *are furious.* **Features** *is embarrassed. The other teams are delighted.* **Yvonne** *blows* **Gary** *a kiss; then herself and* **Lorraine** *and* **Niamh** *laugh.*

Angela Thanks very much.

Noel That's very decent of yis, lads.

Sandra *is collecting empty glasses.*

George Yeh fuckin' eejit, yeh!

Gary (*obviously drunk; but not slurring yet*) Ah, come on.

Martin (*to* **Gary**; *looking at* **Features**) Gobshite.

Features (*gently giving out*) Gary, now ——

Gary Sorry, sorry, sorry; wow.

George (*leaning across, threatening to hit* **Gary**) I'll fuckin' wow yeh.

Denis Question Number Two.

Features (*squashed; defending* **Gary**) Ah now, George ——.

Sandra *dashes out of the way.* **Leo** *enters, and watches to see if anything happens.* **George** *eventually straightens up, glaring at* **Gary**.

George (*not too enthusiastically*) Sorry, Features.

Features Ah, sure.

Martin *hasn't stopped staring at* **Gary**. **Gary** *tries not to, but he belches.*

Denis (*after staring across at* **George**'s *team*) Pop.

Noel Here we go.

Yvonne's *team perks up.*

Denis What is the name ——

Noel (*urging quietly*) Yes, yes.

Denis What is the name of Nana Mouskouri's backing grouuup?

Gary Cliff Richard!

He laughs; surprised that the others don't join in. **Martin** *is thinking about thumping him; looking at* **Features** *to see if he'd get away with it.* **Noel,** *and* **Yvonne's** *team are disgusted with the question.*

Noel *(frustrated; annoyed with the question)* Ah Jaysis!

Lorraine *(across to* **Denis***)* She's not pop.

Denis *shows* **Leo** *the answer, and* **Leo** *looks pleased.*

Leo Now.

Noel *(to his team)* Don't look at me.

Features *(after a bit of thought)* The Athenians.

Gary Wha'?

George *(writing the answer)* Don't tell him.
    (The team leader.) Good man, Features.

Dermot *surprises the rest when he takes the pen from* **Niamh** *and writes the answer.*

Lorraine Jesus!

Dermot *(shrugging)* My ma an' da have one of her albums.

Niamh It's yours.

Dermot It's not —

They laugh when **Dermot** *realises that* **Niamh** *is joking. She leans over and kisses him.* **Yvonne** *pretends to vomit, silently; for* **Lorraine's** *entertainment.*

Denis Question Number Three.

Bertie Shite. Keep thinking, Tommah.

Tommy Okay.

We see **Tommy** *trying hard to think of the answer, and* **Noel** *looking at him scornfully.*

Denis Wha' does —Wha' does a graphologist do?

Noel *(still a bit annoyed)* Pull his wire.

Gary *(quieter than before; then laughs)* Cliff Richard.

George Shut your fuckin' mouth, you, righ'!

Gary Yessir.

Features *wordlessly warns* **Gary** *to cop on.* **Tommy** *whispers the answer to* **Bertie.**

Bertie Is tha' righ'?; good man.

Dermot *(remembering; business-like)* Know it.

Yvonne *(to* **Niamh** *and* **Lorraine***)* Dermot knows it.

George, **Martin** *and* **Features** *are huddled.* **Gary** *tries to join them but* **Martin** *pushes him away, then winces.*

Gary Ah, I want to be in the gang.

Angela (*looking at the answer*) Is tha' a job!?

Tommy Yeah. It was on the telly.

Noel *looks at the answer as if he doesn't believe* **Tommy**.

George Righ', come on. Graphologist —Graphs.

Martin Maps, maybe.

George Good.
    (*Rejecting his own initial response.*) ——No.

Features Charts.

Martin The weather.

Niamh (*indicating* **Dermot**, *who is almost angrily embarrassed*) He's
    great at it, isn't he?

Lorraine Yeah; nearly as good as he is at dancin'.

Lorraine *looks shocked at what she's just said.*

Dermot (*pissed off*) Don't start.

Yvonne (*to* **Dermot**) Don't tell her not to start.

A quiet row between the girls starts, of which we only hear snatches.

Denis Question Number Four.

George (*urgent*) Come on, come on —.

Features I'd say Maps.

George You'd say annythin'.
    (*Unhappy.*) ——Okay.

Gary I know the answer.

George (*eager and hostile*) Wha'?

Gary Not tellin'.

Denis Wha' boxer —

Gary Cliff —

George *thumps him hard.* **Martin** *picks up his Ballygowan bottle.*
Sandra *screams.* **Leo** *enters and is almost at the table before anything
starts.* **Niamh, Lorraine** *and* **Yvonne** *are arguing quietly while the
action below occurs.* **Dermot** *looks at the row at* **George**'s *table.*

Niamh (*to* **Yvonne**) Yis are.

Yvonne We're not, Niamh. I'm not annyway.

Lorraine (*annoyed*) Fuck off, Yvonne.

Leo (*to* **George** *and* **Gary**) None o' that now.

Leo *takes up* **George** *and* **Gary**'s *glasses.*

George (*breathing hard and pointing at* **Gary**) ——You ——.

Noel Cop on over there, will yis.

George Shut your fuckin' mouth, you.

Bertie (*gently but firmly giving out*) George.

Gary *looks scared for a second.* **George** *relaxes a bit.* **Martin** *feels foolish with the bottle in his hand.*

Features Sandra; while you're there, love. Two pints an' a Ballier.
   No Budweiser though.
   (*To* **Gary**.) You're grounded, son.

Gary *tries to look indifferent.*

Sandra (*to* **Features**) Okay.

Lorraine I didn't do annythin'!

Denis (*very indignant*) Leo?

Leo Denis?

George Give us me pint back, Leo.

Denis Can I continue, please?

Leo (*putting the pints back on the table*) Fire away, Denis.
   (*To* **George**.) See now; you're upsetting poor Denis.

George (*still annoyed*) Fuck'm.

Bertie Come on, Denis. Andele.

Dermot (*carefully*) Come on. We're doin' great.

Lorraine (*sardonically*) Yippee.

There is a hostile truce at **Yvonne**'s *table.* **Lorraine** *looks the most put-out, and shifts further away from the rest.*

Denis The boxer, Walker Smith, was better known as what?

Gary, *seemingly in a trance, mouths 'Cliff Richard' to himself.* **Bertie** *and* **Tommy** *know the answer.* **George**'s *team doesn't.* **George** *looks at* **Martin**, *almost aggressively expecting the answer.* **Martin** *shrugs.*

Bertie (*writing the answer*) Oh si!

Tommy (*whispering to* **Noel** *and* **Angela**) Sugar Ray Robinson.

Features A singer?

Martin (*unsure*) No; he means his name —.

Bertie (*across to* **George**'s *team*) Havin' problems, lads?

160

George (*at the same time*) Hang on. ——Denis, we need some clarification over here. Give us the question again, will yeh.

Bertie Objection.

George Wha'!?

Bertie The question was perfectly clear. And Denis's pronunciation was second to none.

George I only want him to read it —.

Angela Don't tell him, Denis.

George Denis!

Denis *feels both* **George** *and* **Bertie** *staring at him.* **Leo,** *pulling pints, is half anxious.* **Sandra** *keeps well away.*

Denis ——Question Number Five.

Yvonne (*supporting* **George**) Ah, that's not fair.

Niamh It is, Yvonne.

Yvonne (*viciously*) Fuck off, you.
(*Out of her seat.*) It's not fair.

George *is out of his seat, furious.* **Features** *also gets up; then* **Martin,** *but not as enthusiastically.* **Leo** *comes out from behind the bar.* **Sandra** *flies offstage with a full tray.* **Bertie's** *team stay seated, thoroughly enjoying themselves but not too obviously.*

Features (*the voice of reason*) Ah now, Denis —.

Denis Wha' character —

George No way!

Martin (*not that loud, but sincerely*) The little cunt.

Gary (*quietly*) Cliff Richard.

He giggles stupidly; then becomes stern, concentrating on not getting sick.

Denis Wha' character —

George *tries to grab the microphone from* **Denis**.

Denis (*ready to die in the mike's defence*) No!

George Give us it!

Noel 'What character' wha' Denis?

Angela It's fuckin' disgraceful.

Bertie (*grinning*) Oh si.

Leo *gets in between* **Denis** *and* **George**; *the flex somehow tangled around his neck.*

Leo Now!
(*To* **George**; *meaning it.*) I'll bar you.

George *makes one more grab for the mike, and nearly strangles* **Leo**. **Angela** *is immediately out of her seat.*

Angela Here!

George Jaysis sorry, Leo. Y'alright, are yeh?

Angela Yeh stupid wanker, yeh.
(*To* **Leo**; *studying his neck.*) There's no marks, Leo.

George (*to* **Angela**) I didn't mean it.
(*To* **Leo**.) I didn't mean it, Leo.

Angela Ah, look what he's done to your fuckin' shirt!

Denis (*back in control of the mike*) Sorry abou' that, ladies an' gentlemen —.

Leo *is rubbing his neck.*

Leo (*testing*) Now.

Features Come on, George.

George Sorry, Leo, righ'.

Leo *smiles bravely.*

George (*just short of pleading*) Denis; will yeh not read it again?

Features (*telling* **George** *to come back to his seat*) George.

George, **Features** *and* **Yvonne** *go back to their seats.*

Yvonne Are yeh alrigh', Daddy?

George *lifts his hand and nods; meaning 'Yes'.*

Denis Question Number Five —.

Leo (*more confidently*) Now.

Denis Wha' character —

Noel Three cheers for Leo. Hip hip.

Some Hurreh!

Noel Hip hip!

Most Hurreh!

Noel Hip hip!

Most Hurreh!

Denis (*outraged, but trying not to sound it*) What —

Bertie The El Supremo of the barmen.

Denis Are yis listening!?

Noel Yeow, Denis!

Denis *waits for total silence.* **Features** *hands* **George** *his biro.*

George (*whispering*) ——Thanks.
    (*On the verge of despair.*) It's happenin' again, Features.

Features Not at all.

Sandra *enters, carefully.* **Angela** *goes back to her place.* **Leo** *goes back behind the bar.*

Denis Wha' character —in the popular soap opera from Australia, 'Neighbours', writes some of the scripts for the show as well as actin' in it?

Features (*trying to be cagey, but pleased*) I think it's, eh —

He leans across and whispers the answer to **George**. **Gary** *looks around him as if waking up, gets up carefully and goes to the Gents.*

George (*cheering himself up as he writes*) Sound.

Bertie's *team expects* **Angela** *to have the answer.*

Angela (*quite happy to tell them*) I haven't a fuckin' clue.

Yvonne (*to* **Niamh**) Oh, I know. The fat one; what's his name?

Niamh *doesn't want to talk to* **Yvonne**.

Dermot Harold?

Yvonne Yeah, him. He was on 'Wogan'.

Lorraine (*remembering*) Jesus, yeah.

Dermot (*to* **Niamh**; *sounding almost like a question*) Great.

Niamh *smiles, and stares at first at* **Yvonne** *and* **Lorraine**; *then smiles.* **Yvonne** *makes a face at* **Lorraine**, *making her smile.*

Tommy Charlene, Scott, Madge, eh, Mrs. Mangle —

Noel No, no, no, —fuck no.

While **Tommy** *goes through the 'Neighbours' cast,* **Sandra** *is collecting empty glasses at* **Bertie**'s *table.* **Angela** *looks at her, wordlessly asking her for the answer.*

Sandra (*whispering guiltily*) ——Harold Bishop.

Bertie's *team is silently and secretly delighted; watching* **Bertie** *write the answer.* **Martin** *sees what happened.*

Martin (*hesitantly at first*) The young one told Angela the answer.

George (*half listening*) Wha'?

Martin (*pointing; almost regretting he's said it*) The young one —.

George (*copping on*) Here!

Sandra *almost jumps.*

Denis Righ'; tha' brings us to the end —

George Denis; Sandra told them the answer.

Sandra I did not!
(*To* **Denis** *and* **Leo**.) I didn't.

Angela She did not, you; get lost.

George (*getting up, but staying at the table*) She fuckin' did. We've witnesses.

Bertie Sit down, George.

Noel Leo; bar the fucker, will yeh.

Leo, *resigned and rubbing his neck, is coming out from behind the bar.*

George They should be disqualified or there should be another question or somethin'. Fair's fair.

Sandra I didn't tell them!

George (*pointing to* **Martin**) He saw yeh. ——Didn't yeh?

Martin Yeah.

George New question, Denis. Come on.

Bertie (*harder*) Sit down, George.

George You should sack tha' young one, Leo. ——Denis.

Noel Sit down, for Jaysis sake.

George Yeh couldn't trust her with the till.

Sandra (*quietly; getting louder*) Yeh fuckin' creep.

Bertie *is out of his seat. Gradually, all stand up.* **Leo** *stands between* **George** *and* **Bertie**.

Bertie She didn't do annythin', so sit down.

George Martin saw her.

Bertie Then he needs his fuckin' eyes tested.

Features Ah now —.

George He heard her as well. Didn't yeh?

Martin Eh —

Bertie There. Apologise.

Martin (*not going to be bullied*) I did hear her, righ'.

We hear **Gary** *getting sick.*

George (*ignoring* **Bertie**) Denis.

Denis Round Six is completed. Sandra will collect the answer sheets from yis.

Sandra I will not. He called me a liar.

George (*to* **Denis** *and* **Leo**) She told them the answer!

Denis *ignores him, and stacks his index cards.* **George** *is outraged, appalled, furious; too furious to be too scared of* **Bertie**. *Some of the others sit down.*

George (*to* **Denis**) You're un-fuckin'-believable, d'yeh know tha'? Yeh wouldn't read a fuckin' question again for us, an' then —then when they cheat an' bribe young ones to give them the answer you let them get away with it.

Bertie (*gentle tactics, but with an edge*) Sit down, compadre.

George Don't fuckin' compadre me, pal. ——It's not fair, Denis. —Denis!

Martin This is fuckin' scandalous.

Angela Sit down or fuck off, the two o' yis.

Denis (*on edge; attempting suavity*) We'll go straight into Round Seven, because we're runnin' a bit late. Eh, Rosemary —. Write your answers on the back o' your Round Six sheets. Then we'll have a break.
(*Attempting humour.*) A well earned break.

Leo *thinks that that's that. He moves away.* **George** *and* **Martin** *stay there. They can't quite believe the injustice of it all.* **Bertie** *gently holds* **George***'s shoulder, to encourage him to his seat.*

Bertie Come on, George —.

We hear **Gary** *getting sick.*

George (*shrugging violently*) Get your fuckin' —!

Lorraine *screams.* **Leo** *is quickly back between them.*

Bertie (*calmly, but angry; going back to his seat*) You're a fuckin' eejit, compadre.

George (*staying where he is*) Am I!? ——
(*Getting more angry as he says it; going back to his seat; to his team; trying to drum up fervour, and almost succeeding.*) It's not a game annymore, lads. This is war, righ'. War!

Bertie (*controlled fury*) Righ'.

Denis Question Number One —.

Yvonne *is the only one at her table who doesn't look as if she wants to* *laugh.* **Bertie** *sits down, and picks up his pen. Without looking* **George**'s *way, he points the pen at him; looking down at the table.*

George (*to the team; then glaring across*) We're goin' to get the fuckers this —
     (*Sees* **Bertie** *pointing at him.*) time.

Bertie Bring me the head of Georgeo Finnegan.

Features Ah now —.

As **Denis** *asks the question the two teams huddle and glare across at each other, some more frankly than others.* **George** *makes his team concentrate on the question.* **Bertie** *hisses.*

Denis (*as the light fades*) Who said —Who said, "Bloodshed is a cleansing an' a sanctifying thing"?

Lights fade.

Act Two

SCENE ONE – THE QUIZ

Kermit The Frog sings 'Lydia The Tattooed Lady'.

In the Kitchen **Briget** *makes sandwiches for the next day's lunches; wraps them, and so on.*

It is about 10.15; the middle of Round Seven.

The teams are at their tables; some hunched, ready to answer, impatient; others in a more relaxed position, listening to **Denis**. **Gary** *seems to be miserably asleep.* **Sandra** *is offstage.* **Yvonne** *is standing, in the middle of a row with* **Denis**.

Denis (*laying down the law to* **Yvonne**'s *team*) You'll just have to bloody well listen like everyone else.

Yvonne (*as* **Denis** *speaks; pointing at* **Bertie**'s *team*) Wha' about them!?

Bertie Sit down ou' o' that.

Noel (*quieter*) Brasser.

George (*across to* **Noel**; *not too loudly*) Wha' did you fuckin' say?

Bertie He said nothin'.

George (*pointing at* **Noel**; *trying not to include* **Bertie**) If you ever, pal, —ever. D'yeh hear me?

Leo *flicks the Pub lights on and off, on and off. Some of the characters, almost in a panic, look at their watches; they think it's closing time.*

Features (*almost terror stricken*) Where's Sandra?

Leo (*getting up on a crate behind the Bar; annoyed*) Listen here a minute —.

Noel (*mimicking* **Leo**) Now.

Angela (*to* **Noel**) Don't start, you.

Leo Listen. I'm warning you now in this corner here. If you don't leave Denis alone and let him get on with his questions, now I'll bar yis all. I will.
(*Pointing out* **Denis**.) Would you do it?

Martin (*quietly*) Do a better job than him.

Leo No, you would not. So, last warning, right.

Bertie (*to* **Angela**) Tha' hombre's a born leader.

Angela Oh, I know.

Yvonne (*quieter, but insistent*) Well, it should be the same for everyone.

Denis (*a little moved by* **Leo**'s *defence*) Thank you, Leo. I'll just say one more thing an' then I'll leave it at that.

George (*impatient*) Come on, come on, for fuck sake.

Bertie (*before* **George** *finishes; supporting* **Denis**) Go on, Denis.

Denis I'm only talkin' about a few —.

Niamh He's goin' to put us on detention.

The girls laugh secretly, but loud.

Angela Shut up, over there.

Denis If yeh don't like the way I run things, well there are plenty of other quizzes you can go to instead.

There's a short burst of ironic applause from **Bertie**'s *table.*

Noel Where's me hankie?

Lorraine Jesus, I only asked him a fuckin' question.

Dermot (*quietly*) Fuckin' spastic.

Niamh Yeah.

Yvonne (*kind of aping* **Niamh**) Yeah.

George (*not too loud*) Come on, before we go fuckin' senile.
(*To his team.*) He's fuckin' hopeless.
(*Rubbing his hands; leading his men.*) Righ'; come on.

Denis Righ' —.

Sandra *enters, with a tray of empty glasses.*

George Here's Mata Hari, look it.

Sandra (*close to tears*) Fuck off!

Yvonne *glares at* **Sandra**, *as if deciding whether to attack her or not.
As* **Denis** *asks the next question the tune of 'Lydia' starts, and as the
scene progresses, speeds up, slows down etc where appropriate.*

Denis Question Number Three. Wha' soccer team —Wha' soccer team did the world famous singer from Spain, Julio Iglesias, play goalie for?

*The teams hunch over their tables, whispering frantically; keeping an
eye on the opposition. They nod, and shake heads; agreeing and*

arguing. **Bertie** *pats* **Tommy**'s *back.* **George** *sees this, and presses his team for an answer.* **Martin** *comes up with one, and* **George** *quickly writes it down. Both teams glare triumphantly across at each other. The girls are pressing* **Dermot** *for an answer: he hasn't a clue.* **Yvonne** *says something disparaging; and* **Niamh** *bites back at her.*

Suddenly, all together, all three teams become alert; listening to **Denis**'s *next question; heads bent towards* **Denis**. **Denis**'s *expression as he reads is a little bit evil: it's a tough one.* **Yvonne**'s *team looks absolutely lost, and frustrated about it.* **Denis** *sorts out his cards.* **George**'s *team, minus* **Gary**, *argue out an answer. On the other side,* **Angela** *and* **Noel** *are aggressively and enthusiastically arguing.* **Bertie** *and* **Tommy** *earwig, obviously, on* **George**'s *team; leaning more and more out over the neutral territory between the tables.* **Tommy**'s *weight pushes* **Bertie** *off his stool.* **Tommy** *tries to look as if nothing has happened.* **George**'s *team, after seeing what has happened, huddle even closer. Then* **George** *very dramatically writes the answer, hiding the paper with his free hand; then gives the fingers to* **Bertie**'s *table.* **Bertie**, *after getting up, has his guns drawn, guarding himself as he sits down. The argument at* **Bertie**'s *table is very heated.* **Noel** *grabs the biro from* **Bertie**. **Angela** *goes for it.* **Bertie** *clicks his fingers: they stop.* **Angela** *gives* **Bertie** *the biro, and they start arguing again.* **George**'s *team looks over, delighted; making silly faces.*

Sandra *delivers three cocktails and a pint to the girls' table. Together the girls go for their handbags, but* **Dermot** *pays.* **Niamh** *and* **Yvonne** *bat their eyelashes at* **Dermot**, *then glare quickly at each other. All together they pick up the cocktails and* **Dermot** *picks up his pint. All four take a sip, and agree, nodding once, that the drinks are lovely.* **Leo**, *behind the bar, appears, disappears under the counter, reappears somewhere else; shakes cocktails Tom Cruise-style; pulls four pints at the same time, one with his mouth; throws bags of crisps offstage, and so on.*

Suddenly again, all three teams become very alert as **Denis** *asks the last question of the round.* **Gary** *wakes up, opens his mouth, as if to get sick; and* **Features** *gets up, grabs him and hauls him offstage.* **Denis**'s *question seems to go on forever. The teams sit stock-still and, only gradually their faces become a bit puzzled, and startled.* **Lorraine** *yawns.* **Leo** *stops to listen.* **Sandra** *tiptoes past him. And still* **Denis** *recites the question.* **Features** *comes back, sits and listens; taps* **Martin**'s *shoulder: Is it the same question?* **Martin** *nods, shellshocked: Yes.* **Denis** *finishes. For a second the teams are stunned; then huddle and consult, frantically.* **Leo** *and* **Sandra** *get going again.*

Briget *exits; and returns with some clothes (part of her 'good' outfit which she will wear in the next scene), and irons them on the table.*

Bertie's *team is first with an answer.* **Noel** *comes up with it, and insists that it's right.* **Tommy** *has doubts but* **Noel** *slaps them down. The others are happy with it, and* **Bertie** *writes it down with a flourish. They sit back and smugly watch* **George's** *team going through agony.* **George, Features** *and* **Martin** *are going through agony as they try to squeeze the answer out of their brains. While* **Bertie's** *team looks across at* **George's** *team's distress* **Noel** *pours some of* **Tommy's** *pint into his own.* **Gary** *enters, and stands at the side of the stage, looking lost, miserable, forlorn.* **Sandra** *enters carrying a tray piled high with empty glasses and has to fly around* **Gary** *twice to avoid bashing into him. She flies offstage.* **Gary** *doesn't know where he is.* **Leo,** *shaking a cocktail, leans over the counter, takes hold of* **Gary's** *tie and leads him offstage; and is almost immediately back onstage, pouring the cocktail into a glass.* **Sandra** *lunges back onstage desperately trying to get to her end of the counter before she lets go of the tray. She makes it; and exits again.* **George** *has a brainwave. A light bulb goes on over his head.* **Features** *and* **Martin** *look to* **George** *eagerly, almost begging for the answer.* **George** *writes it and they, all three together, nod once triumphantly across at* **Bertie's** *team, and fall back, exhausted.*

The round is over. **Sandra** *enters, carrying a pile of answer sheets.* **Sandra** *goes to* **Yvonne's** *table, and* **Lorraine** *goes to take the sheet from* **Niamh** *to give it to* **Sandra.** **Niamh** *doesn't want to give it up yet. They both grab it and tear it.* **Dermot** *stands up, furious; shouts something at them and storms off, but not before* **Yvonne** *pinches his bum on his way past her. He tries to ignore this indignity and dash-walks into the Gents. All three girls mime: 'Men.* ——*Fuckin' eejits'.* **Sandra** *dumps the sheets on* **Denis's** *lap and grabs a full tray. As she is exiting,* **George, Bertie** *and* **Yvonne** *stand up and all shout.*

George, Bertie, *and* **Yvonne** Sandra!

The music stops just long enough for them to shout. **Sandra** *tries to look and go in three directions, almost as if she's been shot by three bullets, then exits.*

The teams relax. The three girls stand, put their bags under their right arms and troop over to the Ladies; **Niamh,** *then* **Lorraine,** *then* **Yvonne.** **Dermot** *comes out of the Gents.* **Niamh** *and* **Lorraine** *turn their faces from him as they go into the Ladies:* **Yvonne** *doesn't: she stares right up into his face.* **Sandra** *flies out of the Gents, still holding her tray. She looks around perplexed; and charges back in.* **Bertie's** *and* **George's** *teams, always aware of one another's proximity, unwind.*

170

They stand up, stretch, rub their eyes, adjust their crotches (including **Angela**). **George**, **Features** *and* **Martin** *look around furtively, and chance a fart, and move away from the scene of the crimes.* **Tommy** *goes to the Gents and* **Angela** *goes to the Ladies; both in a hurry. The girls troop out of the Ladies, in file and go to the bar, ignoring* **Dermot**. **Yvonne** *makes faces at him and sticks her tongue out at him when the others aren't looking.* **Dermot** *hides behind his glass and, when he decides to chance a flirtatious look back at* **Yvonne**, **Niamh** *looks around and nearly catches him. The girls point out exotic bottles to* **Leo** *who pours some of each into his cocktail shaker; then into a bucket as they point to more and more bottles. There is a big umbrella and three huge straws in the bucket.* **Leo** *does his Tom Cruise routine in front of the girls. The girls drink, and admire* **Leo**'*s performance;* **Yvonne** *looking back at* **Dermot** *all the time.* **Dermot** *looks back; pouting, licking his lips, arching his eyebrows, running his hand through his hair.* **George**, *strutting like Foghorn Leghorn, leads his team into the Gents.* **Bertie** *goes over to* **George**'*s table. He unscrews* **George**'*s biro and takes out the cartridge and pockets it.* **Tommy** *is coming out of the Gents when* **George** *is going in.* **George** *shoves* **Tommy** *back in, and* **Features** *and* **Martin** *follow them.*

Angela *comes out of the Ladies, zipping up her fly, and catches* **Leo** *strutting his barperson stuff in front of the girls. He immediately becomes business-like.* **Niamh** *turns, and catches* **Dermot** *opening the top buttons of his shirt and* **Yvonne** *lifting her arm and clenched fist, showing* **Dermot** *what she's going to do to him.* **Niamh** *and* **Yvonne** *are about to fight, when all the characters onstage stop and stare at the Gents door.*

Bertie *strides over to the Gents, and in; holding his pint. First* **Features**, *trying to put his vest, shirt, jumper and jacket into his trousers; then* **Martin**, *fly out, as if thrown out.* **Tommy** *follows, trying to put his tie back into its proper position, and flattening down his hair; looking as if he's been in a fight. All watch the Gents door, and listen. The door opens and* **George** *comes out slowly, back first; followed by* **Bertie**; *forehead to forehead;* **Bertie** *still holding his pint. Moving carefully, their foreheads stuck, they go to centre stage.* **Bertie**'*s face is solid.* **George**'*s isn't quite as sure.* **Leo** *comes from behind the counter and becomes a boxing referee. A microphone is lowered and* **Leo** *introduces the contestants. The teams become the seconds.* **Bertie** *and* **George** *take off their jackets;* **George** *looking less happy behind a brave face. Without looking back* **Bertie** *holds his glass behind him.* **Sandra**, *going by with a tray of empty glasses, inverts the tray (the glasses stay on upside-down) and collects* **Bertie**'*s glass just as* **Bertie**

drops it. **Bertie** *and* **George** *are ready to start fighting when* **Denis** *announces the beginning of the next round.*

Denis (*indignant*) Round Eight.

There is a mad rush to the tables, and the three teams sit, braced.

Denis (*heard over the music*) The scores after Round Seven are as follows: Table 38 have twenty-seven points. Table 36 have thirty points an', in the lead an' out on their own, Table 37 with thirty-one points.

Sandra, *a very reluctant 'Sale of the Century'-style hostess, stands behind each team and holds up scoreboards as* **Denis** *announces the latest scores.* **Yvonne**'s *team looks unhappy with its score, and one another.* **Bertie**'s *team looks aggressively satisfied with its score. But their expressions change when they see* **George**'s *score.* **George** *rallies his troops.*

Round Eight begins fast. **Denis** *asks a short question, and the teams huddle.* **George** *can't get his pen to work. He holds it up and looks up into it, and shakes it; and tries again, and curses it.* **Denis** *asks the second question.* **Features** *gives* **George** *a biro. The pace gets faster and faster. The teams argue, nod, shake their heads, stand up, sit back down as if they are having fits.* **Leo** *gradually disappears behind the counter.* **Sandra** *stands with a full tray and looks as if volts of electricity are going through her. Then the music halts, and —*

Bertie (*getting out of his seat*) No way!
(*Asking for fair play.*) Hey, compadre ———.

Denis I said, 'Domestic rabbit'.

This is a dispute about the answer to the question: What is the world's largest domestic rabbit? The others are gasping for breath after their exertions in Round Eight. **Lorraine** *lifts her arms a bit to let the air get at the sweat.* **Martin** *leans over, afraid that he's going to get sick.* **Sandra** *has to put her tray on the counter.*

George (*to* **Bertie**, *but not too emphatically*) Sit down.

Denis *is about to continue.*

Bertie (*ready to draw*) Don't move, Denis!

George Sit down ou' o' tha'.

Martin (*recovering*) It's fuckin' disgraceful.

Bertie What's wrong with our answer?

Denis (*not going to be bullied*) I said 'Domestic rabbit'.

Bertie ('*so what*' *style*) Yeah?

Features (*almost apologetic*) The Polish Lop is a wild rabbit, Bertie.

George Course, it is.

Angela There's no such thing.

Denis (*repeating the answer; slowly*) The British Giant is the largest known domestic rabbit.

George Course, it is.

Features and **Martin** *both agree, and so does* **Yvonne**.

Yvonne Yeah.

Bertie Come here, Denis —.

Noel Domestic, me arse.

Martin Don't listen to him, Denis.

Niamh *is annoyed and worried that* **Dermot** *won't look at her*.

Bertie Denis. Say if yeh caught a wild rabbit, a Polish Lop say; and yeh trained it —.

Lorraine Ah, this is thick.

George Sit down.

Bertie Yeh trained it. A leetle one, righ'. A bambino. Yeh trained the wild rabbit. What would it be then?

Angela That's righ'.

Features (*quietly, to* **Martin**) He has a point.

Martin (*outraged*) Why don't yeh sit over there then!?

Features *shrugs*.

Bertie Well, Denis?

Denis (*ignoring* **Bertie**; *giving the answer to the next question*) Father Damien lived among the lepers.

George (*aggressively pleased*) Yes!

Bertie Fuck the lepers. Wha' abou' my rabbit?

Angela There's no such thing as a wild rabbit. Would a rabbit bite yeh, would it?

Yvonne It'd bite you.

Angela Go home to bed, you.

Yvonne (*not quite under her breath; turning her back*) Dirt-bird.

Angela (*beginning to get up*) What did she —!?

George *is going to block her way*. **Bertie** *stops her*.

Bertie (*quietly*) Get her in the jacks after.

Angela *sits down.*

Yvonne (*loudly quiet*) No wonder her husband left her.

Lorraine (*expecting murder*) Oh Jesus!

Niamh That's not righ', Yvonne.

Yvonne Ah fuck off, Niamh, will yeh.

Yvonne *raises her eyes to heaven, to* **Dermot**; *as if expecting him to agree with her.* **Dermot** *stares straight ahead.*

Bertie (*sounding quietly threatening*) I'd say a tamed wild rabbit was a domestic rabbit. I'd say annyway. Wha' would you say, Denis?

Noel He's a domestic rabbit.

Leo *enters. He points at* **Noel**.

Leo You're barred.

Noel *looks like a player being sent off.* **Bertie** *goes back to his seat, slowly.* **Leo** *watches him move, ready to bar him.*

Bertie (*trying blackmail*) Remember that video, Denis?

Leo (*to* **Bertie**) You're —

Bertie (*sitting down*) Alrigh', alrigh'.

Denis *looks ghastly after* **Bertie** *mentions the video. He looks hurt, caught, guilty, outraged, defeated.*

Denis (*a shake in his voice; to himself*) Never again ——.

Features (*whispers*) He always says that.

Noel (*amused; surprised*) Did yeh flog it to *him*?

Bertie (*tapping his finger on his nose*) Sil-ence, compadre.

Denis (*after coughing*) An', Question Number Five. Gammon comes from the hind legs of the pig.

The three teams are satisfied with that answer.

Denis I needed 'hind' there.

Lorraine (*protesting*) Ah!

Yvonne (*at the same time*) Ah!

Leo *points at them. They fume, but say nothing.* **Lorraine** *loses interest first. The team is falling apart.* **Leo** *goes back behind the bar.*

Denis Righ'. We'll go straight into Round Nine, the second last round. ——Thank God.

Features Ah Denis.

Denis Table number 37 are now two points ahead of —

George *congratulates and motivates his team.* **Martin** *is beginning to look very uncomfortable, but he soldiers on.* **Bertie**'s *team looks across enviously and contemptuously.* **Bertie**'s *hiss is extra-long.*

Denis —Table number 11 and Table number 36. Right, eh —

George It's our night, lads. Come on.

Denis *is having difficulty summoning the will to carry on.*

George (*to* **Yvonne**'s *team; very loud; unable to resist gloating*) Did I tell yis I was bitten by a rabbit on me way to work this mornin'?

Yvonne *in particular is amused.* **Niamh** *doesn't even smile. Enter* **Gary**, *sobered up, tired and miserable. He plonks down in his chair and studies the floor.*

George (*pointing at* **Gary**) He's not gettin' a kettle, righ'.

Noel Hey, Leo. Am I still barred?

Leo (*more interested in* **Denis**) Your sentence starts at midnight.

Noel Righ'. Sandra; four pints.

Sandra (*on her way offstage*) I'm busy.

George (*re* **Denis**; *looking around*) What's keepin' him?

Gradually, all turn to see what's wrong with **Denis**.

Leo (*quietly*) Denis?

Denis *is slumped on his stool; unable to go on.*

Leo (*very sympathetic; coming out from behind the counter*) Ah now —.

Niamh (*whispering; to* **Dermot**) You're lookin' at her all the time?

Dermot (*sounding 'wronged'*) I'm not.

Yvonne Yes, you are. An' I don't blame yeh.

A furious whispered row starts; **Dermot** *trying to calm* **Niamh**, *then giving up.*

Features *is earwigging, but keeping an eye on* **George** *as well.*

George Our minds'll go cold if we don't get goin' soon. —— Denis!
(*To* **Features**.) 'Jane Eyre'?

Features Eh, —Charlotte —? —Bronte.

George (*turning back to look at* **Denis**) Yeah. ——sound.

Leo *holds* **Denis**'s *shoulders and tries to get him to look up.*

Leo Are you alright, Denis?

George (*to* **Features**) Is he havin' a heart-attack or somethin'?

Martin (*very sorry for himself*) Think I am.

Denis *tries to look at his index cards, but —*

Denis ——I've had it, Leo.

Leo (*very sympathetic*) —Ah —.

Denis I can't —— I —.

Leo Would yeh like a bit of a rest, Denis?

Denis They have no idea how much —
(*Answering* **Leo**'s *question*.) Yeah —— Yes.

Leo *takes the index cards from* **Denis**.

Denis (*reluctant to give up cards*) You mightn't be able to —

Leo You listen now, and make sure I do it right.

Denis *nods his agreement*.

Noel (*to all, including* **George**'s *team*) What's happenin'?

Bertie *looks across at* **George**, *and is cold-shouldered. He smiles grimly.* **Leo** *goes back behind the counter, puts the cards in front of the taps and pours pints as he asks the questions. He places the microphone in front of the taps.*

Leo (*studying the cards*) —Now ——.

Briget *exits carrying the ironed clothes very carefully.*

Leo (*into the microphone*) Now, —Round Nine. ——Denis is taking a short commercial break so —now; Number One —.

George (*concerned about* **Denis**) Is he alrigh'?

Leo Ah, he is.

Niamh (*to* **Dermot**) She's just —.
(*To* **Yvonne**.) You're just tryin' to move in on him. You're just jeal —

Yvonne I did already, an' I didn't have to try.

Niamh *looks lost.*

Yvonne At the party, yeh simple-head yeh.

Niamh's *face crumples for a second, then looks furious; but there's uncertainty there too.*

Leo Oh, and it's a good one alright.
(*Looking at the answer on the back of the card.*) You'll never get it now. What country has 1.5 million registered footballers?
(*To* **Denis**.) That was a powerful one, Denis.

Denis *doesn't react. He's slumped on his stool.*

Niamh (*while* **Leo** *speaks; looking from* **Yvonne** *to* **Dermot**, *and staying on him; angry*) —Did —? —.

Yvonne We wore the faces off each other.
(*To* **Dermot**; *daring him to contradict her*.) Didn't we?

Lorraine *doesn't know where to look.* **Bertie**'s *and* **George**'s *teams huddle.*

Noel (*coming up for air; to* **Leo**) Is tha' soccer footballers?

Leo Oh, —now.

Denis *nods listlessly.*

Leo Soccer; soccer.

Denis *drags himself to the Gents.*

Niamh (*standing up; grabbing at her bag but missing*) You're a slut, Yvonne Finnegan.

Yvonne D'yeh think so, Niamh?

George (*to* **Features** *and* **Martin**) Brazil?

George *sees that* **Features** *is more interested in what's going on at* **Yvonne**'s *table.*

George When you're finished watchin' 'Coro-fuckin'-nation Street' yeh can give us a hand here.

Features (*snared*) Wha'? —eh, —I wasn't —.

George Yes, yeh were, yeh brasser. Italy?

They huddle.

Niamh (*still trying to pick up her bag; getting more angry*) You're a fuckin' tramp. A dirt-bird. I always said it. Didn't I, Lorraine?

Lorraine (*a bit guilty*) I don't know!

Some things have spilled out of **Niamh**'s *bag.*

Angela Tha' place; China.

Bertie Si!

Noel Excellent.

Leo Number Two —.

Features Mexico.

Martin No; Brazil.

Gary I'd say China.

George Would yeh? Fuck off.

Features He might —

George Fuck'm.

Yvonne I never wanked Ju Ju Lips Redmond behind the clinic. Did I, Lorraine?

Lorraine (*embarrassed*) Lay off, will yeh.

Dermot (*half standing up; embarrassed and angry*) Take it easy.

George (*writing*) Brazil. Has to be. They do fuck all else over there.

Leo Oh, it's a holy one. You haven't a hope.

Niamh (*ready to go; to* **Dermot**) Are yeh comin', Dermot?

Yvonne Wha'? Behind the clinic?

Niamh *looks ready to jump on* **Yvonne**. **Yvonne** *holds her glass*.

Leo Who is the Patron Saint —

The teams sit up: they're good at these ones.

Niamh (*to* **Dermot**; *his last chance*) Are yeh?

Dermot *hesitates*. **Yvonne** *shrugs*.

Dermot (*sitting; not looking at* **Niamh**) No.

Niamh (*going*) Righ'.

Yvonne See yeh.

Leo —of the Postal Workers?

Gary *scoffs*.

Niamh (*just before exiting; roars; nearly crying*) You're a fuckin' bastard, Dermot Montgomery!

Leo Now!

Angela (*casually; as if she might have known*) Yvonne.

Lorraine (*scarlet*) Jesus.

Exit **Niamh**, *and comes back immediately. The others look to see who the bastard is; then get back to business.* **Niamh** *looks undecided, contrite; as if she's hoping* **Dermot** *will change his mind; but it's pointless. She exits, running.*

Tommy Saint Gabriel.

Features (*at the same time*) Gabriel.

Both teams are pleased with the answer, and wait for the next. **George** *looks around at* **Yvonne**'s *table.*

George How yis doin', love?

Yvonne Useless. Aren't we?

Dermot ——Eh —.

Leo Number Three —.

Yvonne Daddy, this is Dermot.

George Howyeh.

Dermot *is lost; stunned. When* **Leo** *starts the question* **George** *turns away from* **Yvonne** *and* **Dermot**.

George See yis.

Leo What nationality is Rolf Harris?

Features (*not trusting it*) That's easy.

George It can't be.

Yvonne *and* **Lorraine** *aren't bothering with the quiz any more. They get a fit of the giggles.* **Dermot** *has his head in his hands.*

Lorraine (*beginning to seem drunker than the others*) Ah, it's not funny though.

Bertie Hey, Leo?

Martin (*starting to object*) Here —.

George (*to* **Martin**; *wanting to hear*) Hang on.

Bertie Por favor; do yeh mean wha' country your man Harris was born in?

Leo Oh, I'd say so now.

Bertie Yeh don't know for definite but.

Leo (*into the microphone*) Sandra. Come here now. Do you read me, Sandra?

Noel (*while* **Leo** *speaks*) You'd want to find ou', Leo.

Enter **Sandra**, *dashing and embarrassed.*

Sandra Wha'!?

Leo (*busy at the taps*) Go over and knock on the Gentle-lads door there like a good girl.

Sandra Wha'! I will not! Get lost.

Angela Ah go on, love. It has to be someone neutral.

Sandra, *giving in to* **Angela**, *goes reluctantly to the door.*

Lorraine Scarlet for yeh, Sandra.

Yvonne *waves at* **Dermot**'s *face. He forces a smile, and sits up. When* **Yvonne** *looks away* **Dermot** *keeps looking at her, beginning to look pleased with himself.*

Sandra (*at the door*) Just knock only?

Leo Good.

Sandra *knocks: nothing*.

George (*impatient*) Come on. Come on.

Bertie Give it a good wallop, Sandra; go on.

Sandra *knocks harder*.

Denis Wha'?

Sandra *looks lost*.

Leo Ask him if he means the country Rolf Harris was born in?

Sandra (*to the door*) Do yeh mean the country Rolf Harris was born in?

Denis Yes!

Leo Tell him thanks very much now.

Sandra Thanks very much.

Leo Did yeh hear that now?

Bertie Si. ——Muchos gratiassss.

Tommy He always puts one o' these ones in comin' up to the end. An easy one tha' might be hard but was really easy.

Bertie Australia?

Tommy Yeah.

George Just cos he sings about kangaroos doesn't fuckin' —

Martin Where else could it fuckin' be?

Features Put Australia, George. There's always a trick one near the end.

Leo (*too busy*) Sandra. Read the next one here now.

Sandra (*about to run*) No!

Yvonne (*getting up*) I'll do it.

Sandra No; I'll do it.

Leo *shows* **Sandra** *the question on the card*.

Noel Yeow, Sandra!

Angela *scoffs, and raises her eyes*.

Sandra (*holding the microphone as if it's going to bite her*) Who wrote the best-sellin' book —
(*Appalled at the length of the question.*) Jesus! —tha' also became a widely ah-acclaimed film, —
(*To* **Leo**.) Wha' is it?

Leo (*looking at the card; quietly*) 'Elmer Gantry'.

Sandra 'Elmer Gantry'.

Angela Well done, Sandra.

Sandra (*quite pleased; sitting up on the stool*) Thanks.

Tommy Second time this year.

George (*writing*) D'yeh ever read it?

Features No.

Martin (*lifting his shirt to see if the ulcer is bruising*) Good film. Burt Lancaster an' your woman —.

Gary *leans over to read the answer.* **George** *glares at him, warning him to come no further.* **Gary** *looks at* **Features**.

George Don't tell him.

Denis *comes out of the Gents, looking a bit drained but healthily indignant.*

Yvonne (*to* **Dermot**) Did Niamh ever show yeh her mole, Dermot?

Lorraine (*trying to give out*) Ah, Yvonne.

Lorraine *and* **Yvonne,** *then* **Dermot,** *laugh.*

Leo How are you now, Denis?

Denis Alrigh'. ——Under the circumstances.

Leo Ah great.

Sandra Question Number Five —

Denis *goes to take the cards from* **Sandra**.

Sandra (*disappointed; gripping the cards*) Ah.

Leo (*gentle warning*) Now.

George (*nodding at the answer sheet*) Waste of a question tha' really.

Features Still though. ——nearly there.

George (*worried*) Stop.

Denis (*into the microphone; very formal*) Question —Number Five.

George *and* **Bertie's** *teams applaud.* **Denis** *is a bit moved, but he still tries to look indignant.*

Denis When you're finished —.

George Good man, Denis.

Noel Welcome back, Denis.

Denis *gives* **Noel** *a quick glance of contempt.*

Denis What aristocratic woman —

The teams look worried.

Noel (*under his breath*) He's back.

Denis What aristocratic woman sent clippings of her pubic hair to the famous poet an' ladies' man, Lord Byron?

Lorraine Jesus!

George My Jaysis, wha'.

Features Some floozy annyway.

Denis I'll need the full name there.

Noel D'yeh want the number o' hairs as well?

Bertie's *team laughs.* **Features** *and* **Martin** *start to laugh, but* **George** *stops them.*

George (*urgently*) Don't laugh; don't laugh.

Bertie Pretend we know the answer, compadres.

Tommy (*delighted*) Ah yeah.

George —When about —? Come on.

Angela (*just loud enough*) Yeah; I read it in a book.

Bertie (*pretending to write*) Siii!

Martin They know it.

George Come on; shite!
       (*Desperate; to* **Gary**.) Do you know?

Gary Eh, —no.

George Fuck yeh.

Bertie's *team sits back, looking pleased and mischievous.*

Yvonne (*to* **Dermot**; *re posting pubic hair*) I wouldn't do tha'.

Lorraine You'd deliver them yourself.

Yvonne '*playfully*' *pinches* **Lorraine**.

Bertie (*out of the side of his mouth*) Annyone know it?

They discreetly shake their heads.

Bertie (*loud*) I believe your man, Lord Byron made a doormat out o' your woman's curly fellas.

George (*re* **Bertie**'s *distraction; not turning*) Denis.

Bertie (*loud*) A redhead, she was, by all accounts.

George (*trying to ignore* **Bertie**) Denis. ——The Queen Mother, Princess Anne, eh, Diana, —Fergie?

Martin No.

George Mary Queen o' Scots, eh —eh —Fuck it.

Features Queen Victoria.

George Yeah —No.

Gary She doesn't have to be English.

George Fu —
(*Changes his mind.*) Good thinkin'.

Denis Sandra'll collect your answers. Pens down.

Yvonne We'll help. Come on, Lorraine.

Lorraine (*but getting up*) Ah, Jesus.

Martin Princess Grace.

Features (*aghast*) Ah, no way.

Lorraine *exits with* **Sandra**. **Tommy** *goes to the Gents*.

Yvonne (*to* **George**) Your answers, please.

George Fuck off a minute; sorry, Yvonne love. —D'yeh know?

Yvonne No.

George (*writing*) Shite! —Elizabeth the First, righ'.

Features Ah, fair enough.

Enter **Lorraine**. *She joins up with* **Yvonne** *on their way to* **Denis**.

Lorraine Come here, d'yeh see who's in there?

Yvonne Who is?

Lorraine Ju Ju Lips.

They scream laughing. **Lorraine** *staggers slightly*.

Denis Will yis do the scorin' for me?

Yvonne Ah yeah. Dermot, come here.

Dermot *hops to it*.

Denis Thanks very much. It'd be a great help. It's the only part I
don't ——eh —.

Leo *leans over and whispers into* **Denis**'s *ear*.

Denis (*to* **Yvonne**) You can't do any addin'.
(*Handing her the marker.*) Just writin' in the scores.
(*Indicating* **Bertie**'s *team.*) They might object.

Yvonne (*deciding not to object*) Oh yeah.

Lorraine (*reading the answer sheets; giving out*) Jesus, Yvonne.

Denis (*with a load off his mind*) Righ'; before the final round I'll
give yis the answers to the one yis just did there; Round Nine.

George (*trying to believe it, and comfort himself*) Well, we got four out o' five annyway.

Features That's grand.

Martin (*not convinced*) Yep.

Denis One: the country with 1.5 million registered footballers is, of course, China.

Bertie Siiii!

Bertie's *team is delighted.* **George** *puts his head in his hands. The others are also distraught.*

Noel (*seeing* **George**'s *dismay*) Yeow!

Features (*quietly to* **Gary**) You said that.

George (*to the others*) Yis fuckin' eejits.

Martin Don't start.

Bertie (*across to* **George**) Only one in it now, compadre. (*Showing a lifted finger.*) Uno.

George (*to the others*) Yeh fuckin' thicks, yis.

Features *wants to say something, but is afraid to.*

Denis Saint Gabriel is the Patron Saint of the Postal Workers.

George Thank God. One ahead still.

Martin (*remembering they'd another question wrong*) Your woman's pubic hairs ——.

George (*his world falling apart*) They're level; ah, shite. It's not fuckin' fair. ——Just once —.

Denis (*as the lights go down and Groucho starts to sing*) Rolf Harris is, of course, Australian.

Bertie *is congratulating his team.* **George**'s *team looks beaten and torn apart.*

Lights fade.

SCENE TWO — THE KITCHEN

Groucho sings 'La la laa — la la laa'.

It is a Sunday evening; before the Quiz.

Enter **Briget**, *looking very well in her good outfit; followed by* **Tommy**. **Tommy** *is a bit more neatly dressed than in the Pub scenes. He is carrying a garden shears.*

Briget (*continuing the conversation as she enters*) Ah, yeah. It's nice. For a change, yeh know.
(*Laughing lightly*) Even though it's the same thing every Sunday.

Tommy *is a bit uncomfortable. He won't sit down till he's told to.*
Briget *picks up the kettle to gauge if there's enough water in it: there is. She turns it on.*

Tommy It's somethin' for yeh to look forward to.

Briget Ah yeah —. Sit down, Tommy.
(*As in 'or coffee'.*) Tea?

Tommy Thanks v' much, —Briget.

Briget Or there's a bit o' coffee if yeh —

Tommy Whatever you're havin'.

Briget (*putting two bags into mugs*) Tea.

Tommy Have you enough for the mornin'?

Briget Ah, I'll use these ones again.

Tommy (*almost frightened*) Ah God, Briget —!

Briget (*feeling a bit guilty*) I'm only messin'. I've loads. I'd want to have. My shower wash themselves with tea. ——Yeah; I like my Sunday nights. Yeh know Trudy? Feature's —? Ah, she's gas. Mad.

While **Briget** *and* **Tommy** *speak* **Briget** *gets a box of Cornflakes from a shelf, takes it to the table and, after looking out into the hall to make sure that the kids aren't around, lifts the inner packet out of the box, and takes out the Jaffa Cakes. She takes out some of the cakes and* *quickly puts the Cornflakes back on top of the Jaffa Cakes.* **Tommy** *is startled and confused, but tries not to look it.* **Briget** *gives him two cakes.*

Briget Two. Cos it's Sunday, wha'.

Tommy (*not getting the joke*) Thanks v' much, Briget. Lovely. —— I don't like Sundays that much.

Briget Ah; why not?

Tommy Ah ——I like some of it. The mornin's, I like. I watch the match; the soccer. I help out a bit, yeh know. Your Gavin's comin' along very well, so he is.

Briget (*pleased*) Ah, is he?

Tommy Ah, he is. He's goin' to be a useful little footballer. —— We have a couple o' pints then; the lads from the club. It's gas sometimes. Always, nearly. ——I like me Sunday dinner as well, I must admit now.

Briget Ah yeah.

Briget *is thoroughly enjoying herself, and* **Tommy** *is beginning to.*

Tommy I look forward to tha'. The gravy an' the roasters.

Briget An' the sweet after, wha'.

Tommy No, not really now. ——I eat it, but —cos it's there just.

Briget That's often the way.

Tommy (*getting to the point*) I watch the telly with me mother. She likes the Sunday stuff. An' yeh know the way she's a bit deaf? I tell her wha' they're sayin'. We watch the 'Antiques Roadshow'. D'yeh watch it yourself, Briget?

Briget Ah yeah; sometimes I do.

Tommy Ah, it's very good. I think annyway. We guess the prices of the things before they say how much they're worth an' sometimes we get it righ', nearly exactly.

Briget Ah, do yeh?

Tommy Sometimes only.

Briget Still.

Tommy I took her to see it when they were over here, the 'Antiques Roadshow'. They were over here. In the Royal Hospital there in Kilmainham. We didn't bring annythin' with us though.

Briget You should've brought the shears.

186

Tommy (*getting the joke after a while*) Ah yeah; very good. (*Serious; holding up the shears.*) We have these fifteen years though, Briget. ——Me father, God rest him, got them for me mother for her birthday.

Briget (*enjoying both the sentimentality and the absurdity*) Ah. —— Wha' d'yeh do after the antiques, Tommy?

Tommy I stay in to watch the telly with her. (*Reluctant to rat on his mother.*) I don't mind. She loves 'Glenroe'. Ah, she thinks they're brilliant. I think it's a bit borin'.

Briget Yeah.

Tommy Sometimes I'm not concentratin' on it, yeh know, an' she says, 'What's he after sayin' there?', an' I just say, 'He says he's goin' ou' to milk the cows'. An' she thinks that's grand. It doesn't seem to matter, yeh know. But, come here, sometimes it's terrible. We were lookin' at 'Eastenders' there. Ah, a few months back, it was. When your woman, Cath, was in court abou' tha' fella tha' raped her; d'yeh remember it?

Briget Ah, yeah.

Tommy An' your man —your man tha' done it was in the —dock, yeh know, givin' his evidence. It was shockin'; d'yeh remember it?

Briget I do, yeah.

Tommy It was terrible now. ——An' she kept sayin' to me, "What's he sayin'? What's he sayin'?". An', God, Briget, I couldn't tell her "He says he's goin' ou' to milk his cows".

Briget *laughs, and then* **Tommy** *laughs as well; enjoying himself. Enter* **George***; carrying a putter and an eight-iron. When he sees* **Tommy** *his expression falls just short of a sneer.* **Briget** *remains relaxed, expecting* **George** *to join in; but* **Tommy** *looks a bit snared. He begins to get up, hesitates, sits back down; grips the shears, as if about to go.*

Tommy How-howyeh, George.

George (*forcing himself into a good humour*) What's the story here; wha'?

George *puts his golf clubs in a corner.*

Briget (*to* **George**) Did yeh win?

George (*the same question, with a slight edge*) What's the story?

Briget Tommy's collectin' his shears. We had them for ages.
Sorry, Tommy.

Tommy Ah.

George Wha' were we doin' with his shears?

Briget I borrowed them off him.

George (*to* **Tommy**) Yeh have them now, do yeh?

Tommy (*very uncomfortable*) Yeah. Here —

George (*before* **Tommy** *can finish*) Good.
Have yeh finished your tea?
(*Looking into the cup.*) Yeah; yeh have.

Tommy (*getting up*) Yeah. I'll —eh —

Briget *is determined to make* **Tommy** *stay; because she has been
enjoying herself and she won't let* **George** *away with being so rude.*

Briget (*getting up quickly*) There's more tea in the pot here,
Tommy.
(*Ordering him.*) Sit down. ——D'yeh want one, George?

Tommy *sits down, as if on a hot plate.*

George (*as if his tea is a fundamental right*) Yeah.

Briget (*pouring*) We'll serve our guest first, then we'll see if there's
any left for you.

George'*s face says 'There'd better be'.* **Tommy** *feels* **George**'*s eyes
burning him.*

Tommy Just a half of a cup'll do me.

George (*to* **Briget**) D'yeh hear tha'?

Briget (*ignoring him; handing out the tea*) Wha' d'you watch after
'Glenroe', Tommy?

Tommy (*very aware of* **George**) ——Depends, —Briget.

George On wha'?

Tommy If there's a film on. ——She likes the cowboys.

George Does she? Where does she go to meet them?

Tommy *doesn't get it.* **Briget** *nudges* **George**, *to leave* **Tommy** *alone.*
George *is more relaxed.*

Briget (*trying to get* **Tommy** *going again*) Does she like John
Wayne?

Tommy Loves him; she loves him. Funny; she can always hear
him. Randolph Scott as well, she likes. But he's never on on
Sundays.

Briget (*surprised*) Randolph Scott?

Tommy Yeah. Her mother, like, had a cousin tha' married a fella called Scott an' they went to America an' she thinks we're prob'ly related to him, Randolph Scott.

Briget Ah, that's nice.

Briget *looks at* **George**, *to make sure that he is enjoying himself. He is, but his expression is very sardonic. Also,* **George** *is noticing how relaxed* **Briget** *is, how much she's enjoying herself.*

Tommy I don't think he is. He's dead now annyway. We watched one on Channel 4 there last week, with those subtitle yokes.

Briget Did yeh?

Tommy (*a bit guiltily*) I thought tha' with the subtitles she wouldn't need me to tell her wha' they were sayin', so I could get ou' for a pint, yeh know like, but —.

George (*unwillingly impressed*) That was good thinkin'.

Briget Yeah.

Tommy Only she couldn't find her glasses so I had to read the subtitles for her.
(*Wanting to go.*) I'd better —.
(*Standing up; explaining.*) 'Glenroe'.

Briget Ah yeah. Milkin' the cows, wha'.

Tommy Yeah.
(*Going; holding up the shears; unable to look at* **George**.) Thanks v' much, —Briget.

Exit **Tommy**.

Briget (*shouting after him*) Bye bye, Tommy.

Briget *laughs silently, then louder; expecting* **George** *to join in. He does, but half-heartedly.*

George *goes to the fridge and takes out a bottle of milk.*

Briget Ah, he's gas, isn't he?

George Yeah. ——fuckin' eejit.

Briget (*fondly*) Ah, he's not. Yeh should've heard him about 'Eastenders'. His mother —

George (*with an edge*) Yis get on well annyway.

Briget Ah yeah.
(*Noticing something wrong; indicating the clubs.*) ——Did yeh lose?

George (*after taking a slug from the bottle; putting it back*) No, I didn't lose.

Briget *looks at* **George**, *trying to see what's wrong with him; not wanting to start a row.*

Briget (*after a pause; attempting cheerfulness*) Are yeh ready to go out?

George I haven't heard yeh laughin' like that in ages.

Briget (*reasonably*) Ah, yeh have.

George (*as if out of nowhere*) He's not to come into the house again, righ'.

Briget Wha'?

George Fuckin' Randolph Scott. I don't want to see him in here, righ'.

Briget (*lost*) Tommy!?

George Yeah! Tommy! Buy a fuckin' shears.

Briget What's wrong with yeh?

George (*not answering*) What're yeh dressed up for?

Briget We're goin' out.

George *looks at her as if he knows why she's really dressed up.*

Briget (*seeing his look*) Ah now, hang on. Cop on, George. Tommy!?
(*Attempting humour.*) Jesus, don't insult me.

By now **George** *has made himself feel wronged and justifiably sorry for himself.*

Briget (*aggressive, but worried*) What's wrong with yeh?

George (*moving to beside* **Briget**) There's nothin' wrong with me. With *me*.

Briget (*getting up*) I'm not listenin' to this. Yeh eejit.

George *pushes her back down, and immediately feels a bit thick. But when* **Briget** *insists on trying to get up again he pushes her back down, really losing his temper.*

Briget (*trying to remove* **George**'s *hand*) Let me up, George.

George *grabs one of the golf clubs, but puts it back down. He clenches his free fist.*

Briget (*frightened; angry*) Leave me alone!

George I'll kill yeh; I'll split your fuckin' head for yeh!

Briget (*terrified*) Don't hit me!

George *stands over* **Briget** *for a while, breathing deeply, feeling a bit foolish, and embarrassed, guilty; but also thinking that she was looking for it.* **Briget** *is afraid to look up.* **George** *steps away.*

George ——Righ'. ——Do yourself up.

Briget *wipes her eyes.*

Briget (*quietly; carefully, but determined*) You don't think tha' at all. Sure yeh don't?

George (*aggressive, but a bit guilty*) Wha'?

Briget Me an' Tommy —.

George (*not very loud*) Shut up, will yeh.

Briget Jesus. You know fuckin' well I wouldn't —.

George (*still aggressive and guilty*) D'yeh want me to hit yeh; is that it?

Briget It's just an excuse.

George (*sneering; hiding behind it*) Is it?

Briget Yeah. It is.

George (*scoffing*) Shut up.

Briget I'm sick of it.

George Are yeh?

Briget Yeah, I am. You've some fuckin' neck, you have. ——It's always the same.

George Shut up.

Briget Always, it is. When I wanted tha' job. When —when I wanted to go to Liverpool with the girls. When I did tha' English night class.
(*Triumphantly.*) An' I passed it, yeh bastard. Even when I just have a bit o' crack with someone else, yeh put me down.

George Shut your fuckin' mouth, will yeh.

Briget Always, yeh put me down. Yeh do, George. Even for laughin' at Tommy, because it wasn't you. Cos you're afraid I'll —

George *stands closer to* **Briget**, *over her. He clenches his fist and draws it back.*

George Shut up!

Briget *half screams, and cowers.* **George** *relaxes, and steps back; and hitches up his trousers.*

George (*after sniffing; quietly gruff*) Righ'. Come on. ——Let's go; come on.

Briget (*standing; not looking at* **George**) I will not. I'm not stayin' here.
(*Vaguely.*) I'm goin'.

George (*digging into his pocket and putting his money on the table*) Here. Here. Here's your bus fare for yeh, look it. Go on ——. Go.

Briget (*picking up the money; fumbling*) I will. You're not goin' to bully me.

George (*after a slight pause*) I just did.

Lights fade.

SCENE THREE — THE QUIZ

Groucho sings 'La la laa —la la laa'.
It is 10.55; just before the start of Round Ten.

The Kitchen is empty and **George** *is back at his place in the Pub. The teams and the other pub characters are as they were at the end of Scene Two.* **Lorraine** *is drunker than* **Yvonne**. **Dermot** *is beginning to look a bit creased.* **Denis** *is reading the answer to the last question in Round Nine.* **George** *is looking into his pint, shaking his head; grieving.*

Denis An' the aristocratic lady tha' sent the, eh —unusual present to Lord Byron —

Lorraine (*as she works with* **Yvonne** *and* **Dermot**) Slut.

Denis —was, of course, Lady Caroline Lamb.

Martin (*contemptuous*) Who was she!?

Angela (*waving to* **Sandra**) Four pints, Sandra love.

Sandra Righ'.

Leo *has put the pints on her tray when she turns to give the order.*

Sandra Four —Oh Jesus!

Leo Now.

Yvonne Hey Leo; are yeh givin' us annythin' for doin' this?

Noel (*to* **Tommy** *and* **Bertie**) Know wha' I'd give her.

Angela (*scoffing*) A good laugh.

Leo (*to* **Yvonne**) Ah now.

He puts three packets of crisps on the counter.

Yvonne (*insulted; disappointed*) Ah Jesus.

Lorraine (*indignant*) Don't touch them, Yvonne.

Yvonne (*taking up her pack*) Better than nothin'.

Denis (*supervised by* **Dermot**; *pleased*) Righ'. ——The scores as we go into the last and final round are —

The teams listen; **George** *still staring at the table.*

Denis Table 11 are in third place by themselves but they've fallen back a bit. Come on now, lads. Yis have thirty-six points; two behind Table 36, so it's not over yet. Yeah —Table 36 are in second with thirty-eight. An' Table 37 are still in the lead, but only by one point: thirty-nine. An' that's top class scoring. ——Righ —.

George sits up during **Denis***'s rundown of the scores: he's confused. So are* **Features** *and* **Martin**. *They should be level with* **Bertie***'s team.*

Features (*very quietly*) We should be level.

George (*out of the side of his mouth; afraid of being heard*) Is he after makin' a bollix of it?

Features Don't know —.

George is trying not to look too pleased, in case the point is taken back off them.

Martin (*tense; excited*) I need a Ballier. ——Sandra.

Bertie Lady Caroline Lamb. That's your woman with the ears tha' works in the chipper, isn't it?

George (*torn between fury and delight*) Yeh cunt yeh, Bertie. (*Not quite believing his luck; hardly able to stay sitting.*) We're still winnin'.

Martin (*to* **Sandra**) A Ballier, two pints an' — (*Looking at* **Gary**.) —that's all.

Denis Righ'. Round Ten.

George No; here. Come here. No drink till after.

Martin It's only water.

George We're a team. If we're not drinkin' you're not fuckin' drinkin'.

Sandra (*going*) Please yourselves. I know where I'm not wanted.

George Righ'; come on. We have it for the takin'. Come on. (*To* **Gary***; sternly.*) You as well.

Features *is pleased to see* **Gary** *back in the fold, and so is* **Gary***, though he tries not to show it.*

Denis Righ'. Just before we enter the final phase of the competition I'd like to thank yis all on behalf o' the Barrytown Wheelies for comin' out an' supportin' us tonight. It's the last quiz I'll be in charge of, so —

Eyes are raised to heaven and secret grins are exchanged: they've heard **Denis** *say this before.*

194

Noel Yeah yeah yeah.

Denis —I want to —

Leo Closing time now, Denis.

Denis (*after a deep breath*) Righ'; last round. Here we go.

Bertie (*pretending nonchalance*) We don't really need a new kettle but, sure —.

George (*who isn't really following his advice*) Don't listen to them.

Angela Yeh don't want F-Troop to win them, do yeh?

George (*to* **Angela**) If you win one the Vincent De Paul'll take back your old one.

Denis Question Number One.

Angela An' they'll take back your clothes while they're at it.

Martin Yeah; an' give them to you.

Denis What was the name —

George Don't listen to them.

Denis Are yis listenin'!?

George (*to* **Denis**; *aggressively defensive*) It wasn't us. It was Winnie Mandela over there. An' fuckin' Stompie.

Bertie (*laughing*) I'll stompie his bollix for him.

Denis (*to himself; promising his retirement*) —Definitely —. Wha' was the name of the actor tha' played 'Robin' in the very popular nineteen sixties cult crime —?

George (*interrupting* **Denis**) We know!
(*Less loudly.*) Jaysis; what else could Robin've been in? 'The fuckin' Riordans'!?
(*To his team.*) Righ'; who was it?

Denis (*livid; determined to finish*) —series, 'Batman'!

Leo Good man, Denis.

Gary leans over, and whispers the answer. **George** *nods his thanks grudgingly.*

Tommy Burt Ward.

Noel No; Dick Grayson.

Tommy No; that's his name in —

Noel Look; I'm a fan, righ'.

Bertie (*writing down*) Burt Ward.

Angela Definitely.

Denis Question Number Two.

George (*trying to be cheerful*) Four to go only.
   (*To* **Gary**.) You're sure about' tha' one now?

Gary Yep.

George (*afraid to contemplate victory; willing* **Denis**) Come on.

Denis Who is the guitarist —

Noel (*sitting up; to his team*) Red alert, red alert.

George (*worried and sardonic*) Hope he's not commercial.

Denis Who is the guitarist with the very popular grouuup, The
   Smiths?

Gary (*announces; determined to advertise his knowledge*) They broke
   up years ago.

George Yeh fuckin' eejit, yeh!

Gary They did.

Leo (*seeing* **Denis** *beginning to panic*) 'Was', Denis.

Denis *Was* the name of the guitarist.

Gary *leans over and tries to give* **George** *the answer but* **George** *won't
meet him halfway.*

Yvonne Do yeh know it, Dermot?
   (*Leaning much closer to him; which surprises him.*) Tell us it.

Lorraine (*imitating* **Yvonne**) Tell us it.

Yvonne *gives* **Lorraine** *the fingers without looking at her.* **Lorraine**
puts an empty crisp bag over **Yvonne**'*s hand.*

Gary D'you want to know the fuckin' answer or don't you? I
   mean, I know it; yeah?

George (*drowning the urge to kill* **Gary**) ——Wha' is it?

Denis Question Number Three.

Gary *leans over and whispers.*

George (*muttering*) Fuckin' better be.

Noel Em, ——I knew it before they broke up.

Denis Who painted —

Noel It's somethin', eh —.

Bertie (*angry*) I speet on somethin'.

Denis Who painted the world-famous painting, 'Guernica'?

George (*seeing the row at the next table*) We're two ahead. ——Who
   was it?

They don't know. They think hard. **Gary** *thinks that he should know the answer.*

Martin (*muttering*) Can't be tha' fuckin' famous.

Angela *knows the answer, and whispers it to* **Bertie**.

Bertie Si!
  (*Whispering across to* **George**'s *table.*) Picasso, Picasso, Picasso.

George (*trying to think; about to confer*) Fuck off ——Fuck off —— Fuck off!

Leo (*warningly*) Now!

Denis Question Number Four.

George (*aggressively pleading*) We need more time, Denis. We're bein' put off over here.

Noel You should change your socks more often then.

Martin Fuck off, Larry Gogan.

This insult takes a lot out of **Martin**.

George We need more time, Leo.

Denis I'm in charge.

Bertie Well said, compadre.

Denis Question Number —

Yvonne Ah, that's not fair.

Denis Four.

Yvonne Yeh can do your own addin' then. ——Yeh thick.

Yvonne *goes back to her table, bringing* **Dermot** *and* **Lorraine** *with her.*

Lorraine (*being dragged*) Jesus, Yvonne!

George (*distressed; furious; fearing defeat*) Shite! Me head's gone empty.

Features (*mildly giving out*) Ah God, George. Yeh always fall for it.

Denis What are —

Features (*comforting* **George**) One ahead still.

George (*trying to shake himself*) ——Yeah.

Denis What are peptic, gastric and duodenal varieties of?

Martin (*nearly choking on a mouthful of Ballier*) Jaysis!

Gary *knows the answer as well but* **Martin** *gets to* **George** *before he does, and whispers the answer.*

George Good man!
  (*As he writes.*) Sound.
  (*Confident again; rubbing his hands.*) Yaah —hah —!
  (*Suddenly worried again.*) Come on. Last one.

George's team tries not to celebrate too early.

Lorraine (*to* **Yvonne** *and* **Dermot**) Wha' are they?

Yvonne Don't know. Do you, Dermot?

Dermot Eh, —no.

Yvonne Do yeh not? Jesus.

Lorraine *and* **Yvonne** *laugh.*

Bertie (*coming out of a team huddle; writing; loud*) Spuds.

Features (*not too sure*) They don't know it.

George He's messin', the cunt.

Denis Last question.

George Last question.

Yvonne Come on, Daddy.

George Fuck —! ——Shhh, love.

Yvonne (*whisper-roars*) Come on, Daddy!

Denis What arm —

George Jaysis, I can feel me heart.
  (*Quietly.*) Come on, yeh cunt.

Denis (*after a longer delay*) What arm an' eye did Admiral Nelson lose?

Noel His own.

Bertie's *team laughs and then gets down to business.* **Angela** *takes the pen from* **Bertie**.

George Righ' or left ——.

Features *closes one eye and puts a hand inside his sleeve.*

Features I'd say the righ'.

Martin One of each —.

George No. —Which?

No one is prepared to give the answer.

George (*taking a coin from his pocket*) Ah here, fuck it. Heads the righ'.

Denis Sandra will now collect your answers.
  (*To* **Yvonne**'s *team.*) Will yis help her?

Yvonne (*pulling Lorraine back down*) No.

George *tosses the coin. No one is willing to say which.*

George Do I have to do everythin'? ——Heads.
(*Looking down at the coin.*) Heads.
(*Writing.*) The righ'. ——Maybe though ——No, fuck it.

George *smiles and shakes hands with his team.*

George We did our best annyway, wha'.

Martin (*getting up*) Fuck the ulcer. I'm havin' a pint.

Enter **Sandra** *with a bundle of answers.* **Angela** *gives* **Sandra** *her answer sheet.*

George (*to* **Sandra**; *not too harshly*) It's the spy who came in from the cold.

Sandra Ah, snap ou' of it, Mister Finnegan.

Denis I'm on my own again, —
(*Glaring across at* **Yvonne** *who glares back.*) So I'll give yis the final answers before I do the addin' up.

George This is it.

Denis Robin was played by ——Burt Ward.

George Yeow!
(*Worried again.*) Shhh! Shhh!

George *glances across to see if* **Bertie**'s *team got the right answer.*

Bertie (*meeting* **George**'s *glance; coldly*) Si.

Denis The Smith's guitarist, eh, used to be Johnny Marr.

George Yeow!

George *gives* **Gary** *the thumbs-up.*

Noel (*disgusted with himself*) Yeh fuckin' eejit, Noel.

George Two ahead. Come on, Denis.

Denis Picasso painted ——'Guernica'.

Bertie's *team congratulates* **Angela**.

Bertie (*to* **George**'s *team*) Did yis get tha' one, lads?

Features *wants to point out that* **Bertie** *had given them the right answer, but decides not to.* **George** *and* **Martin** *are about to explode.*

George (*steadying himself*) Okay, okay. Still one.

Denis Peptic, gastric and duodenal are, of course, varieties of ——ulcers.

George Yess!

George *looks desperately across at* **Bertie**'s *table.*

Angela (*to* George) Me daddy has one of each o' them.

George Fuck. ——One ahead still. Last one. Oh Jesus ——.

Denis Admiral Nelson lost his right —

George *is up out of his seat.*

Denis —arm an' his —

George *sits back down, ready to jump up again; in agony.*

Denis ——right eye.

George *lifts his hands to heaven; a religious moment. The others are overjoyed; even* **Gary**. **Bertie**'s *team look on contemptuously and enviously.* **Bertie** *checks that his gun is loaded.* **Dermot** *puts his arm around* **Yvonne**. *She looks at it, and shrugs, indifferent.*

George (*to* Bertie) Gotcha, compadre.
 (*To* Features.) Three years, wha'.

George *punches the air.*

Martin I think me ulcer's fucked off.

Denis (*innocently*) I'll need two rights in tha' last answer. One for his arm an' one for his eye.

George (*confused*) Wha'?
 (*Realising; like a question.*) One'll do yeh, Denis.

Denis (*to himself; as in 'not again'*) Oh no.
 (*To the public.*) No.

George (*standing up*) Ah Jaysis —.

Gary That's crazy.

Bertie (*quietly to* Angela) Did we put down two?

Angela Course we did!

Bertie (*to* George) Sit down. Sit down there.

George Yeh shouldn't have to write it twice. It's not necessary.

Martin No.

Denis (*looking up from his counting*) I'm afraid it is.

Bertie Sit down ou' o' tha'.

George *looks as if he's going to destroy* **Denis**. *Then* —

George (*trying logic*) Look, Denis; listen. If I said, 'Denis, do you work five days a week?', would you say, 'Yeah, yeah, yeah, yeah, yeah'? Yeh wouldn't.

Noel He might.

George Fuck off, you.

Bertie (*warningly*) Hey.

Denis (*not looking up*) Right arm an' right leg.

Martin (*muttering*) You're a righ' bollix.

George Hang on, Martin —.
(*Quietly to* **Denis**.) They always win, Denis —Denis?

Gary He lost them in the same battle.

George (*clutching desperately*) That's righ'.

Tommy He didn't.

Noel He lost his pillar as well, wha'.

George Fuck off!
(*To* **Denis**.) One battle, one righ', Denis. ——Denis.

Denis *ignores him.*

Noel (*sings*) Are yeh righ' there, Nelson, are yeh righ'.

Bertie's *team is delighted.* **Leo** *comes out from behind the bar.*

Yvonne That's not fair. Wha' happens now?

Martin (*to himself; wincing*) It's back.

Features (*to* **Yvonne**) A tie breaker.

Lorraine Oh brilliant!

Yvonne (*giving out*) Lorraine!

Leo (*getting between* **George** *and* **Denis**) You sit over there, George, now.

George (*becoming firm*) Righ'. Fair enough.
(*Sitting down.*) Righ', lads. No sweat.
(*To* **Features**.) 'The Naked An' The Dead'?

Features Eh, Norman Mailer.

George (*to* **Martin**) Lester Piggott's Derby winners?

Martin Nine.

George (*to* **Features**) 'To The Lighthouse'?

Features Virginia Woolf.

George (*to* **Martin**) Rugby Grand Slam, 1984.

Martin Scotland.

George We'll fuckin' gut them.

Noel Here, listen.
(*Continuing the song.*) Yeh lost your arm an' eye in the one fight,

> Then yeh crashed your scooter,
> An' yeh fell an' broke your gooter,
> Are yeh righ' there, Nelson, are yeh righ'.

During **Noel**'s *recital* **George**'s *team sits proud and dignified.* **Leo** *watches both teams, ready to step in.*

Denis (*as the lights fade*) Righ'. It looks like we have a Tie-break Situation.

Yvonne This is brilliant, isn't it?

Lorraine (*giving out*) Yvonne!

Lights fade.

SCENE FOUR — THE KITCHEN

Groucho goes 'La la laa —La la laaaaaa.'

It is evening; some time before the Quiz.

Briget *is sitting at the table, writing into a copybook. The radio is on low, playing pop music. She looks up, and at the door; almost nervously. She stops writing, and reads over what's written; looking pleased but uncertain. She stands up and presses down on the cover of the copybook, to make it stay shut. As she is doing this she hears* **George** *approaching and gets away from the table, but without looking worried or panicky. She picks up the kettle, to be doing something when he walks in.*

Enter **George**, *in a clean, very white vest. He is holding a shirt.*

George Here, Briget. Stitch a button on for us, will yeh.

Briget Righ'. Which one is it?

George *shows* **Briget** *a buttonhole at stomach level.*

George This one; look it.

Briget (*mildly sardonic*) Ah; yeh don't want people to see your belly.

George (*not bad-humoured; a bit caught*) Don't start.
    (*Taking the shirt from* **Briget**; *the decent man.*) No; make your tea first. ——An' I'll have a cupful while you're at it.

Briget There's a surprise.

She makes the tea.

George (*picking up the copybook*) Don't start.

George *reads, a few pages in.* **Briget** *is horrified at first when* **George** *starts reading, but not too obviously. She is nervously pleased when he likes what he reads.*

George (*reads*) 'By the time I got to our gate there'd be nothing left. Only the crust.'
    I used to do tha' as well.
    (*Reads.*) 'I'd hide under the stairs when my mother cut the

bread and found out she's nothing for the tea, only a long
hollow crust.'
(*Laughing lightly.*) Ah, that's very good.
(*Looking at the cover.*) Whose is it?

Briget (*just in time*) Joanne.

George It's very good. Isn't it?

Briget (*not wanting to boast; even to herself*) Yeah.

George (*reads the cover*) 'Hard Years, Happy Years'.
(*Glancing through the other pages.*) —An', look it; pickin'
blackberries ——.

Briget Where's the button?

George (*still concentrating on the copybook*) ——Wha'? ——Fair
play to Joanne. Her handwriting's fuckin' terrible though. It's
like an oul' one's.

Briget (*sterner*) Where's the button?

George Wha'?; there isn't one.

Briget *puts the copybook up on a shelf. She takes an old sweet tin full
of buttons from a shelf, sits down and starts searching for a button.*
George *squeezes the teabag.*

George ——Pickin' blackers, wha'. ——I'll never forget one dose
I got ——. My Jaysis. Me poor mother had to keep the
windows open for —.
(*Turning up the radio.*) Hang on.

Herman's Hermits are playing 'I'm Into Something Good'. **George** *is
delighted.* **George** *nods his head; then gets a bit braver. He pretends
he's singing, holding a microphone, patting his thigh to the rhythm.
Then he sings along, deliberately making his voice quavery, tapping his
adam's apple.* **Briget** *can't help laughing as she searches for and finds a
button.*

Enter **Yvonne**, *in her dressing-gown. She catches* **George** *doing his
Peter Noone impression.* **George** *grabs her, and they do a twirl. He lets
her go. Laughing, she opens the fridge, takes out her jeans and exits,
dashing.* **George** *tries to pull* **Briget** *up, to dance; but she won't stand
up.* **George** *pulls her again, harder, beginning to look annoyed.* **Briget**
is determined to stay sitting. **George** *gives up, suddenly looking as if
he's made a mistake; almost apologetic. The song ends, and* **George**
turns off the radio just as a current chart song starts.

George (*after a short, awkward pause*) Herman's Hermits, wha'.
They were the best. ——Fuck The Beatles; I always said it.

Briget You always said Fuck somethin' anyway.

George *is amused, but not sure what* **Briget** *is getting at.*

Briget You even said it when you asked me to marry yeh.

George I did not!

Briget You did so, George. I remember; God. You said, "Will yeh fuckin' marry me?"

George Tha' was only cos yeh didn't hear me the first time I said it.

Briget Yeh big liar. You were sittin' on me, so why wouldn't I'ave heard yeh the first time. There was no one else talkin' to me!

George Yeh weren't concentratin'.

Briget Concentratin'! Will yeh ——! You were sittin' on me. An' yeh roared it righ' into me face.

George *chuckles, remembering.*

Briget All o' Finglas heard yeh. When I was walkin' home Mrs O'Keefe was out at the gate askin' me did I say 'Yes'.

George Don't start. She was the skinny oul' one tha' gave us the bottle o' Lourdes water for a weddin' present, wasn't she?

Briget That's right.

George Mean ol' bitch.
(*Imitating Mrs O'Keefe.*) "It'll be a friend to you wherever you may roam."

Briget What happened it?

George We ran out o' tonic the Christmas before last, d'yeh remember?

They laugh. They are both very relaxed. **Briget** *is sewing the button onto the shirt.*

George (*about the holy water*) I don't know. ——Yeah; I was sittin' on yeh ——. That's righ'. In the field.

Briget *almost cringes when she's reminded of the field.*

George You told me tha' Lar McEvoy'd told yeh he'd got two tickets for Bob Dylan in the Adelphi an' would yeh go with him an' you said —
(*Mimicking* **Briget**.) —you were thinkin' abou' it.

Briget I didn't say it like tha'.

George Nearly. ——Lar McEvoy, wha'. ——Yeh could've been stuck with him now, Briget.

Briget (*before* **George** *finishes*) He never said it.

George (*casually*) Wha'?

Briget He never asked me to go to Bob Dylan with him.

George *doesn't understand.*

Briget I just said it to see what you'd do.

George (*still a bit confused; not at all annoyed*) ——I asked yeh to marry me.

Briget I know.

Briget *laughs, a bit nervously.*

Briget ——Sorry.

George (*just about to see the funny side*) ——Fuckin' hell.

Briget Still; yeh were goin' to ask me annyway, weren't yeh?

George Eh, yeah. ——Yeah.

Briget There then.

George An' here we are, wha'.

Briget (*not a bit sarcastically*) Yep.

George (*after a pause*) Wha' happened Lar McEvoy?

Briget Don't know. ——He went to India, I think it was.

George India!? Tha' cunt couldn't find his way to Butlins.

Briget (*slagging, but pleased*) Ooh, you're still jealous.

George No. ——No. He owes me a fiver. We had a bet on. The first one to ride you —.

Briget *looks up and studies* **George**, *to make sure that this isn't true.* **George** *turns before* **Briget** *can get a good look at him and takes the teabags out of the mugs. He hums 'I'm Into Something Good', innocently.*

Briget It's Eric Schweppe should be gettin' the fiver so.

George Wha? ——Wha!?

Briget *studies the button, pulls it, and hands the shirt to* **George**.

Briget There.

George Thanks.
(*Just a bit worried, and affronted.*) —Eric Schweppe!? You're messin'. ——Aren't yeh?

Briget *is trying not to laugh.*

George (*more confident*) When he was a baby the fairies came an' took his chin away.

Briget Ah, that's terrible.

206

George (*relieved*) I knew it.

(*Scornfully; giving out to himself.*) Eric Schweppe.

(*Looking at the button.*) ——Thanks —very much.

George *starts to leave, his reason for being in the Kitchen gone; but he stops and stands there a while, unwilling to go.* **Briget** *sits, but seems to want to do something. They both look awkward.*

Briget (*quietly; as if finished one thing and unsure about what to do next*) ——Well —.

Lights fade.

SCENE FIVE — THE QUIZ

Groucho sings 'La la laa —La la laa'.

It is 11.15 pm; before the final, sudden-death Round.

In the Kitchen, **Briget** *takes the copybook from the shelf, and writes for a while. She then exits, and re-enters wearing the outfit she wore in Scene Two. She takes a bottle of gin from a shelf, adds tonic from the fridge, sticks a little paper umbrella into her glass and sits down and drinks while she continues doing the crossword she started in Scene Two.*

Denis *is doing a final check of the scores.*

Denis Righ' ——.

Features *is standing, being friendly and being ignored;* **Gary** *is sitting, reading the lists* **George** *had in Scene Two; memorising them;* **George** *and* **Martin** *are in the Gents.* **Angela** *is at the Bar talking to* **Sandra***, making her laugh;* **Bertie** *is sitting down, his feet on the table;* **Tommy** *is beside* **Bertie***, looking eager, and about to put his feet on the table, like* **Bertie***;* **Noel** *is offstage.* **Yvonne***,* **Lorraine** *and* **Dermot** *are at their table.* **Lorraine** *is sitting a bit apart from the other two. She isn't merrily drunk anymore; just drunk.* **Yvonne***'s delivery, when drunk, is business-like and clipped.*

Dermot (*continuing a difficult conversation*) So are ye doin' anythin' on Saturday?

Yvonne (*nodding, as if again*) Yeah.

Enter **Leo**.

Leo (*not looking at* **Bertie**) Feet now.

Bertie *draws his gun but puts it back in his holster and takes his feet off the table.*

Denis Eh ——righ', ——yeah —.

Dermot (*unsure, but suspecting the worst*) So, ——what? D'you not want to go out with me or somethin'?

Yvonne No, Dermot; I don't want to go ou' with you or somethin'.

Dermot *isn't completely sure what* **Yvonne**'*s answer means.*

Denis Righ'. Ready.

The team members onstage go to their places. **Martin** *comes out of the Gents. There's a pint waiting for him at his table.*

Yvonne I think the way you treated Niamh was fuckin' disgraceful.

Dermot You —!?

Yvonne I don't like her; that's my excuse. What's yours? I'll tell yeh: You're a fuckin' bastard.

Enter **Noel**. *The teams are at their tables; except* **George**.

Noel (*secretly to the 'lads'*) I'm away there.

Features Denis, would you ever mind givin' George a shout, like a good man.

Denis (*as if unwilling*) George.

George (*from the Gents*) I'm comin'!

Yvonne You've been hoppin' round after me all night like a fuckin' poodle. I hate tha'.

Dermot (*attempting sarcasm*) You're somethin' else, d'you know that?

Yvonne D'you think so, Dermot?

George *comes out of the Gents.*

George (*passing* **Denis**) Can't go to the fuckin' jacks without the Neighbourhood Watch investigatin' yeh.

Denis'*s face at this moment could do justice to an Amnesty International poster.*

Yvonne I'd say a night ou' with you would be very borin', Dermot. Very borin' indeed. You're a ride, Dermot, but women look for more than that in men. You should read Cosmopolitan, Dermot. Seeyeh.

Yvonne *moves away from* **Dermot**, *and nearer to* **Lorraine**. **Lorraine** *looks lost and miserable.*

Bertie (*standing up as* **George** *passes*) George.

George Wha'?

Bertie *puts his hand out.* **George** *accepts it.*

Bertie (*grasping* **George**'*s hand; after a pause*) You're fucked.

George Let go o' me fuckin' hand. Let go!

(*Freeing his hand; shouting at* **Denis**.) That's intimidation, tha' is!

Dermot *shakes his head, forces himself to chuckle; then stands up.*

Dermot (*leaving; to* **Yvonne**) Fuck you.

Yvonne (*smiling*) Bye bye, Dermot.

Angela (*without looking*) Jesus; Yvonne again.

Exit **Dermot**.

Lorraine (*confused; to* **Yvonne**) Wha'?

Yvonne I —
(*Blowing*.) —blew him ou'.

Gradually **Lorraine** *starts to cry*.

Yvonne (*as if this has happened before*) Ah Jesus, Lorraine.

George *is shaken. He sits down. The teams are bracing themselves.*

Martin (*staring at his untouched pint; defeated*) I'd better not.

Features Ah, God love yeh.
(*Trying to be cheerful*.) Seconds away.

Denis Righ'. As two teams have both got the same score —

George (*trying to regain control*) We know. Come on.
(*To* **Gary**.) All set?

Gary *nods, and* **George** *nods*.

Denis (*insisting*) As two teams have both got the same scores —

George (*muttering*) Fuckin' eejit.

Denis —After all the rounds are over we have to have a tie-break. A sudden-death round.

George (*over his shoulder*) Come on, will yeh.

Denis (*to* **George**) Not everyone knows the rules, yeh know. Not everyone has managed to get this far an' lose nearly every month for the last three years!

George Don't mind him, lads. It's his time o' the month.

Denis (*very determined*) That's it. I'm goin'.
(*To* **George**.) I'm not lettin' anyone say —*that* to me.

Noel Ah, not again.

Denis *is off his stool, picking up his books.*

George Righ'. ——Sorry. Sorry.

Denis *ignores him as he looks around, making sure that he has everything.*

Bertie He said he's sorry, Denis.

Exit **Denis**. *They watch as he goes; some obviously waiting for him to come back.*

Features (*after a long pause*) He's gone.

Enter **Leo**. *He looks to where* **Denis** *was. The teams look lost.* **Bertie** *stands up and looks offstage, and shrugs.*

Leo Now?

Sandra He's gone.

George Did he leave his questions?

Sandra (*looking*) No.

Angela Leo; you do it.

Leo Ah now. No. It's over. Come on.
   (*Picking up the microphone*.) Time now, ladies and
   gentlemen —

George Ah here!

Bertie Leo. ——Leo!

Leo *stops*.

Bertie The quiz, she is not over. Now, it ends, righ', tonigh' or
   nonc of us here will come an' drink in this canteena annymore;
   comprende?

George (*backing* **Bertie**) Yeah.

Bertie An' we'll break every table, chair an' bit o' glass on our way
   ou'. Comprende, Leo?

Leo Si.

George Good man, Leo.

Angela Just one question, Leo; that's all, love.
   (*To* **Yvonne** *and* **Lorraine**) Hey, girls. ——Give us a hand
   here, will yis.

Yvonne Wha'?

Angela Come here.

Yvonne (*to* **Lorraine**; *grabbing her hand*) Come on, Lorraine.

Lorraine, *still sobbing, follows* **Yvonne**.

Angela (*to* **Lorraine**) You stand behind them. An' you stay here,
   Yvonne.

Lorraine *stands behind* **George**'s *team and* **Yvonne** *stands behind*
Bertie's *team.*

Leo, *still behind the bar, is trying to think of a good question.*

Bertie Righ', Leo. Shoot.

Leo One question?

Bertie That's it.

Leo (*into the microphone*) Now. Who wrote 'Wuthering Heights'?

George Hang on. ——Leo; this is like a cup final, righ'. We're the best two teams out o' more than fifty nearly. It's like the F.A. Cup. Liverpool versus Everton. Now, would you ask Ronnie Whelan a question as easy as tha', would yeh?

Leo No.

George Then cop on, for fuck sake, will yeh. Give us a decent one.

Leo Right, ——now ——. How many packets of crisps do you get in a box?

Martin Oh my Jaysis.

Noel Tayto or King?

Leo (*looking under the counter*) Tayto.

Bertie (*to his team*) A ton.

Noel Too obvious.

Bertie A ton.

Angela Yeah.

Bertie *writes the answer and hands the sheet back to* **Yvonne**. **Martin** *looks quickly around at* **Lorraine**, *as if distracted by her sobbing. This doesn't stop her.* **George**'s *team come out of a close huddle, and* **George** *writes the answer.*

George Fuckin' better be ——.
(*Handing the sheet back.*) There y'are, love.

Both teams look tense and worried.

Leo (*to* **Yvonne**) Now?

Yvonne (*reading*) A hundred.

Lorraine A hu-hundred an' tw-twenty-two.

Leo No. Way off. Fifty-five.

Bertie (*standing up*) We're nearest. We've won.

George No way! ——Leo!?

Leo *is coming out from behind the bar, and sits on* **Denis**'s *stool, enjoying himself.*

212

Leo (*as in 'be reasonable'*) Ah now.

Bertie (*sitting down*) It was worth a bash.

Features Another one, Leo.

Leo Who is the —
(**Denis**-*style*.) Who is the —General Secretary of the barman's union?; The Irish National Union of Vintners, Grocers and Allied Trades Assistants.

George (*to himself*) Oh fuck —

Features It's a hard one annyway.

Expressions on faces tell that no one knows the answer. They study each other's faces and discreetly shrug, and look across at the opposition, worried.

Bertie (*looking at* **George**'s *team to make sure that they don't know the answer; to* **Yvonne**) ——Nope; don't know.

Yvonne Good. ——Oh Jesus, Sorry.

George (*looking at* **Bertie**'s *team to make sure*) Don't know.

Yvonne They don't know it.

Lorraine Y-yeah.

Leo Thank God for that now. I don't know it meself. ——I've a good one now though.

Noel (*quietly*) How many pints in a keg?

Angela (*quietly*) Eighty.

Leo Who was told —Who was told, 'You'll go down in history'?

Noel (*quietly*) Shite.

The teams huddle.

George Hitler, Thatcher, ——Stephen Roche ——Someone tha' shot someone ——

Features *is trying to think of the song he's heard those words in. He thinks, hums, and stops; hums, and stops.*

Bertie Thatcher, Hitler ——

Noel No. Someone yeh never heard of.

Bertie I don't know the ones I never heard of!

Noel Yeh know wha' I mean.

Angela He's righ'.

Tommy The fella tha' shot the Pope.

Bertie May ——be —.

Bertie's *team argues.* **Features** *thinks of the song. He hums it through. He doesn't believe he's right at first.*

George (*about to write; looking for clearance*) Lee Harvey Oswald; yeah?

Features Eh, ——George.

He whispers the answer into **George**'s *ear.*

George Wha!? Fuck off, Features, will yeh.

Features *sings the song into* **George**'s *ear.*

Bertie Ah fuck it. Thatcher.

Noel Yeah, righ'. They don't know it either.

Bertie (*handing back the answer*) Signorita.

George's *expression remains sceptical as* **Features** *whisper-sings into his ear; then* —

George (*writing*) Fuckin' hell, Features, ——wha'.
(*Handing the answer to* **Lorraine**.) There y'are, love.
(*To* **Features**; *doubtful*.) Yeh sure?

Features I think ——yeah.

Leo Now?

Yvonne (*reading*) Margaret Thatcher but it's not spelt righ'.

Bertie's *team is about to riot.*

Leo Now now.

Lorraine (*reading; still sniffling*) Ru-Rudolf the R-Rednosed —— Reindeer.

Bertie Wha'!

The teams look to **Leo**; **George** *looking particularly anxious.*

Leo (*after a pause; sings*) You'll go down in hiss —torreey. —— Now.

George (*unsure*) We've won; have we won? We've won. We've fuckin' won! Jesus!

George's *fists punch the air as he stands up. The team members hug one another.* **Yvonne** *joins in.* **Martin** *wolfs his pint.* **Bertie**'s *team look on, getting ready to go.* **Bertie** *looks amused. He shrugs at his team; going 'Hey'.* **Noel** *looks very envious.* **Angela** *can't believe what she's seeing.* **Tommy** *shrugs when* **Bertie** *shrugs, and forces himself to smile.*

Groucho sings 'Lydia', but not too loud.

Leo (*into the microphone*) Time now, ladies and gentlemen, please. Ladies and gentlemen, please, we're well past closing time now.

Sandra, *beside* **Leo**, *very officiously presents* **George** *with a kettle.* **George** *kisses it, and holds it aloft like a cup. He puts the lid on his head. The others hold their kettles; delighted.*

Martin (*to his kettle*) I'll only boil Ballier in yeh!

Bertie *claps as he stands up. He pats* **George***'s back.*

Bertie Next month, compadre.

George (*thrilled*) Ah, yeah. Good luck, Bertie.

Bertie *and his team exit;* **Bertie** *as if on his way to the OK Corral.*

Leo Time now, ladies and gentlemen, please. Ladies and gentlemen, this pub will self-destruct in five seconds.

The lights dim as **George***'s team and* **Sandra**, **Yvonne** *and* **Lorraine** *exit, shifted by* **Leo** *as he speaks into the microphone.* **Leo** *is now alone. He clears the tables, humming 'Lydia'.*

Towards the end of the scene **Angela** *enters and stands near the wing, waiting for* **Leo***.* **Leo** *is aware that she is there, but says and does nothing.*

In the Kitchen, **Briget** *hears 'Lydia' on the radio and goes over and turns it up. She loves it. She laughs. Then she has an idea: she takes her biro from the table and uses it as a moustache. The salt cellar becomes Groucho's cigar; and* **Briget** *does a Groucho impression.*

Leo *walks up to* **Angela***. He smiles, a bit shyly.*

Leo Now.

Angela Now.

They exit together, and the lights in the Pub go down.

Briget *does a bent-knee walk, like Groucho; going 'La la laa —la la laa'.*

Offstage, the front door slams. **Briget** *dashes to turn down the radio. She takes the salt cellar and biro back to the table, still dashing, and sits down; and waits, looking at the door; wondering what state* **George** *is going to be in when he enters.*

Briget (*quietly; worried; for herself*) Please God, he didn't lose again. Please.

Lights fade.

Suggestion *A large poster/notice in the foyer beside the exits on which is printed, 'Sinclair Lewis wrote 'Elmer Gantry'.*

A Selected List of Titles Available from Minerva

While every effort is made to keep prices low, it is sometimes necessary to increase prices at short notice. Mandarin Paperbacks reserves the right to show new retail prices on covers which may differ from those previously advertised in the text or elsewhere.

The prices shown below were correct at the time of going to press.

☐	7493 9030 1	**Books of Bale**	John Arden	£4.99
☐	7493 9044 1	**Book of Evidence**	John Banville	£4.99
☐	7493 9077 8	**Kepler**	John Banville	£4.99
☐	7493 9076 X	**Dr Copernicus**	John Banville	£4.99
☐	7493 9178 2	**Collected Poems**	Christy Brown	£5.99
☐	7493 9179 0	**Down All the Days**	Christy Brown	£4.99
☐	7493 9177 4	**My Left Foot**	Christy Brown	£4.99
☐	7493 9182 0	**A Promising Career**	Christy Brown	£4.99
☐	7493 9181 2	**A Shadow On Summer**	Christy Brown	£4.99
☐	7493 9183 9	**Wild Grow the Lillies**	Christy Brown	£4.99
☐	7493 9801 9	**The Commitments (Film Tie-In)**	Roddy Doyle	£4.99
☐	7493 9125 1	**The Snapper**	Roddy Doyle	£4.99
☐	7493 9045 X	**New Book of Dubliners**	Ben Forkner	£4.99

All these books are available at your bookshop or newsagent, or can be ordered direct from the publisher. Just tick the titles you want and fill in the form below.

Mandarin Paperbacks, Cash Sales Department, PO Box 11, Falmouth, Cornwall TR10 9EN.

Please send cheque or postal order, no currency, for purchase price quoted and allow the following for postage and packing:

UK including BFPO
£1.00 for the first book, 50p for the second and 30p for each additional book ordered to a maximum charge of £3.00.

Overseas including Eire
£2 for the first book, £1.00 for the second and 50p for each additional book thereafter.

NAME (Block letters) ....

ADDRESS...

....

☐ I enclose my remittance for ....

☐ I wish to pay by Access/Visa Card Number

Expiry Date